" 'Paris Remembers' is a great story!"

—PETE SEEGER

"*Acoustic Stories* is a wonderful, enchanting read. Bassist Bill Amatneek has an engaging way with a story, grabbing the reader's attention right away in a nicely understated, yet captivating style that keeps you wanting more. If you've ever wanted that something more you just couldn't put your hands on about the artists, a closer look at a musician's life, this book is a must have, an entertaining read and, with many excellent photos throughout, a fine addition to the music collection of any acoustic music fan."

—JOE FALLETTA, *Bluegrass Now*

"Your stories are MUSIC to my ears."

—MARY CARTER SMITH, AFRICAN GRIOT

"Your fine writing and keen insight have made my job a delight. I wish there were 40 of you."

—ED ENRIGHT, EDITOR, *Down Beat*

"It is the highest testament to Amatneek's excellence as a raconteur that praise for his efforts have come from both storytellers and fellow musicians alike. He has had a major impact on the world of acoustic music, and in turn it has had an impact upon his development as a major talent in the storytelling community."

—ROBERT RODRIGUEZ, *Storyline*

"Reading your book was entertaining, enlightening and enjoyable. But there were moments when it sang. At those times, I wasn't aware of reading, but was there, in that story, experiencing it, with a smile on my face or lump in my throat.

—MICHAEL BREMER, *UnTechnical Press*

"What makes Amatneek's book special is his funny, vivid, and always affectionate portrayals of a pantheon of many of the world's best musicians. *Acoustic Stories* beautifully illustrated with photos by some of the best musical photojournalists, would be a worthwhile read for almost anyone, but those familiar with the California acoustic music scene really owe it to themselves to seek it out."

—Michael Parrish, *Dirty Linen*

"I'm going on record as having been totally unsurprised at the writing skill Bill showed in this book. I was his editor at *Rolling Stone* in 1970, and it's extremely rare to find someone who knows his way around music and a typewriter. Bill, to an editor at a music magazine, was a dream come true."

—Ed Ward, rock historian, *Inkwell*

"During my near twenty years at Sweetwater, there were only a small handful of performers whose sheer poignancy made me cry: Watching John Lee Hooker walk on stage; Elizabeth Cotten, at age 88, forgetting the words to her song 'Freight Train,' and the audience singing the lyrics for her; Ralph Stanley singing so lovingly about his departed brother, Carter; Allen Shamblin telling how he came to write 'I Can't Make You Love Me,' which became a huge hit for Bonnie Raitt; and Bill Amatneek, when he finished telling 'Paris Remembers.' It was so touching I burst into tears."

—Jeannie Patterson, owner, *Sweetwater, 1979–1998*

Affiliations are listed for identification purposes only.

ALSO BY BILL AMATNEEK

Acoustic Stories: Playing Bass with Peter, Paul & Mary, Jerry Garcia, Bill Monroe and 18 Other Unamplified Tales
The first edition of *Acoustic Stories* · Vineyards Press · 2003

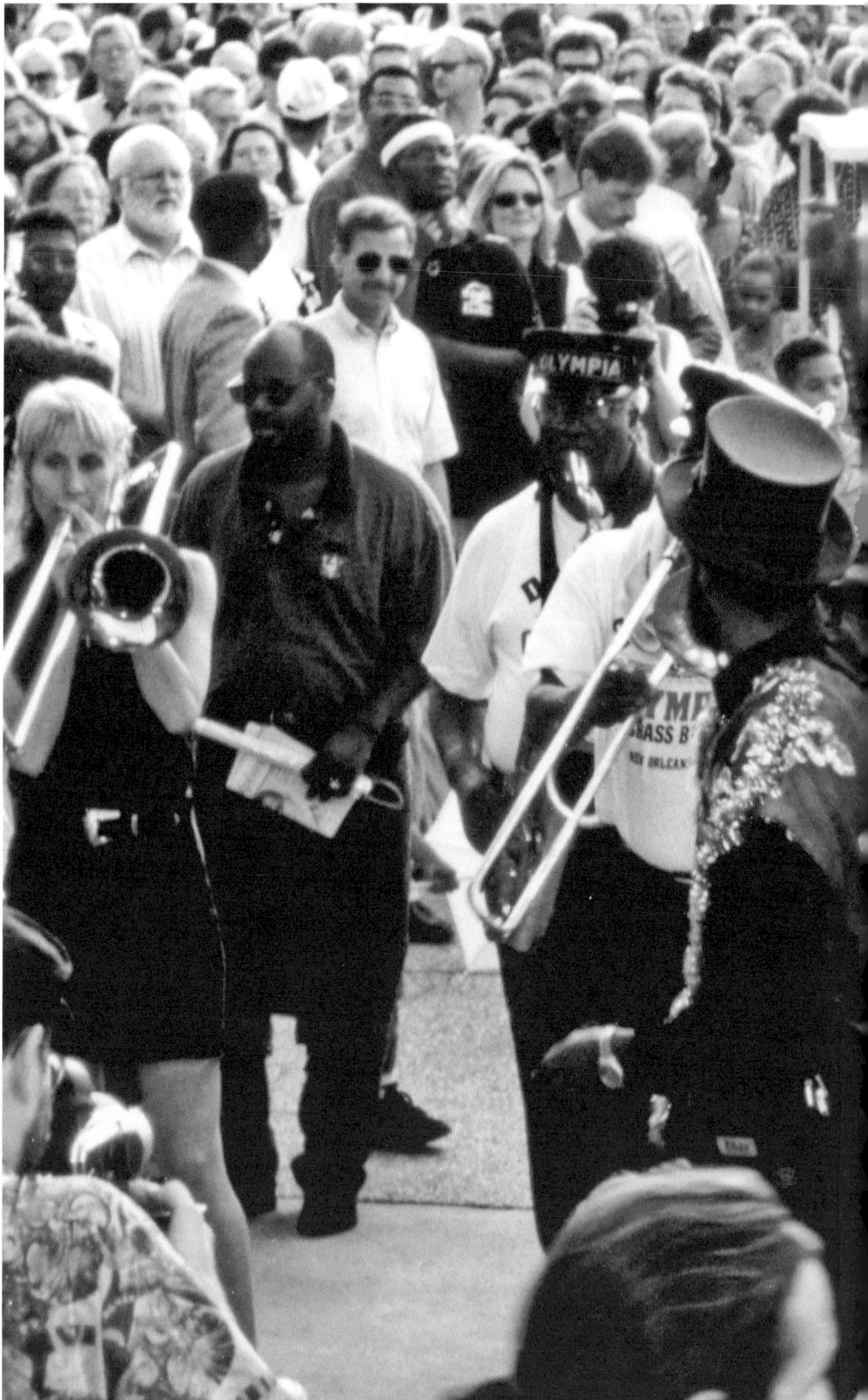
OLYMPIA

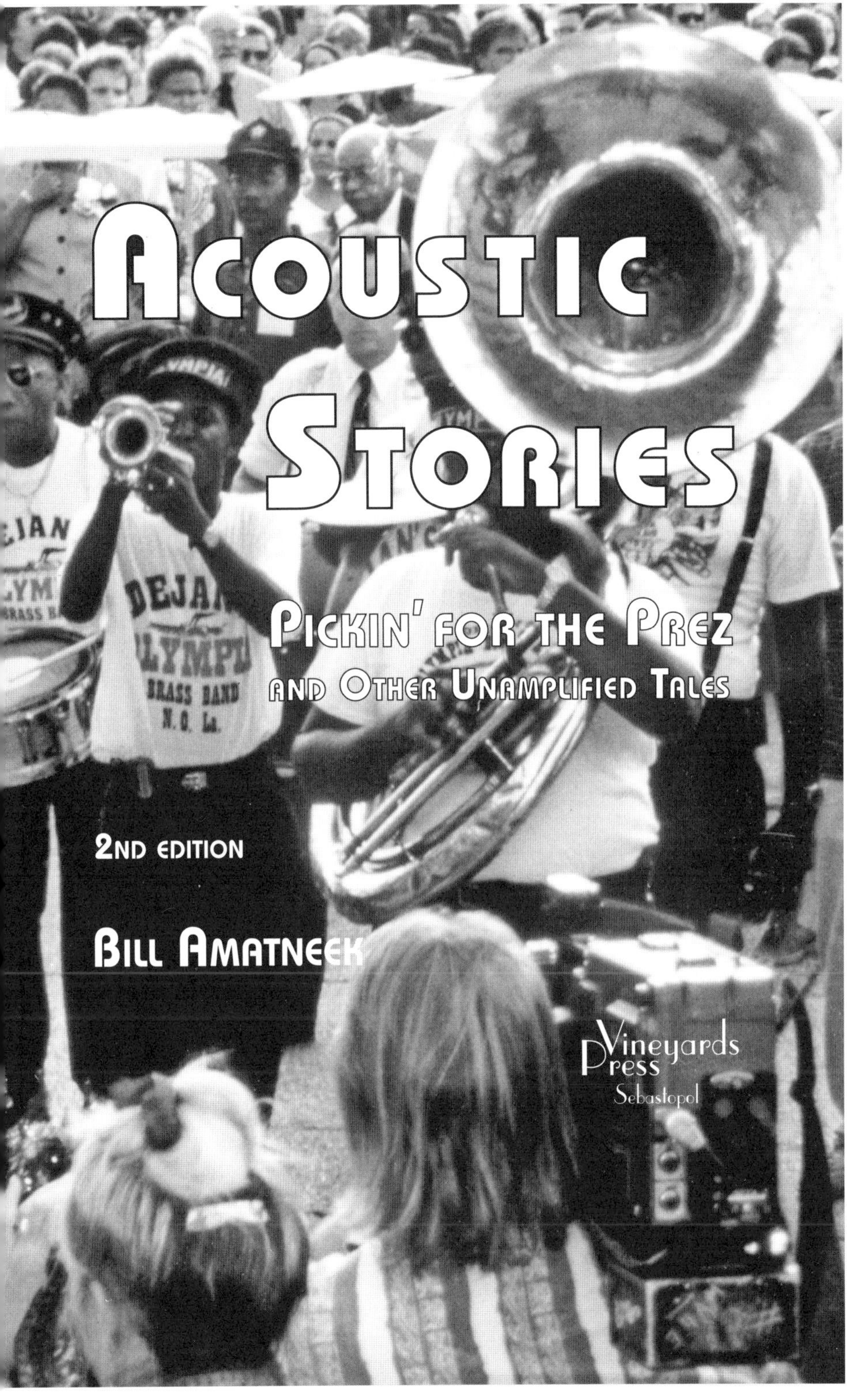
ACOUSTIC STORIES
PICKIN' FOR THE PREZ
AND OTHER UNAMPLIFIED TALES
2ND EDITION
BILL AMATNEEK
Vineyards Press
Sebastopol

Vineyards Press
P.O. Box 716, Sebastopol California 95473
VineyardsPress.com

Portions of this work appeared previously in different forms in the magazines *Bluegrass Unlimited, Yoga Journal, Down Beat, First Leaves~2002, The Dickens, Bass World,* and in the book, *Encounters with Bob Dylan: If You See Him Say Hello.* The stories in this book are based on actual incidents. Some facts may have been changed, ignored or forgotten in creating these stories, and in some cases names have been changed to protect the privacy of the individuals in question. *Acoustic Stories* is not affiliated with, sponsored or endorsed by anyone named in this book. Acknowledgments and permissions are in the back of the book. Dust jacket, cover, book interior and all unattributed photos are by the author.

Publisher's Cataloging-in-Publication
Amatneek, Bill
Acoustic stories : pickin' for the prez and other unamplified tales/ Bill Amatneek —
2nd ed. p. ill. cm.
ISBN 978-1-928578-12-3 (cloth bound)
1. Amatneek, Bill. 2. Folk musicians—United States—Biography. 3. Double bassists—United States—Biography. 4. Musicians as authors. I. Title.

ML418.A5 A3 2013 787.5/092 B
Library of Congress Control Number: 2013930622

9 8 7 6 5 4 3 2 1 Second edition · First printing

Printed in the United States of America

To my wife, Noni

My life's song

ANYONE WHO BLOWS IS

OUTTA SIGHT!

—Dizzy Gillespie

Contents

Preface

These are thirty-three stories from my life as a string bassist and 5-string banjo man in American music bands, presented in rough chronological order. The music here arches blues to bluegrass, old-timey to new acoustic music, and the Great American Songbook to the great American big band. And there is a tale about a recent passion: playing bass in a Middle-Eastern band for belly dancers.

Some of these pieces began their lives on the written page. But most started as tales that I told to friends, and at story swap groups and storytelling festivals.

Storytellers differentiate between facts and truth. Journalists supposedly pursue facts, the absolute reality. But storytellers seek the truth, the fundamental reality, also known as the story's heart. If a teller has told the heart of a story as he feels it, he has told its truth, even if alleged facts have been stretched or ignored. Although most of these tales are straight-ahead fact based, some take a dogleg towards the not-so-factual. You'll know them by the smiles they wear.

A couple of these stories, though swimming in an ocean of fact, surf on a current of fiction; I hope you catch them, because I've forgotten which they are. There's a tall tale in here, wearing a tall hat, a few long-standing myths that have been perpetuated if not outright amplified, and some names that have been changed to protect the guilty.

Moving a told story to the printed page presents some difficulties for the typesetter. The storyteller's facial expressions, gestures, body language, and melody of speech are not easily manifested with print, though you may notice that some word painting has been applied to this book's Epigraph and Colophon.

The rhythms of a told story are also tricky to convey. I have tried to suggest some of them with as much punctuation as my editor let me get away with, shorter paragraphs, ellipses, section breaks of various sizes and types, drop caps, blank pages between some stories, and other typesetting devices. Sometimes you'll see a switch from past to present tense, a jump that most of us take as we arrive at the heat of a told story. And sometimes you'll see text frames that have been shifted so that reading about an event precedes a page turn and a photo of that event.

In sum, you may see some unconventional typesetting, punctuation, and grammar on these pages, all in the service of recreating the rhythms and pauses of a told story.

All but one of the tales from the first edition of this book, *Acoustic Stories: Playing bass with Peter, Paul & Mary, Jerry Garcia, Bill Monroe and 18 Other Unamplified Tales,* have found their way into this edition, and most of them have been updated. Some people who appeared in the first edition have passed on, and their stories, particularly those of Ali Akbar Khan and Mary Travers, merited a coda. Others have died and I have not mentioned it, wanting to avoid making this edition of *Acoustic Stories* a roll call of souls passed.

A friend, having heard me tell "Jesus Loves this Mandolin Picker," remarked, "That story isn't about Frank Wakefield; it's about Frank and you."

Yes, all these tales represent brushes I've had with various people. Please read them as stories about my encounters with them, and not an attempt at biography or even profile, though some biographical information has sometimes been included.

You may be tempted to browse the table of contents and page to the story of a favorite musician or band. May I suggest you resist that impulse. Some people materialize in two or more stories. I introduce them the first time, but subsequent appearances assume you've already met them; jumping into the middle of the book might leave you unclear as to just who these characters are. Similarly for certain music-related words and phrases: the first time they appear, I briefly define them; subsequent uses assume you know them. To further dissuade puddle jumping, I've omitted an index. So in reading this book, may I suggest you take it "from the edge," as music directors say, that is, from the very beginning.

Acoustic music has always been my favorite. The sound of real instruments, totally un-electrified, has always appealed to me; it was the music I was brought up on. It's also easier on my ears; even playing in a shouting big band fills but never overloads my senses. It is for this reason, my love and appreciation of unamplified music, that I call these tales "Acoustic Stories."

In the midst of interviewing Aretha Franklin for *Rolling Stone* four decades ago, I saw that I wanted to be on the other side of the note pad, playing music, not interviewing someone who was playing music. When I went home to write up our meeting, I realized I didn't have much to say because I hadn't done much in my life. I put down the typewriter and re-focused on playing; writing could return later.

I have been blessed to witness and participate in some extraordinary music events since then, and fortunate to have played and hung out with many talented artists. Writing and telling about these events and these people constitute the realization of a long-term goal. As a soldier in one of the stories you'll read here, "Brotherhood of the Stick," said, "It's a nice feeling I'll have for the rest of my life."

I hope you enjoy these *Acoustic Stories.*

SEBASTOPOL, CALIFORNIA
MAY 1, 2013

Introduction

Our family lived at 178 Bleecker Street in Manhattan's Greenwich Village during the 1940s, when the Village was largely an Italian neighborhood that enfolded a small, close-knit bohemian underground. Dad was an engineer for *Consumer Reports* magazine, so we were the first on the block to have tape recorders and televisions, borrowed from his test bench at work. I remember watching TV at night and waking in the morning to the sounds of the iceman on the street hawking his frozen wares to families that could not afford refrigerators.

Village musicians would hang out at our house so they could hear themselves played back on recordings dad made of them. Pete Seeger and the Weavers were frequent guests, as were Paul Robeson and Charity Bailey.

Pete once came by with a small vocal group that he directed, facing them, with 5-string banjo. They were maybe half a dozen singers. One, I remember, was a blond teenager, not impossibly Mary Travers, later of Peter, Paul & Mary. If this is the case, it was a group called the Song Swappers.

I remember Paul Robeson singing in our living room while mom accompanied him on piano. He sang, "No more driver's lash for me, no more, no more," and spat out the word "lash" like he meant it making me aware that he was expressing the lyric, not just singing it. Even then I felt that Robeson was a giant: an actor and singer of staggering talent, an outsized human being. It was a thrill to hear him sing in my father's house; his voice vibrated the apartment.

I started playing violin at the age of six, taking lessons at the Turtle Bay Music School on 52nd street in Manhattan. One day, after I had spent weeks sawing scratchy scales and arpeggios, my teacher gave me a simple duet for violin and piano. Mom, who had graduated in piano from Juilliard High School of the Performing Arts, sat down that evening to play the piece with me. She counted it off and we began. A dozen measures into it, intent on my own playing, I started running away with the tempo.

My mother stopped playing. "Bill, when you play music with other people, you must listen."

It was the first music lesson I remember, and the first music lesson every player should receive: *Listen.*

Thanks, mom.

Dad played the piano accordion – the squeezebox, he called it – and the mandolin and mandola. My sister played piano and guitar. For years our family would sit around the piano after dinner and play down the *Fireside Book of Folk Songs.*

That songbook was my introduction to folk music. I'm looking at the copy we had back then, the first edition, given to me by my mom before she passed. It is beat up, the cover faded to bare legibility and the spine separated from the text block. Although the color printing on each page has bled onto the opposite page, the music, "Oh Susanna," "Wayfaring Stranger," "Careless Love," remains.

Frequently, when you do something or see someone for the last time, you don't realize it at the moment. Sitting around the piano with my family and playing the *Fireside Book* for the last time was one of those moments, now much missed.

The musicals of Rogers and Hammerstein, especially *South Pacific,* played on our turntable frequently. I remember that my dad bought tickets to see Lerner and Lowe's musical, *My Fair Lady,* early in its run with the original cast that included Rex Harrison and Julie Andrews. It was the hottest ticket on Broadway, and a much-anticipated show that our whole family enjoyed.

When I was in single digits, my folks took me to see Toscanini, then in his eighties, conduct the NBC Symphony Orchestra. A brass railing surrounded the conductor's podium on three sides.

"Why is that railing there?" I asked my folks.

He is old, they said. He gets so excited when he's conducting that he must hold on to the railing to keep from falling down. They told me to remember this evening, that Toscanini was the greatest orchestra conductor of our time.

I understood, and tried to be very still and listen very hard.

Mom and dad sang in the 150-voice Interracial Fellowship Chorus. They dragged me to their weekly rehearsals where I squirmed in my seat the entire time. But despite my fidgeting, it gave me an appreciation of choral music. Every December the chorus performed Handel's *Messiah.* Sitting quietly in a church pew while they sang this monumental oratorio was a monumental bore. But through the years I started appreciating the outsized power and beauty of this inspired piece, and to this day listening to it or singing it gives me chills.

I continued playing violin through our move to Sunnyside Gardens in Queens and continued disliking this instrument. It was not me. Now, when parents I know foist music lessons on their children, I ask them if they are sure the imposed instrument is the right one for their child. (Maybe I should be asking their kids that question.)

We moved to Springfield Township, a Philadelphia suburb, where I entered Hillcrest Junior High School and joined the student orchestra there. After the first rehearsal, the music teacher, Mr. Lilly, approached me and said, "You have the largest hands in the violin section. How would you like to play string bass?"

I said, "Yeah, sure!"

As it turns out, the violin-to-bass pathway is well traveled, and not a few string bassists started out their double-bass lives as large-handed violinists. Thank you, Mr. Lilly.

In high school I played bass drum and clash cymbals in the marching band, and string bass in the orchestra, and better yet, in the big band. Under the inspiring leadership of our band director, Joe DePolis, I remember playing "Intermission Riff," "Stardust," and "Moonlight Serenade." I've played in big bands almost continuously since, and love this ear-bending experience, as you will read.

During my high school years I played and taught bass with the Philadelphia Folk Workshop. When we had weekday afternoon gigs playing at local high schools, I had to get written permission from the teachers whose classes I'd be missing.

I remember playing the first Philadelphia Folk Festival in 1961, backing the Greenbriar Boys – Ralph Rinzler, Bob Yellin, and John Herald – on string bass.

And I remember Peter, Paul & Mary.

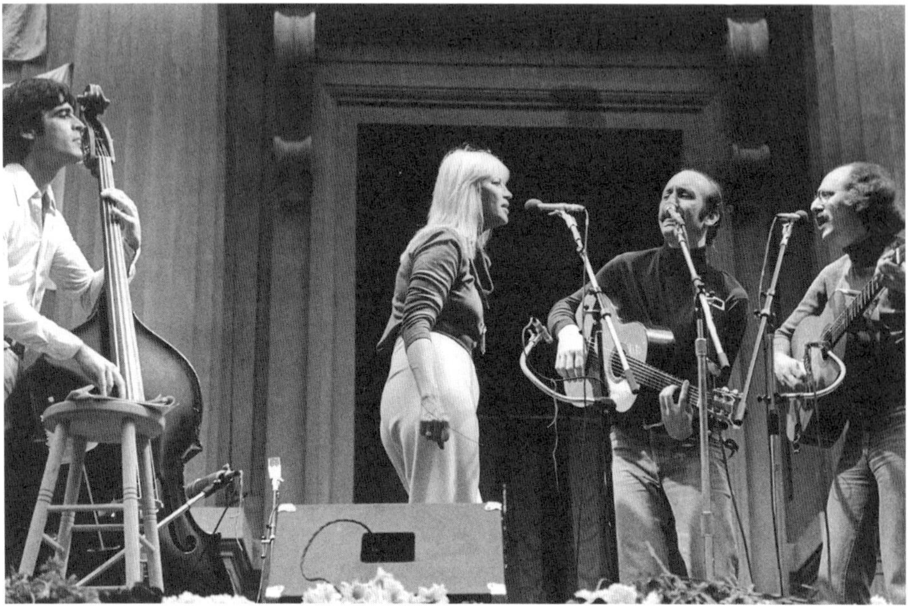

Mary Travers, Noel Paul Stookey & Peter Yarrow
accompanied by the author
Greek Theatre, Berkeley · October 7, 1979
By Jon Sievert

MARY,

... Peter & Paul

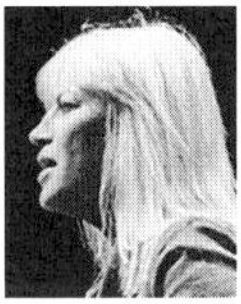

Into the 1962 American folk-music arena of bluegrass pickers, blues shouters, gospel preachers, trad balladeers, and singing songwriters, entered a trio of singers – a girl, and two boys playing guitars – with a new style, forward-looking repertoire and social zeal that made all America take notice. They called themselves "Peter, Paul & Mary," and they were an unexpected blessing, a balm for our soul.

Peter, Paul & Mary set a new standard for American folk music groups in the polish of their ensemble, arrangements, and stage presentation. Their singing arrived tight, their contrasting voices blended by untold hours of practicing their bright arrangements. Their harmonies were more complex than most folk groups', and more engaging.

Peter and Paul's guitar work, also honed by long hours together in the woodshed, added to the group's sparkle. Paul played a nylon-strung classical guitar to Peter's steel-strung Martin. On any given tune, one of them usually capoed up, playing the same chords (but with different fingerings), higher on the neck. This nylon-against-steel combination, plus the broader tonal range that came from playing on different stretches of the fingerboard, added to their unique sound.

Their stage performance was novel: the three crowded a single microphone stand with two, and later in their career, three mics, and moved around within the setup's audio halo, taking turns at the center spot. This gave their audiences a dynamic image to watch, engaging our eyes as well as ears.

The trio introduced their fans to new songs by new songwriters, most importantly those of Bob Dylan, John Denver, and Pete Seeger. Their tunes became so well known over the trio's 47-year career, that their multi-generational audiences – toddlers to grandparents at every concert – would join in all the choruses. To attend a live Peter, Paul & Mary show was to become part of a love-fest. Everyone adored this trio.

A music reviewer at the time of their first album, it is storied, referred to the group's two guys, Noel Paul Stookey and Peter Yarrow, as "two cellos playing guitars." A sweet image, I thought.

But to my eyes, the sweetest image was of their girl singer, Mary Travers. With her long blond hair, bangs to her eyebrows, the warmest smile and bluest eyes, Mary was a chorus of curves, radiating femininity. She sang sweetly, her harmonies shimmered.

Mary sang the lead on some of the trio's best-known songs, including "Leaving on a Jet Plane," "Blowing in the Wind," and "Where Have All the Flowers Gone." On these tunes, Mary was the voice of Peter, Paul & Mary, her singing the perfect foil to Peter and Paul's harmonizing and guitar work.

She made the group's "look" as well. When I eyeball any photograph of them, any video, my gaze goes straight to Mary. The camera loved her as it loved Marilyn Monroe.

Smiling at me from the cover of their debut album, a garland of freshly cut flowers in her hands, Mary was young as springtime, and sweeter yet. I was a seventeen-year-old folk music fanatic when their album was released, and, like many guys of my age and music interests, I had a teenage crush on Mary.

Mimi Fariña of the Bread and Roses Festival of Music called me in 1979. By that time I had migrated to the coast and settled in Mill Valley, California. She said that Peter, Paul & Mary were going to play the festival that year and had asked for my services as the festival's house bass player to back them for their performance. Rehearsal would be the day before their first show, backstage at Berkeley's Greek Theatre, at one o'clock sharp.

I was ecstatic.

The group over-nighted me their set list, I walked over to Village Music and bought the three Peter, Paul & Mary albums needed to cover the songs, and started studying the bass parts. All of their tunes were fairly straightforward, as far as the bass player goes, with one exception, and that was their big hit, John Denver's "Leaving on a Jet Plane."

The bass player starts this song playing a melodic bass lead. So he kicks off the tune, sets the tempo, sets the groove, and sets the mood of "Leaving on a Jet Plane" with a bass line that is part melody and part bass vamp. As the lone bass, new boy on their block, opposite three people who had been playing together for almost a quarter century, when it came to kicking off "Leaving on a Jet Plane," I was scared witless.

Finally the big day of the big rehearsal arrived and I got to the theatre at twelve o'clock, in plenty of time to get real nervous.

Then, at one o'clock sharp, in walked Mary!

... ... and Peter and Paul.

Mary was more beautiful and enchanting than her album cover shots revealed. My jaw dropped as she walked in.

Exuding confidence, Mary strode directly to me, introduced herself – "Hi, I'm Mary Travers" – and gave me a hug.

Yes!

Then she introduced me to Peter and Paul. We shook and howdied.

Then the four of us found a rehearsal nook back stage, took out our instruments and tuned up. Peter, it became clear, was their M.D., their Music Director. He took charge of the rehearsal and called the leadoff tune for the afternoon.

"Let's try 'Leaving on a Jet Plane' first," he said.

An acid churn swarmed the pit of my stomach as I realized he'd called this tune as a test for me.

Then he turned to me – not Mary or Paul – he turned to me and said: "Ready?"

I knew what "Ready?" meant. It meant, "You do know why I'm calling this tune first, don't you kid?"

" 'Leaving on a Jet Plane.' You guys recorded it in the key of A major, but it opens in E major. Peter, … I'm ready."

Peter counted off the song: "One. … Two. … One, two, three, four."

I played the bass part the way I had practiced it, leading as boldly as I could under the circumstances.

The three of them looked up at me with big, pleased smiles. Mary stood up, walked straight over to me, looked me in the eyes, and sang:

All my bags are packed, I'm ready to go,
I'm standing here outside your door,
Hate to wake you up to say good-bye.

Mary, you can wake me up any time.

But the dawn is breaking, it's early morn,
Taxi's waiting, he's blowin' his horn,
Already I'm so lonesome I could cry.

You and me both, Mary.

So kiss me and smile for me,
Tell me that you'll wait for me,
Hold me like you'll never let me go.
I'm leaving on a jet plane,
Don't know when I'll be back again.

Then Mary looked at me longingly, and sang:

Oh babe, I hate to go.

It was a sweet and deep feeling to be on the bass-bottom of this classic acoustic harmony, surrounded by the singing of the voices that had created it, an exquisite and unforgettable moment. Although we would play this song to eight thousand people the next day, it was our playing it that afternoon at rehearsal that stands out most vividly for me.

I understood then that Peter, Paul and Mary mean what they are saying and singing. Peter, Paul and Mary *are* who they sing they are.

The rest of the rehearsal went very well, as did our performance the next evening. It's a funny thing about shows, though. A show can go by in a moment, but there are moments in the show that seem like they last forever.

I remember one of those moments. Towards the end of their concert, Peter stepped to the center mike to sing the first two verses of a ballad as Mary sauntered back to where I was playing bass. She came up on my right side, and laid her hand on my shoulder.

I broke into a hot sweat.

Then she rested her head on my arm.

More sweat.

Then she looked up at me … real slowly.

I looked back at Mary, my heart thumping in my throat, my bass slipping away from my sweaty hands.

She looked deep into my eyes.

I looked deep into her eyes.

And that's when it hit me: Mary loved me. I could tell. Mary loved *me!*

I was floating, blissed. I don't know how I finished the tune. I don't know how I finished the set. But three tunes later their concert was over, and they left immediately … on a jet plane no less. I didn't even get to say good-bye to Mary. I didn't even get to see her again for a year and a half.

Finally, I read in the paper that they would be playing the Circle Star Theatre in San Carlos. So I bought a ticket and waited impatiently for the date, still a long month away.

At last the big night of the big show arrived, and I drove out to see them. Stepping up to the stage door, I knocked loudly, and who opened the door, but Mary! And she gave me a big hug and a kiss.

Terrific!

But, they were about to go on stage, so I said, "OK babe, I'll see *you* after the show," and I rushed to the back of the theatre to watch them from there.

They put on a dynamic concert for an enthusiastic, mixed-age crowd; the audience sang along all night. Peter, Paul and Mary are consistently excellent performers and their performance that evening sparkled.

But towards the end of the show, Peter stepped to the center mike to sing the same two verses of that same ballad. And Mary sauntered back to where their regular bassist, Richard

Kniss, was playing bass. She came up on his right side, and she put her hand on *his* shoulder.

Then she rested her head on *his* arm.

She looked up at *him* real slowly.

He looked down at her.

And that's when it hit me: Mary didn't love me. She looked at *all* her bass players that way!

Mary had used me ... as a prop ... in her act.

I played a rehearsal, a sound check, a pre-show warm-up, and a show with them, all in the course of a couple days. But in that short time I feel I had touched the Peter, Paul & Mary experience, as it certainly had touched me.

It was an honor and a thrill to play with them on stage, a cherished experience. I must remember to thank them all for it and, when I see her next, to tell Mary:

So kiss me and smile for me,
Tell me that you'll wait for me,
Hold me like you'll never let me go.

I'm leaving on a jet plane,
Don't know when I'll be back again.

Oh babe,
I hate
to go.

Mary? ... Babe, ... all is forgiven.

The Philadelphia Folksong Society

Presents

BOB DYLAN

In Concert

Friday, May 3, 8:30 P.M.

Ethical Society Auditorium – 1906 Rittenhouse Sq.

Donation: $1.75 Members: $1.50

TICKETS AVAILABLE:
Gilded Cage, 261 S. 21 St. and at the door

Dylan Plays Philly

Back in 1963, I was a string-bass poppin', banjo-pickin', Philadelphia folkie. The folk scene was small then, and Philly was just a two-hour drive from New York, so what went on in the Big Apple was known soon and known well in the City of Brotherly Love.

Bob Dylan was what was going on in Gotham. *Sing Out!* magazine tracked Dylan's rise from early on, and everyone in town was talking about him, though most of us had never seen him.

The folk music scene, then as now, had its camps. The bluegrass boys, old-timey folks and traditional balladeers often hung in the same circles. The ragtime fans and blues folks seemed to share an affinity. And certainly the political singers and ethnic music fans were into their own worlds.

But Dylan, it was said, was none of these, but maybe all of them.

Dylan, it was said, was something else.

Everyone, in every corner of the Philly folk scene, was looking forward to his first local gig.

On a sunny May day in 1963, Dylan arrived for his first Philly concert, just weeks before his second album was released.

Some would testify that he arrived on his motorcycle, a pre-release copy of his new album tucked under his black leather jacket. His girlfriend, Suze Rotolo, rode pillion, her arms wrapped around him like a circle 'round the sun.

Others said that they themselves drove to the 30th Street Station to pick him up. He arrived alone, no album.

Dylan's gig was at the Ethical Culture Society hall on Rittenhouse Square in downtown Philadelphia. The seating was 300. That's what the sign over the front door said. But even at a ticket price of $1.50 for Philadelphia Folksong Society members and $1.75 for the general public, Bob had that hall filled.

The 8:30 show time came and went, and Dylan had not stepped on stage. Having arrived early, I had a front row seat. There was a door ten feet in front of me that led backstage. So I decided to see what was happening, see where Dylan was. I stepped through the door and into the Ethical Culture Society's backstage area. A hallway led to the wings, some steps led up to the catwalk, and a staircase led down. I went down.

After some staircase twists and blind corridors, I spotted Dylan. There was no manager, no agent, no entourage. Just him, his guitar, and his harmonica. At the moment I set eyes on him, he was backing out of what appeared to be a janitor's closet, having wisely decided that this was not the way to the stage. He looked vibrant and bright-eyed, inner-driven … and lost.

So I said, "Lookin' for the stage, Bob?"

"Yeah."

"Follow me." I led him up to the stage level and pointed him to the wings.

As he walked by me to the stage, he said, "Thanks, man."

There were two sets that evening with a good break between, so we all went outside. And we all recognized, no matter which folk camp we called home, that what Dylan was doing that night had not been done before.

First off, no one who wrote songs was also performing them. There were singers and there were songwriters; the twain rarely lived in one person. Sure, Woody Guthrie wrote his own material, but most of my peers had never seen Woody. Everything Dylan did that evening was his own work, and his work was deeply personal. His lyrics exposed who he was and how he felt, and he felt passionately.

No one sang like Dylan. His shouted vocals, harangued with a nasalized twang, were ear searing. His Midwesternese, now widely copied, had never been heard before. Sometimes he'd squeeze more words into a line than its meter could handle, or put an odd number of lines in a verse, and get away with it poetically.

A harmonica? No one was putting a harmonica in a holder and playing it along with guitar. No one. Most harpists back then played cross-harp style, sucking in on the notes to bluesify them. But Dylan mostly played blow harp. He blew out to play, and the melodies he blew were his own jingle-jangle.

His absorption in each song was transfixing, and put you in to the Dylan haze. He made no introductions or small talk. He didn't try to charm or entertain. He dove into each song and executed it – tore it up. Dylan was ferocious. With a bouncing harmonica, pushed vocals, and hypnotic guitar accompaniment, Dylan was a three-piece, one-man band.

It seemed as though Bob had questioned the major

cornerstones of folk music, from creation through performance, and come back with a new thing.

Yes, there were some who said that Dylan was a strummer, not a picker. But his strumming was hammering, and he drove his songs into you.

And there were some who said he could not sing. Certainly Bob broke the rules of singing. He'd take a breath in the mid–dle of a word, fergoshsakes. Even folkies knew you didn't do that.

What we all knew was that Dylan had been riveting.

I remember seeing his new album, *The Freewheelin' Bob Dylan,* in a record shop window a few weeks later, the cover showing him and Suze walking through Greenwich Village snow, her arms yet wrapped around him. And I remember thinking that a sea change was taking place. A new era was beginning: the era of the songwriter as performer, the "singer-songwriter."

After Dylan, if you wanted to make your mark, whether you were country, folk, R 'n' B, rock, blues or bluegrass, when you walked on stage, you sang your own song.

Bob Dylan has enjoyed a long and prolific career, and we are the lucky beneficiaries of that. His well-spring of songs, apparently fed by an infinite aquifer, has influenced every contemporary songwriter, and his book, "Chronicles: Volume One," is as creative as any of his tunes. Everyone dances beneath the diamond sky of a favorite Dylan song or lyric – or more likely, many favorites.

I have lived in an age that has seen an explosion of hyper-talented artists: Aretha, Ella, Jimi, Miles, Pete, Basie, Dolphy, Ellington, Pavarotti, Sondheim, Ray Charles, Bill Evans, Ali Akbar Khan, Niels-Henning Ørsted Pedersen, Marc Russo, Stevie Wonder, the Beatles, a hundred others, and certainly, Bob Dylan.

"It had been almost like a marriage between three people. We all cared for each other very much – true friendship stands the test of time."

—Dionne Warwick
on working with songwriters
Burt Bacharach and Hal David

Dionne Sings

For most folks, their twenty-first birthday is a fairly important one. If you're over twenty-one, you probably remember what you did that day. If you're under twenty-one and you remember your twenty-first birthday, welcome to California. My twenty-first trip around the sun was in the 1960s, so I would have faint memory of it were it not for Dionne Warwick.

As an undergraduate at Penn State University in State College, Pennsylvania, I was also treasurer of "the world's largest jazz club," as we were fond of boasting, with thousands of dues-paying members.

How did we get that membership?

Every spring the club's board of directors would convene and decide on the acts that we would hire for the following fall's concerts. We'd try to book two headliners on the popular side of jazz; acts that could pull a mainstream crowd and fill the 7,500-seat rec hall.

We'd have folks like jazz flutist Herbie Mann. Mann singled on the charts in 1961 with "Comin' Home, Baby." We brought in jazz pianist Ramsey Lewis who had a crossover hit in 1965 with "The In-Crowd." We hosted Dave Brubeck, with Paul Desmond on alto sax,

Joe Morello on drums, and Ray Brown playing bass. Brubeck was the first jazz artist of his day to appeal to a non-jazz audience, and succeeded wildly with an instrumental in 5/4 time called "Take Five." It appeared on his 1959 album, *Time Further Out,* the first jazz album to sell over a million copies.

On the opening day of fall semester, when the student body trooped into the gym to sign up for clubs and activities, the jazz club had a booth. We'd sell tickets to the headliner concerts we had booked and we'd sell memberships in the club.

This was the deal. If you bought a membership in the jazz club, you got a reduction in ticket price. The reduction was so substantial that if you were buying only two tickets to one show, it was cheaper to pay for membership and get the two reduced-priced tickets than it was to buy two regular-priced tickets without membership. This was the original no-brainer; even the MBAs got it.

The revenues from these blockbuster shows enabled us to present many other, harder-core jazz and blues artists for concerts that were not always profitable. Over the years we hosted Muddy Waters; Thelonius Monk; John Coltrane; Cannonball Adderly with his brother, Nat, and saxist Charles Lloyd; Archie Shepp; Horace Silver with Wayne Shorter; Mose Allison with melody drummer Paul Motian; Andrew Hill; and Bill Evans with bassist Eddie Gomez and drummer Marty Morrell.

The jazz club was always profitable. At one point we had accumulated so much cash that, at my urging, we started giving it away to needy causes such as the Committee to Rescue Italian Art shortly after Florence and Venice experienced catastrophic flooding in 1966.

On my twenty-first birthday in October 1966, Dionne Warwick came to sing. Her show was sold out. Dionne was hugely popular in the '60s with lushly melodic and haunting hits that were written by Burt Bacharach and Hal David. "I Say a Little Prayer," was her best-known recording from that era, and the Grammy award-winning "Do You Know the Way to San Jose" her most popular. Dionne charted with "This Girl's in Love with You," and "Walk On By." She was the ideal interpreter for Bacharach-David's compositions, and their tunes the perfect settings for her silken voice. The three produced some long-memorable music.

I awoke on my birthday and was hardly aware that it was my birthday. The day of a major show is busy for folks involved in producing it. Everyone on the board was running around, and I don't recall going to a single class. But I also recall, as the day wore on, that neither mom and dad, nor my sister had phoned in to sing "Happy Birthday," a longtime family tradition and something they usually do before noon.

The show that evening was a wild success. Dionne's band was tight and her singing was top notch. She had superb communication with the crowd and sang every song we wanted to hear. By the time her performance was over, only one person, my girlfriend Susan, had said happy birthday to me all day.

After our concerts, the jazz club's board of directors had a tradition of hosting a party back at our apartment. We'd always invite the featured artists to join us. If you were a single musician staying overnight in State College following your gig, there was not a lot going on, so you might fall by and take a chance on a party with unknown college kids. And if you weren't in that position, well, probably not.

We approached Dionne after the show and invited her to the party. Dionne was with her mom, Lee, herself a well-known Gospel singer, and it was around midnight. Dionne is a regal and classy lady, and we didn't believe she would be interested in partying with us hippie jazz-club college students … but she was.

So we all went over to our place – a dozen folks were already there when we arrived – and commenced having a fine old time. Dionne was sociable, chatty, and supremely relaxed after her concert. This was remarkable in itself. Putting on a two-set show to a large crowd is exhausting, physically and emotionally. The energy reflected back from the crowd won't set you on a ten-mile jog, but it will keep you awake for at least two hours. Dionne was more than awake. Her effervescence and relaxed poise, at that time of night and following a large show, was impressive.

At half-past midnight, I was standing in the living room talking with Dionne and her mom, and I saw the president of the jazz club, Stan Lathan, the vice-president, Steve Gorn, and a half dozen other members of the board bringing a cake with birthday candles out of the kitchen. And I thought, "Well, that's nice. I wonder whose birthday it is? Because it sure isn't mine anymore."

And as they were bringing the cake over, Dionne started singing "Happy Birthday" to me!

She led everyone in singing happy birthday … to me!

That was Dionne and me. Me and Dionne! Cake. Dionne. Me. Dionne. Candles. Dionne singing, everyone singing "Happy Birthday." To me … with Dionne.

It was a shimmering slice of twenty–first-birthday heaven.

At about two in the morning, Dionne was sitting next to me and I was sitting next to the phone. She turned to me and said, "Bill, we'd like to go home now. Would you please call us an airplane?"

I'd never been asked to call anyone an airplane, or to call an airplane for anyone. But in a moment I went from thinking, She must be joking, to realizing, She's not.

So I said, "Sure, Dionne," picked up the local yellow pages and started looking under "A" for "Airplane."

Please understand that State College was a small town back then, with one tiny airport. The airport was so small that if a pilot was going to do a night landing, he had to radio ahead to the tower so they could run out and fire up the Tiki torches that lined the dirt runway.

Finally I found an air charter service, although I could tell by the mini-listing that it was a one-man shop: a single guy with a single-engine, four-seat Cessna, trying to make a buck. It was 2:00 AM Sunday morning, and I called the number. After eight rings a sleepy voice picked up.

"Could you fly two people to Philadelphia?"

"Hang on, I'll get my appointment book."

"They'd like to leave in twenty minutes."

"OK, I'm actually free then."

"How much?"

"A hundred dollars."

I turned to Dionne and told her that he wanted one hundred dollars – at that time the price of a first class, round trip ticket to Paris – and she said, "Fine." So we bundled up into the car and drove Dionne and her mom to the airport. Sure enough, someone had gone out and lit the Tiki torches. The airplane was tiny, and the pilot looked funny sitting at the controls in his pajamas and bathrobe, but we understood.

Dionne's mom got into the plane, and then Dionne. As I said good-bye to them – I was about to close the door –

Dionne waved to me and called out "Happy birthday, Bill!" over the engine's drone.

So Dionne, although other events from the '60s have slipped my mind, this one has not. Thank you so much for a glistening, twenty-first birthday. I don't believe I've heard "Happy Birthday" sung to me so sweetly since.

I sent this story to Dionne in August, two months before my birthday, asking for her blessing in publishing it. A few weeks later, I received this note from her:

Dear Bill,

Good luck with your book, and thank you for including me.

It'll soon be that time again so "Happy Birthday" in advance.

Dionne

What a thoughtful and sweet soul Dionne Warwick is.

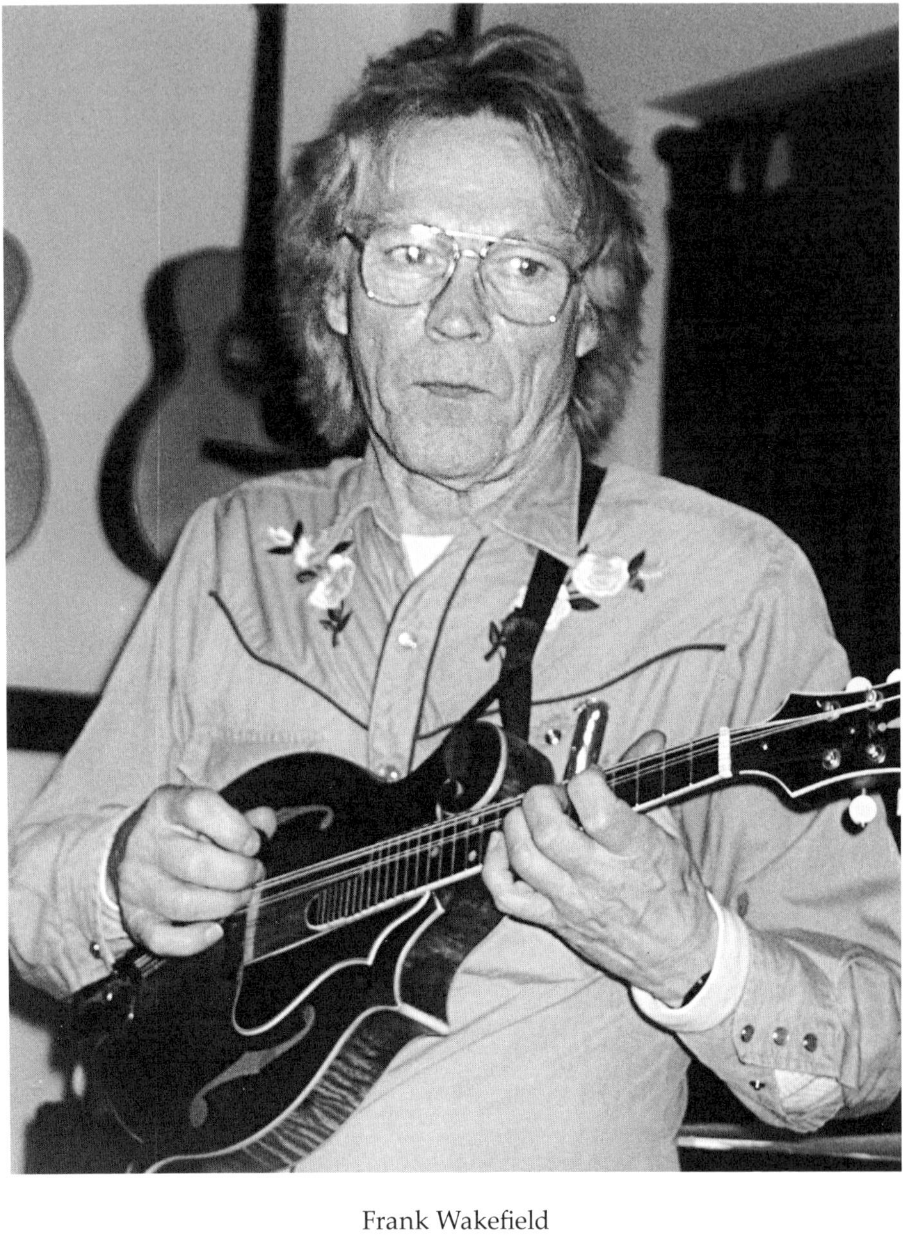

Frank Wakefield

Steve Swan Guitars, Kensington · November 16, 1997

Jesus Loves His Mandolin Player

I can still remember the first time I heard him play, forty-five years ago. His music physically hit me as I turned the corner to the theatre. The sound of his mandolin rang out against the red brick walls, hopped over some New England poplars, bounded up the streets of Providence Rhode Island, and stuck right in my ears.

His sound cut. It was woody, it was raw, and even a block away it was blazingly bright.

My ears popped. By now an avid, 22-year-old bluegrass banjo picker, I had come just to hear him play. I chased his sound 'round the side of the theatre and found him outside the stage door leading his band.

His scraggly blond hair framed a ruddy and well-traveled face. He was bent over his mandolin, pickin' and *gleefully* grinnin'. This was Frank Wakefield, the notorious and hellacious mandolinist.

His band was rehearsing one last tune, "Blackberry Blossom," before going on stage. Frank's group was tight, though I realized I played banjo a lick or two better than his banjoist. I didn't say anything of course; I just stood there, smiling broadly, enjoying the music.

They came to the end of the tune, and Frank's banjo man made a big mistake: he put his instrument down and wandered off to find the bathroom. I asked Frank if I could play a tune with him on the kid's banjo, and he said, "Sure, go ahead."

Frank's playing soared. Standing there pickin' with him, I realized that this was the first time I had played with anyone who had music in his veins. Frank was burning up with music. Melodies overflowed the *f*-holes of his old Gibson mandolin.

By the time the tune ended, Frank knew that I cut his banjoist. When the guy came back from the bathroom, Frank eased him out of the gig, and then talked him into letting me borrow his banjo to play the concert. I rehearsed one more tune with Wakefield's group, and then they called us to go on stage.

As we walked to the wings to be brought on, Frank asked me what I did and if I would like to go on the road with his band. I told him I was staying in Brown University graduate school to beat the Viet Nam draft, but playing with him sure beat that.

We shook on it.

In that moment I quit one graduate school and started another, got my first professional music job, walked on stage to play a sold-out concert with a musical fireball, and oh yes, exposed myself to the wartime Viet Nam draft.

That afternoon on stage, Frank taught me a lot.

A traditional bluegrass group's performance involves a stylized choreography with its roots in live stage shows and radio. With only one microphone for the entire band, players have to map out their moves in advance. You don't want to be stepping up to the mike to sing a verse at the same time the banjoist is swooping in, peghead first, to take a solo. You could get your eye poked.

But we didn't have time to rehearse the tunes or the moves. During the show Frank hovered in the back of the group and gestured me in and out of the lineup as my entrances came. Before each tune ended he would lean over and tell me the name of the next tune and the key it was in.

When a song was done and the applause had died, he'd turn to the audience and say something like:

"Thank ya s'much. Y'all make us feel so good when you give us a good hand like that, I swear ya do. And now we'd like to sign up for one that we're gonna put a hurtin' on. It's called 'John Hardy.' "

BAM! I had to nail my introduction as he said "Hardy," in the right key and tempo. On stage that day, Frank made it clear that this was what he expected of me.

After the third song, Frank introduced his band to the audience. When he came to me he said: "And on the 5-string banjo we got an ol' boy who's gonna be pickin' with me till our men come home from Viet Nam, cause that's the only way he's a gonna beat the draft. But why don'tcha make him welcome anyway … Bill Matnick."

What was that? It didn't matter. The flush of a hot spotlight hitting me and the crowd cheering felt terrific.

The audience ate us up and brought us back for an encore. Frank decided on the Bill Monroe instrumental, "Rawhide."

Everyone takes a solo on "Rawhide." So when my turn came I played my solo, and as I was putting the last four bars on it, I felt Frank come up behind me. As my chorus ended, he pushed my left hand off the banjo neck. I couldn't play with that hand! And Frank started fretting my banjo with his left hand while I was still picking the strings with my right.

It worked! The crowd broke into applause. They'd never seen anything like this.

I'd never seen anything like this, and I was doing it.

But it wasn't over. Still fretting my banjo and strumming his mandolin, Frank maneuvered his instrument so it was within my reach. And he gestured for me to play his mandolin with my free left hand.

Mind you, Frank didn't know if I played mandolin or not. He was relying on the bluegrass tradition that every picker picks a little on the three fretted instruments: guitar, banjo and mandolin. Fortunately, Frank was right. My dad was a mandolinist and there have been mandolins in my house all my life. So I reached under Frank's mandolin, grabbed the neck with my left hand and started fretting the notes that Frank was picking. This locked us in a schizophrenic embrace that split me in half: I was a banjo man on one side of me and a mandolinist on the other. I'd known him for only a couple of hours, but Frank had already taken me to a place I had never been before.

As we hit the first beat of the last sixteen bars, Frank pulled one more surprise. He spurred the tune into double-time tempo, hell-bent-for-leather. We galloped to the ending, harmonized on a shave and a haircut, and ended the tune with a chop that exploded the crowd. We exited to thunderous cadence clapping and two-fisted whistling, the cap to a thrilling concert.

~

I went on the road with Frank's band for about a year. We played East Coast coffeehouses, college concerts and folk music clubs. In New York, we headlined at the legendary Gerde's Folk City for a week; Emmylou Harris opened for us. As I got to know him better, I saw why Frank himself is as legendary as his mandolin playing. He is well known for a kind of talking, "Frank-talk," which relies heavily on double negatives, non-sequiturs, and plain ol' nonsense.

For instance, I might pick up the phone one day and hear Frank on the other end saying, "Good-bye Frank, this is Bill speakin'. Let's not have dinner with Smoke Dawson tonight at the Cafe Lena. Hello?"

My response would have been, "Good-bye Bill, this is Frank speakin'. OK, let's not have dinner tonight at eight o'clock. … Hello?"

Frank can also twist the facts about an event until his telling of it may be somewhat at odds with reality. Here is an example:

There is a well-known story about Frank and his priceless, 1923 Gibson, Lloyd Loar-signed F-5 mandolin. (Loar contracted as a master instrument designer at the Gibson Mandolin-Guitar Manufacturing Co. in the early 1900s; he famously signed and dated the F-5 model mandolins whose tops and backs he hand tuned.)

At a recording session many years ago, Frank, frustrated over how the work was going, allegedly threw his mandolin to the floor … hard.

It must have been electrifying to have been there. Acoustic musicians coddle their instruments, clean them after each playing, and sometimes talk to them. Throwing an axe (as an instrument is referred to) is unheard of, and speaks to just how broken up Frank must have been about the session.

But the session's producer just bent down, picked up the instrument, which miraculously had landed undamaged, and handed it back to a chin-on-his-chest Frank.

Recently, I saw Frank and the producer together, and I heard Frank say to him: "You remember that time I was at

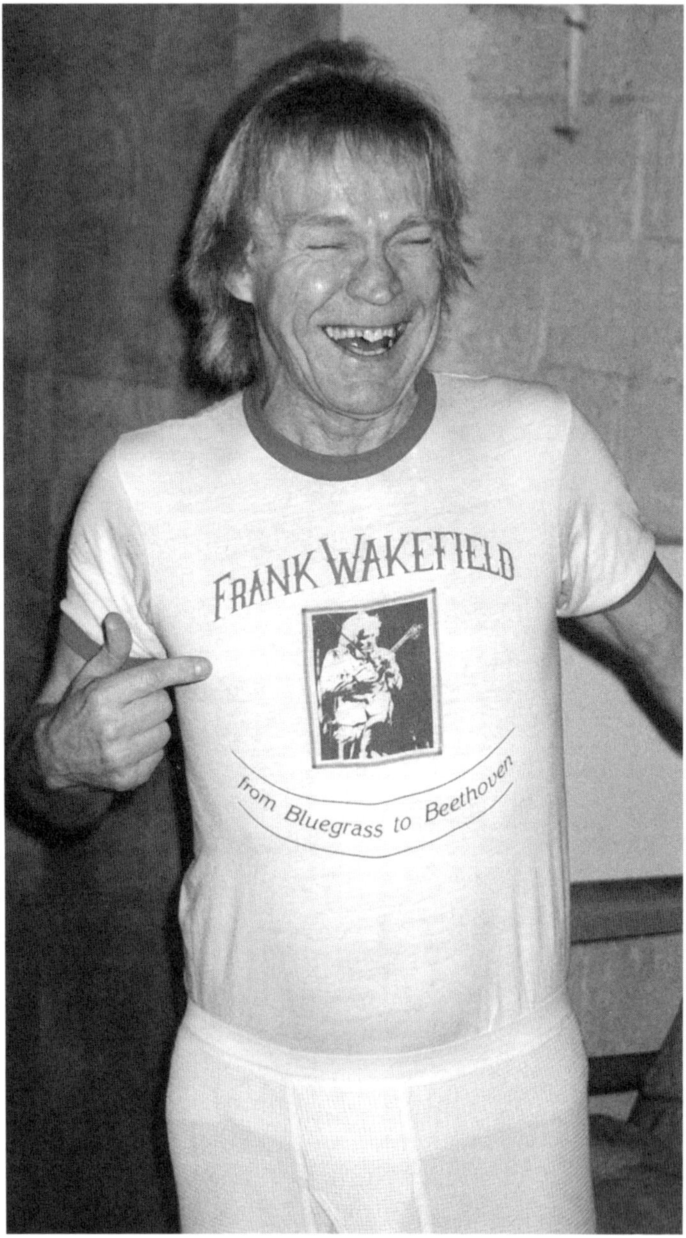

Frank Wakefield Revealed

Freight & Salvage, Berkeley · November 18, 1997

your house and you threwed your guitar down the staircase?"

Well, this is Frank talking "Frank-talk."

As I told Wakefield the first time I met him, I was in Brown University's graduate school with a student deferment. Joining his band ended that. I was draft-eligible the entire year I played with him. (A week after I left Frank's group to discover California, Uncle Sam sent me a notice to come in for my physical exam, which I flunked.)

But Frank, who I reckoned was pro-war, got it in his head from our first talk that I had joined his group to evade the draft. Frank had it that right up there on the government's list of bona fide, draft-deferrable gigs, along with "Napalm Bomb Design," was "Pickin' Banjo In Frank Wakefield's Group."

It was such an outlandish claim that I never tried to straighten him out on it. I was Frank's draft-dodger banjo-picker from that first concert until I left his group, and I will admit, sometimes his ribbing got to me.

In the many years since, I've rarely seen Frank Wakefield; mostly we've lived on opposite coasts. But in 1991 he came to play Mill Valley's own Sweetwater, an internationally renowned nightclub, Mill Valleyians want you to know.

Now it may seem to you that Frank is in his own little corner of the music world; the mandolin tunes he has written are uniquely his. Fiercely bluegrass at their core, some have also been called "classical." His tunes can stop, ... and start up again on an offbeat. Some of his compositions can change time signature for a few measures and then go back to the original time. This is fairly unusual for bluegrass.

He wrote a song cycle he called "Jesus Loves His Mandolin Player." And surely He must, Frank, because some of those tunes, and I mean this in the highest complimentary sense, are from somewhere else.

A number of rock and pop stars were brought up on bluegrass and have a direct connection to Frank. In the house that evening were Maria Muldaur, who famously sang "Midnight on the Oasis," David Grisman, Wavy Gravy, and David Nelson of the Jerry Garcia Band and the New Riders of the Purple Sage. All have performed with Frank at one time or another, as have Emmylou Harris and Linda Ronstadt.

There were two sets that night at Sweetwater. In the first, Frank played a number of mandolin instrumentals. Some were classics by Bill Monroe, the father of Bluegrass music, and some, like, "New Camptown Races," were classics by Frank. Wakefield lifted the crowd out of their seats and got them dancing in the aisles. The applause was deafening as the band exited the stage. The set was a tribute to Frank's power with his mandolin.

Back stage during the break, Maria Muldaur rehearsed an old-timey song with Frank, his group, and me sitting in on string bass. It was written by Rosa Lee Watson, Doc Watson's wife, and is called "Your Long Journey."

Maria related that "the song came to Rosa Lee one day as she was cleaning house. The thought struck her as to what would happen if her husband Doc was called to heaven before she was." One of the most haunting songs in the American old-time repertoire, "Your Long Journey," usually sung as a male-female duet, goes like this:

God's given us years of happiness here,
Now we must part.
And as the angels come and call for you,
The pangs of grief tug at my heart.

Oh my darling,
My darling,
My heart breaks as you take
Your Long Journey.

Oh the days will be empty the nights so long
Without you my love.
And as God calls for you I'm left alone,
But we will meet in heaven above.

Oh my darling,
My darling,
My heart breaks as you take
Your Long Journey.

Fond memories I'll keep of happy ways
That on earth we trod.
And when I come we will walk hand in hand
As one in heaven in the family of God.

Oh my darling,
My darling,
My heart breaks as you take
Your long journey.

When the last note of the tune had died, the greenroom went silent. Finally someone said, "What an incredible song."

And someone else echoed, "Amen."

Then it was time for the last set at Sweetwater. I gave Frank a big hug and thanked him for all he had shown me: burning artistry, spontaneity, fiery performance, and a few licks on the 5-string to boot.

We had just started up the stairs – he was carrying his mandolin; I was two steps behind him toting my bass – when he turned around to me and said:

"Ya see. It was good that ya played with my band all them years and stayed out of the draft until the war was over."

I couldn't believe that a quarter century later, Frank was going to get on about Viet Nam again.

This time, I had to say something. I warily looked up at him and asked, "Oh really, Frank? Tell me, why is that?"

He said, "Well, ya didn't go die in some gol-dern war. And now you're here with us tonight to play beautiful music."

I played with Doc Watson once, at San Francisco's Great American Music Hall when he was passing through town backed by Bobby Kimmel, the bass player with Linda Ronstadt and the Stone Poneys. In the dressing room between sets I played a tune or two with Doc, and then again on stage. It was an honor.

Doc passed on May 29, 2012, taking his long journey before his wife, Rosa Lee, just as she had sung he would, decades before. She died six months later, on November 22, 2012. I'm sure Rosa Lee walks hand in hand with Doc in heaven.

Frank Wakefield has been living in Saratoga Springs, New York, for some time now. He's seventy-eight. His lungs collapsed a few years back, which was followed by an operation, so he's not much on the road.

When I asked him if he was still pickin', he said, "If I quit doing that I'd die right away."

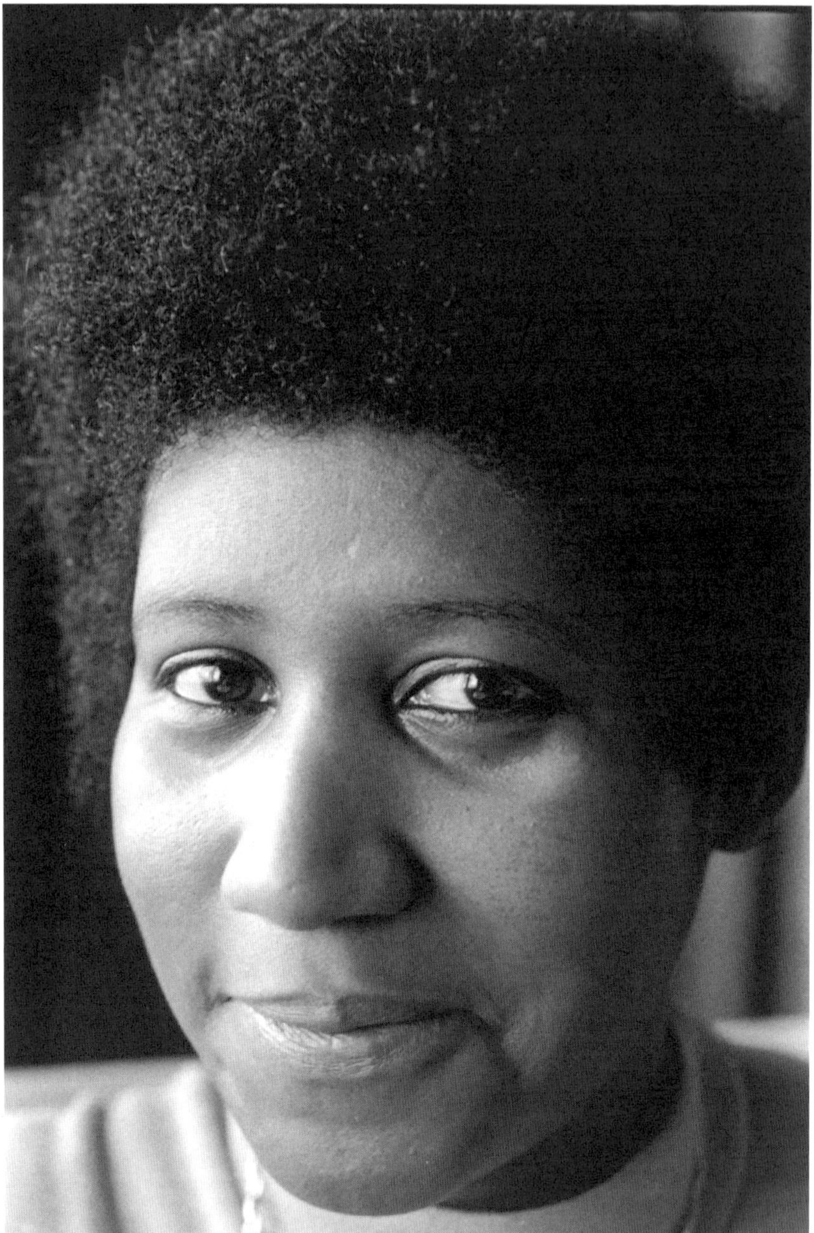

Aretha Franklin

Magenta Suite, Fairmont Hotel, San Francisco · February 1971

By Annie Leibovitz

Aretha Speaks

There are some people in California who are so deeply into astrology they can tell your sign by the shape of your face. They *know* that Johnny Carson was a Libra, because Johnny Carson's face had that "Libra" shape.

Well, I just don't see it.

And then I met Aretha Franklin.

I was free-lancing for *Rolling Stone* in 1971 when I heard that Aretha was coming to play the Fillmore Auditorium. Aretha defined the soul sound of that era with hits such as "Respect," and chain, chain "Chain of Fools." There was the wailing "Dr. Feelgood" in the morning, and the women's anthem, "Do Right Woman," among many others.

I asked my boss, Jon Carroll, if I could interview her for *Rolling Stone.*

He laughed at my request. He told me that Aretha was said to be a tough interview; it was not easy to get her to open up. Rumor had it that she felt mistreated by a 1968 cover story in a major weekly magazine, and she was talking to the press even less than usual.

That didn't bother me; I idolized Aretha and asked Jon to set it up.

He set it up.

Jon sent the renowned photographer Annie Leibovitz to do the shooting. I was glad he was sending a pro like Annie, because as I stood outside the Magenta Suite of the Fairmont Hotel where Aretha was staying, my knees were literally shaking.

But I had done my homework. I had chased down a dozen Aretha Franklin albums, listened to them carefully and drawn up a list of questions to ask her: questions about her recordings, her music, … her life, in a well-prepared, two-hour interview.

Annie and I knocked and were let in by someone who was probably hired to do just that. Immediately, our eyes were assaulted by magenta everywhere we looked. Rugs, walls, furniture … everything was a shade and design of magenta.

And there was Aretha, seated in a magenta lounge chair, surrounded by an entourage of twenty people. I had never seen an entourage before, but as soon as I saw this group of people hanging on Aretha's every word, I knew: *this* was an entourage.

Annie and I made our introductions and while she started clicking away furiously, I got out my notebook, switched on the tape recorder, and started to interview Aretha Franklin, the Queen of Soul.

Whatever my boss had said about Aretha was wrong. She was not a tough interview; for me, she was impossible.

I asked easy questions, like, "How are you enjoying San Francisco?" and she said:

" … Good."

I asked open-ended questions, like "Tell me about your six years of recording at Columbia Records."

And Aretha said, " … Good."

The only thing she wanted to talk about was her soon-to-be-released album, *Young, Gifted and Black*. This was the only album Aretha had made in the last decade that I hadn't been able to get a hold of. Sure, it hadn't been released yet.

I went through my two-hour list of questions in seven minutes flat. Each elicited a one-sentence answer, max. Annie tried to help me out, she was a trouper, but I never got the momentum going with Aretha.

I closed my notebook, turned off the tape recorder, and stood up, indicating the interview was over. Instantly, Aretha dropped her guard and started talking nonstop about the sightseeing and shopping she'd been doing in San Francisco. Since the entourage was glued to her every word, the room soon got into a group discussion, and the topic moved to astrology.

Then, as we did in those heady days of the early '70s, everyone started asking everyone else, "What's your sign? … What's *your* sign?"

Aretha turned to me. She said, "I know what your sign is, Bill."

The room went dead. For the first time since we had arrived, Annie put her camera down.

I smiled. It takes most people twelve tries to hit that I'm a Libra. I was sure she didn't have a clue.

"What sign am I, Aretha?"

"Bill, you're a Libra."

"Aretha, no one ever gets that! How could you tell?"

"By the shape of your face."

"The shape of my face?"

"Why yes," Aretha said. "It's just like Johnny Carson's."

"You don't love someone because they're perfect, you love them in spite of the fact that they're not."

— Jodi Picoult
My Sister's Keeper

What's a Girl Like You . . .

Our big band rock group, Fried Soup, had a one-week gig in Atlanta in 1971. As we drove into the parking lot of our hotel, we saw a working girl, working the street. Ultra mini-skirt, black fishnet stockings, black stilettos, tight blouse popped open, the way she held her body, the way she sashayed – a blind man couldn't have missed it.

But Tom, our songwriter and guitarist, missed it. As soon as he saw her he said, "Whoa, baby! Would you look at this gal! Is she a sight or what? Hey guys, dig this gorgeous chick!"

We rolled our eyes, not believing that he wasn't seeing her for what she was. But Tom had spent most his life in a West Virginia hollow and had emerged a tad naive. No one felt like educating him on this one, so we egged him on, "Yeah Tom, she's one heck of a woman. Look at her strut. Oh yeah, gorgeous."

At the hotel's front desk, they divided our ten-man group into five rooms spread out over the second and third floors. We all crowded into the elevator where we met Pops, the elevator man. He knew where it all was in the hotel. Girls? Floors three and four. Their pimps? Same floors. Drugs? Which ones? Coke? Pot? Heroin? Pops knew it all and got tipped big to make connections. He was quiet as fog, and knew more.

Returning to the hotel at 3:00 AM after our first Saturday night at the club, we ran into our parking lot lady in the lobby. Tom, my roommate, wanted to invite her to our room for a glass of wine.

"Her name's Linda," he said, "and she's real nice."

I was reluctant, but he was excited about the prospect of hanging out with her, so I said "Sure."

The three of us talked about this and then that, and towards the bottom of the wine bottle she told us her story.

I was born in a town in Iowa. It was so small that if you looked for it at the end of summer, with the crops in and the wind blowing the topsoil around, well, you'd miss it altogether. And if you said that there was nothing to do in my town, you'd have said too much.

My dad was a drunk. Mom tried to hang onto him, and drank with him just to keep him from running off. I was in high school, waiting tables in the coffee shop, waiting for my life to begin, and just … waiting.

Then one day a man came in for breakfast, a salesman, said he sold tractors and combines. He was wearing a white shirt, and a blue vest and tie that matched. He had black loafers with tassels on them, and I just knew he hadn't bought them at Sears and Roebuck, that they must have come from a real store in a big city. He was not at all like the meatheads I went to school with. He was a real man.

I remember when I came over to his table to take his order, why, right off he was actin' real sweet to me and askin' my name and telling me how pretty I was and telling me he had never met a girl like me before.

When I brought him his breakfast, he didn't touch it at all for talking with me. He wanted to know all about me and where I lived and how old I was. I was almost sixteen, but I told him I was seventeen. And I could see that he liked me a lot.

Then I had to wait on another customer. But when he had finished his breakfast, I came over to his table and asked him if he wanted anything else.

He said yes, there was something else he wanted to know. "What's a girl like you doin' in a town like this? You look so fine dear, you're wasting time here. This ain't no life for you, miss. Let me take you away, away to New York town. Silks and satin, gold and platinum, dress you in a Gucci gown."

Well, no man had ever said that to me! It sounded like poetry.

So right then and there, I untied my apron, tossed it on the counter, and walked out the door with him. Didn't say goodbye to nobody, just walked out. We were so wrapped up in each other, I don't think he even remembered to pay the check.

We got in his car and drove straight east, all the way to New York City! I had never been out of Iowa; I'd never been out of the county, and here I was in New York City. I couldn't believe I was there. It was like out of a dream.

He took me to a fancy hotel that looked out at a big park smack in the middle of Manhattan, and that's an island, ya know. Well, there was a doorman at the front door, all dressed up like it was England or something. The lobby was just like in the movies, only bigger. He got us a bunch of rooms all together – he called it a sweet – and there was a huge bed in every room and the windows went from the floor to the ceiling and they all looked out over the park.

We went down for dinner and the restaurant was just like in the movies too, with these white starched tablecloths and white starched linen napkins that were standing up at each setting like a grain elevator. When we sat down at the table, well, the waiters were all over us like hounds on a hare, and one of them even took the napkin and opened it up and put it on my lap. Can you imagine?

Then they brought us this menu and the menu looked like … well I don't even know how to say. It was huge and printed on thick, creamy paper and there was gold letters all over it. And the things they had on the menu! There were snails on the menu, and I didn't even know you could eat snails. There was a steak from New York and I didn't even know they raised beef cattle in New York City. He told me I could order whatever I wanted and not to mind how much it cost, and that he'd take care of it. He ordered a bottle of wine and when it came I couldn't even read the label cause it was all in some other language or something.

But when we came to leave the hotel the next morning we left real early. He told me to be real quiet 'cause we didn't want to wake no one up. But as we tiptoed out of the elevator and across the lobby, why there was some ol' boy at the front desk, and he must have seen us 'cause all of a sudden he says in a real loud voice, "Is monsieur checking out?"

And Rob was real cool. He just walked over to this guy and he said, "Yes, we're leaving."

And the guy said, "Will monsieur be paying in cash, check, or credit card?"

And Rob said, "I won't be paying at all, cause I don't have a dime on me."

Well, I about peed in my pants.

Rob laughed like this was a big joke, but the guy behind the counter wasn't laughing at all, and in two seconds flat two big guys took us by the arms into the manager's office and the manager said we owed him five hundred dollars.

Five hundred dollars? Can you imagine! I'd never heard

of so much money. Rob said he didn't have five hundred dollars and could we work it off in the kitchen?

Then the manager laughed. He said, "Work it off in the kitchen? You can work it off in jail."

Faster than that they got the New York police in there and they hauled us out to two paddy wagons. They threw me into one with a dozen gals in it. And they all got heavy makeup on and red red lipstick and short skinny skirts. I looked at them real funny, and they looked at me real funny.

And then one of 'em said to me, she said, "What's a girl like you, doing in a dump like this? Country bumpkin, I'll tell ya somethin', this ain't no place for you miss. They're takin' us away, away to a dirty cell. Rats and bugs there, no hugs or love there. It ain't no place for you, miss."

So I told 'em my story, just like I'm tellin' you. I told them I needed five hundred dollars to get my man outta jail, and I needed it real fast. Some of 'em laughed; they laughed at me. But I'll tell you, it wasn't funny to me. It wasn't funny at all.

The other gals, they hushed them up, and then there was this quiet. They started lookin' at me real funny like, lookin' at me from head to toe. And then these gals they started lookin' at each other.

And then one of them, the oldest girl there, she said to me, "I know how you can get that money, honey. Stick with me and I'll turn your money green."

And that's how it all got started, right there. And ya know, it's funny, but I never saw that boy again.

"How did you end up here?" Tom asked. He had understood her story, but it didn't matter. He was nuts for this girl.

"I had a big fight with this man that was runnin' me in New York. He said he was gonna kill me. So I lit out of there fast as I could. The next bus that was leaving was going to Atlanta, so I got on it and here I am."

It was getting early, the sun would be coming up soon,

and I was ready to crash. But when Linda went to powder her nose, Tom asked me if I would bunk in one of the other rooms that night, and I said sure.

Well, the other guys had locked their doors, gone to sleep, so I grabbed a couple of blankets and a pillow from the hall linen closet and made a pallet on the floor outside our room. As I drifted off, I heard Tom pickin' on his guitar, and singing to her,

What's a gal like you,
Doing in a dive like this?
Carrin' on an'
Honkey-tonkin' an'
It ain't no life for you miss.

Let me take you away,
Away to our sunshine home.
Lacy curtains,
And I'm certain,
A baby of our own.

No man had ever said that to Linda either, I imagined.

~

When I got up late next morning, Tom and Linda were gone. They had scrawled a message with Linda's red red lipstick on the bathroom mirror: "Gone home. Love, Tom and Linda." On the sink, Linda had left the lipstick, and Tom, his favorite flat-pick. We finished the gig without him, sad that he was gone, happy for where they were going.

The band broke up after Atlanta and we all went our own ways. Every now and again I get a letter from Linda and Tom. They settled in upstate Vermont, a change in scene for both of them. They had a boy, Dan, and two years later, a girl they named Patti. Tom pretty much gave up the road, though he does play local gigs. So he's still pickin', still grinnin', and he sings a song to her every night:

What's a girl like you,
Doin' with a guy like me?
I feel so happy,
With Dan and Patti,
And you babe here with me.

You just take me away,
Away to our happy home.
Milk and honey,
And it's funny,
A family of our own.
A family of our own.

Subplot ~ Judy Davis

Judy Davis was a legendary American voice teacher. She coached – ready for this? – Sammy Davis Jr., Frank Sinatra, Barbra Streisand, the Kingston Trio, Peter, Paul & Mary, Judy Garland, Mary Martin, Jerry Garcia, Grace Slick, and other not-famous folks such as me. I took lessons from her because, though I loved to sing, I didn't know anything about the technique of singing and was concerned that I might be abusing my voice.

Judy put me at ease on my first lesson. "I'm a plumber," she said. "I fix pipes." She was able to help her students fix their pipes because Judy had fixed her own. When she was nineteen, a tonsillectomy damaged her vocal cords, fogging her speech. To overcome this, she studied the vocal apparatus, starting with *Gray's Anatomy*. She researched the mechanism of the voice, and came to understand it thoroughly. But she gave up on singing as a career.

Taking what she had learned from her studies, Judy started teaching voice. In this she became legendary, holding forth at her studio on College Avenue in Oakland, across the street from a supermarket. Her mother was the receptionist, and sat in an office on the left. Judy's studio, with a 5′ 7″ Yamaha baby grand piano, was on the right. Down the hall was a dance studio with wrap-around mirrored walls and ballet barres.

Judy guided me through every step of her singing program. She started tearing my voice apart by getting me in touch with every organ involved in singing. I became so conscious of my tongue, lips and teeth, my diaphragm and breathing, that I became tongue-tied. I had to re-learn how to use the vocal apparatus that I had taken for granted.

As she started reassembling my voice, she gave me vocalises (singing exercises) to practice, all her own creations. The exercises combined speaking carefully enunciated vowels with singing scales, modulating the vowels *en route*, creating sounds that grated the ear and contorted the face.

Judy taught me how to move sound creation out of the throat (where it scuffed the vocal cords) and into the mouth. I was finally able to make all the vowel sounds with just the tongue, lips and teeth, and to flow from the sharpest aa's and ee's to the broadest oo's.

Soon she had me singing songs such as "Blue Moon," "Embraceable You," and "Moonlight in Vermont" as exercises in articulation, breathing, and phrasing. But Judy did not want me, or any of her students, to actually perform these tunes. And that was fine with us, because by the time *Judy* was done working you through those songs, *you* were done with them too. Any nightclub singer who will not indulge a request for "Blue Moon," even though the promised tip is generous, was probably a Judy Davis student.

Judy was particularly obsessed with vowels, their correct enunciation and placement (where the vibrations hit the hard palate). She drilled me incessantly on how to exactly create vowel sounds. Here's one early homework assignment: "Practice saying 'He' eight times at a shot, one hundred times a day, at a modest spoken pitch. Direct the vibrations into the ridges of the gums. SMILE! Tongue relaxed against teeth. Rattle the teeth for a BIG VIBRATION."

A hundred times a day.

If you couldn't sing the assigned exercise at the next lesson, she gave you the lesson again instead of moving forward, and her private lessons were not cheap.

She encouraged me to work at all aspects of the business of singing, and to play out (perform publicly) as much as I could, wherever I could – piano bars, clubs, weddings, picnics. She urged her students to be entertaining and learn performance skills. "Remember to smile!" she always said. She wanted us to be professional singers, and the more money we made from it, the better.

Singing involves the entire being: body, spirit, heart, and mind. This whole-body devotion to singing usually has an extroverting effect on the singer, and these lessons had that effect on me.

Judy's most stunning lesson was on subplot. She primed you about that session for months. You were in the Judy Davis big-time when she gave you this lesson, and in September 1973, it arrived for me.

She started by saying, "Have you ever read a reviewer who said that a singer had 'done her homework'?"

"Of course."

"What do you think it means?"

"I'm not sure."

"It means the singer had constructed a subplot – a story – to help her express each lyric. In other words, she had 'done her homework.' "

Judy said that a singer must create a replicable path into the song that will enable her to consistently convey the emotions of that song each time she sings it. The singer does not want to bring the trauma of her dog's dying that day, or any other emotion she is going through, into the song. To accomplish this, she must study the song's lyrics and create a story that will answer Who, What, When, Where and Why about the lyrics.

The story leads into the song; its last words segue into the first words of the lyric. The subplot starts in the past and continues into the present as the singer sings the words of the song.

The story has at least two characters, the person singing, and the person being sung to. It is the singer's personal subplot that specifies the "who" and "to whom." Is a girl singing this song? How old is she? Who is she singing to? A boy? How old is he? What does each do for a living? Where are they? What led her to this moment and this lyric? The more the singer knows about this, the better, because the subplot's characters and narrative must fit every word of the lyric.

Through subplot, the singer *becomes* the character who is singing the song. Mastery of subplot creation, Judy said, is what enables singers to make successful transitions to acting more frequently than actors transition to singing. A great singer knows that the way to inhabit a song is to become the song's character through subplot.

The accomplished singer tells a story to the audience, a story that begins with the subplot. This was an important rule for Judy, one she repeated many times: "You don't sing *at* your audience. You tell the song *to* them."

"The music may begin here" – Judy held her left hand in front of her left shoulder – "and end here" – she held her right hand in front of her right shoulder – "but the singer begins way over there and ends way out there" – and she extended her hands until they were a yard apart.

For her first subplot homework assignment, Judy had me write out the lyrics for the Ruby and Bloom classic,

"Give Me the Simple Life," a song about the singer's longing for family, love and laughter. At the next lesson I was to tell her my subplot and then segue into telling her the song's lyrics in one long story.

"She won't like your first try," all her advanced students cautioned. "Forget about bringing in your 'Simple Life' subplot and her falling for it. That ain't gonna happen."

Inspired by this challenge, I worked hard on "Give Me the Simple Life," and told my subplot to her with sweaty confidence.

Judy tore it apart. I can't remember what she said; it was too painful.

An example of a subplot? Here, with a tip of the hat to Judy, is my take on a song you may know.

"Hey, babe. Open the door, would ya please? I know I said we were going to get married next month. But I'm pushing thirty, and this tour with the Stones is the biggest opportunity I've ever had, maybe the best offer I'll ever get. I can't turn it down. Look, I've got to get us out of Georgia, babe. You don't want to be waiting tables all your life, do you? Yeah, I know this tour could go on for months, maybe a year. I know that. But we can get married when I get back, if you would just open the door and talk to me. Look, the taxi is pulling up. My bags are packed. I'm ready to go. I'm standing here outside your door. ..."

You get the picture. Somewhere in there, the story seamlessly became the John Denver lyric. (Well, hopefully it was seamless.)

I never dreamed that the great singers prepared for performance by creating subplots. As I left Judy's studio in a daze, I walked across the street to the supermarket without looking for traffic, and almost got hit from both directions.

Judy Davis didn't teach classical or operatic singing; she taught American popular voice. Get full control of your vocal apparatus, she preached. With your diaphragm supplying air, create sound with your tongue, lips, and teeth.

Build a subplot for every song you perform and address it in your mind before you begin singing. Above all, do not sing at the audience. Tell the lyrics to them.

But in all the voice lessons I took from Judy, I never once heard her sing.

"For three hundred years, classical music has been Schubert, Brahms, Bach, Beethoven, Mozart. Today's classical composers are Cole Porter, Jerome Kern, Irving Berlin, George Gershwin.... Three hundred years from now this music will still be played."

—Stéphane Grappelli

Standing Room Only ~ Jack Brooks

This story, about my love affair with the American musical, begins with my introduction to the art form by one Jack Brooks, and follows my education in this genre, pausing for discourse, personalities, and anecdotes along the way. Hopefully, by the story's conclusion, when I return to Jack, you will understand my love of this uniquely American art.

Jack Brooks married more times than any other man I've ever known: He stood at the altar six times.

More importantly, he always had a line of women waiting to be the next Mrs. Jack Brooks. At one point he was married to soon-to-be-divorced wife *x*, had soon-to-be fiancé *y* in the wings, and girlfriend *z* out on the loading dock. It was standing room only. Jack couldn't make love to a woman unless he was married to her, and fortunately, he committed easily.

To a man's eye – but what do men know about these things – Jack was not a particularly handsome guy. Musicians in the band marveled that in spite of his apparent unattractiveness, he attracted *many* women. We didn't see what the ladies saw in him, and it was important that we did. How to succeed with gals is crucial single-guy lore. If Jack had an angle, it would be a good one to know.

The story I recall is that Jack was a matinee star of the Broadway musical stage. That is, he filled in on those Saturday or Sunday matinees that the star couldn't, wouldn't, or just didn't want to perform. So he played some big Broadway shows such as *Camelot,* where during the 1960's he understudied Robert Goulet as Sir Lancelot. Some time after that he made his escape to the Coast.

I met Jack when I played in his cabaret group that he named Standing Room Only. "SRO," as we called ourselves, opened the Holiday Inn Golden Gateway. That is, we were the first entertainers to play the hotel's main room when it debuted in 1974.

SRO was four actor/singers on stage in costume, a piano trio in the pit, plus a sound and light man. Importantly, Jack had rounded up "angels," as backers are called in the theater business. So the show's costs – the eight-person troupe, arrangements, props, costumes, and a secretary – were all paid for in advance. The backers were well rewarded for their risks, as I recall. For the year or so that we were at the Golden Gateway, SRO filled the 500-seat room on most nights we played.

What did Standing Room Only do? During any one-hour show, we presented the essence of one Broadway musical. The troupe acted out the show's plot and sang all its hit tunes that would fit, while Jack supplied narration as needed. When the plot called for more than four characters, one or more of the actors would duck off stage for a costume change. We had forty musicals in our repertoire starting with Rudolf Friml's 1924 hit operetta, *Rose-Marie,* and ending in 1970 with the first rock musical, *Hair.* We did two musicals a night, one at 9:00 PM and another at midnight.

At the 10:30 show we took requests, boasting that we could perform at least one song from any Broadway musical that had enjoyed a run of five hundred or more performances. To Jack's credit, the crowd never stumped us. An animated, passionate guy – passionate about the theater – his large love of the American musical was contagious. Everyone who worked with him caught the fever, me included.

Before Standing Room Only, I dismissed the American musical as American pap. I was way wrong. The Broadway musical tells the American story and bares the American soul. It gives us the most memorable and lyrical American popular songs, created by our country's most skilled composers and lyricists.

Jack became my Broadway guru, and taught me about the musical and its foremost songwriters, starting with Irving Berlin. Called the "Dean of American composers," Berlin wrote some 1,500 songs, including "God Bless America" and "Easter Parade."

Cole Porter was one of Jack's favorite composers. A genius of witty and bright, Cole penned the iambic tetrameter, "*We settle down as man and wife, to solve the riddle called married life.*"

Amen, Cole.

George and Ira Gershwin wrote *Porgy and Bess,* the premier American opera of the early 20th century. Jerome Kern wrote some seven hundred tunes, including the classic "Old Man River," a number that Jack loved to sing. Learner and Lowe wrote the delicious *My Fair Lady,* while Rogers and Hammerstein wrote almost everything else – *Oklahoma, Carousel, South Pacific, The King and I, The Sound Of Music* – during the 1940s and '50s, the "Golden Age" of the American musical. Jack put every one of their hit shows in SRO's repertoire.

West Side Story, with music by Leonard Bernstein and lyrics by Stephen Sondheim, also figured in our master set list. Sondheim is the most celebrated and will be the most enduring musical theater composer and lyricist of our era. His writing changed the sound of the American musical. At least two of his creations, *Sweeney Todd* and *Sunday in the Park with George,* are American masterworks, and stand shoulder-to-shoulder with *Show Boat, South Pacific,* and *Carousel.*

The music of American stage and screen shows from the 1930s to the '60s – the era that Standing Room Only performed – is known as the "Great American Songbook." Cabaret singers call it by its acronym, the "GAS." Jazz musicians refer to these tunes (with the addition of some jazz classics) as "standards."

The ballads of these Songbook composers – recall your favorite version of Harold Arlen's "Over the Rainbow" – bring chills every time you hear them. Their songs of good cheer – listen to Ray Charles singing "Oh what a beautiful morning!" – are exuberantly sky-high. Their expression of the human condition surpassed that of the greatest poets, as these writers were themselves bards who wedded their verses to music. In this vein, it was Cole Porter who asked, in a poignant marriage of words and music, *"What is this thing called love?"*

The GAS composers created a new music genre of melodic finesse, harmonic sophistication, and lyrical depth, one that, for many people, has not been surpassed.

Through Jack Brooks and Standing Room Only I became interested in writing a musical about a big band, and started scouring the library for books on creating musicals. There were very few at the time, most of them written by one Lehman Engle. The books noted that he taught show writing at his Musical Theatre Workshop through the auspices of Broadcast Music, Inc. I called BMI's headquarters and found that Lehman was still offering his workshops in New York and Los Angeles. With Jack's encouragement –

he told me that Lehman was a legendary Broadway figure – I made half a dozen trips to L.A. to sit at the master's feet and learn about writing musicals.

Lehman was a Broadway show conductor for decades, and directed Cole Porter's comeback hit musical, *Kiss Me Kate,* as well as *Li'l Abner* and *Wonderful Town.* Incredibly, he also conducted the original production of *The Cradle Will Rock,* an historical show in New York theater that had a legendary opening night. (Tim Robbins recreated that evening in his film, *Cradle Will Rock,* with actor Steven Tyler playing Lehman.) In all, Lehman won four Tony Awards for "Best Conductor and Musical Director." Then they discontinued the award.

During those years that Lehman waved a baton at the pit orchestras he led, he was watching the show in all its dimensions: book, lyrics, acting, dancing, and music. He watched what made one musical a hit and what made another a flop.

Lehman recorded what he learned in the books he authored, and taught it at his workshops. He told us that although the rewards of a hit musical were immense, writing one was the toughest task a person could undertake. For this reason he said that a show should always be based on a pre-existing book or play, preferably a successful one. To attempt writing a show's book – its script – from scratch would be to add difficulty to an already difficult job. Hollywood knows this; most American movies we see have scripts that are based on pre-existing books, plays or shows, usually successful ones.

Lehman also believed in the time-honored plot of boy meets girl, boy is separated from girl, boy pursues girl, and boy and girl are reunited. Why? Because it worked.

One of Lehman's lessons was that the lyrics, melody and chords of a song had to be tightly coiled. If the lyric speaks of happiness or sadness, triumph or defeat, the melody and chords must support those emotions exactly, note for note.

One of his first workshop assignments was to write a song that expressed and supported one given emotion, one that he chose. Another was to write a love song that didn't use the word "love." Jack Brooks told me this was a classic exercise.

Lehman taught us this central truth about why we sing: we break into song when spoken words cannot express the emotions we are feeling. Sinatra, some have suggested, could have sung down the phone book and made you cry. But Sinatra would have known better: a list of names, void of emotional content, is just not worth singing. So, one of Lehman's toughest assignments was to write a song for the character Frankie Adams in Carson McCullers' *The Member of the Wedding* at a point in Act I where there was nothing to suggest that Frankie had much to sing about.

Lehman would pepper his workshops with stories about famous Broadway personalities. Michael Bennett, his best-known student, directed and choreographed the Broadway hit musical, *A Chorus Line,* and had a large hand in creating it. He was so thankful for Lehman's workshops, that on the teacher's 60th birthday, in 1970, Michael gave him 60 crisp, 100-dollar bills, fanned and framed.

We lived a few stories of our own at Standing Room Only. SRO gained a reputation for itself after a while, and theatre personalities would stop by the Golden Gateway to see a show, or to sit in and sing a song or three. One night, Gerome Ragni and James Rado, the librettist and lyricist of *Hair,* came by to catch our performance of their show.

And one evening, with much fanfare, a well-known Bay Area chanteuse came by to sing a few songs from the GAS. Possibly Jack was eyeing her as his next fiancée. He seemed eager for her performance to go well, and called the trio in to review her songs with her before the show. There was no piano in our suite, so she talked us through her charts, pointing out the twists and turns that we had to negotiate. There was nothing too difficult, and our trio was confident, even at ease, about backing her.

At 10:30 we took our places in the pit, the lights dimmed, our drummer, Marc, pressed a roll on the snare, and Jack brought the lady on with much ado. La Diva slid into the spotlight to fulsome applause, and as it died she turned to the trio and, *sotto voce,* said: "Oh, did I mention? Everything is up a minor third." Then she counted off the tune.

She was telling us that her songs were to be played in a higher key than was written, higher by an interval of a minor third. We were being asked to transpose the tunes on the spot. All the challenges of sight reading music – fast tempos, difficult or changing key and time signatures, tricky stops and starts – all pale next to the horrors of real-time transposition.

Learning to read music is learning to put the fingers of the hands precisely here, when you see that note there. Hammering in those associations for all the notes on the staff is what reading music is about: see this; do that … automatically and without thinking about it.

When you transpose music, you throw those associations out. Your mind and body must process each note you see to produce a different pitch than what is written. To our drummer, Marc, who played no pitched notes, there was no transposing to be done, so it was not an issue for him. But Bob, the pianist, and I were gaping into an existential maw; we could die in here. Every note we saw was wrong.

Marc looked over at us and laughed as he played us into the first measure. Bob jammed his face into the sheet music, opened his eyes wider than I'd ever seen, and – hats off to him – played very well. For myself, I put my left ring finger on the note that was written, but played what was under the left index finger on the adjacent string of my Fender bass, which is a minor third higher than the ring-finger note.

This worked most of the time, I hope.

We gasped a sigh of relief when our nightingale flew the stage. She never sailed into our spotlight again.

Another SRO story: One night, as we stepped off the stage at the conclusion of the first show, the tuxedoed headwaiter wheeled over a serving cart with an ice bucket that held a magnum of the hotel's finest Champagne cradled inside. Even in those days, a magnum of French bubbly must have cost the patron an injurious three-figure sum.

Our troupe was delighted, and we asked the headwaiter to show us to the donor of this generous gift. He led us to the table of a distinguished-looking couple from New Orleans, both in their seventies and having a rollicking good time. They were delighted that we dropped by and asked us to join their party.

We made our introductions, and then, in a legato Bayou drawl, the gentleman said, "Thelma and I were in N'awlins this morning having brunch on the veranda, and I said to her, 'Thelma, let's go to San Francisco and take in a show.' … And here we are!"

A gypsy breathes in the soul of all who ply the arts for a living. Casting your fate to your own creativity is a quantum jump of faith to a potentially wild and always unpredictable life that can impoverish or enrich you in many ways. Our troupe of gypsies recognized the gypsy in this man and wife. Having the financial resources for the undertaking, plus devotion to the arts and good times, they had taken off on a tear to a faraway city. To do what? To see a show, by God! What a capricious and delicious adventure.

When the gentleman declared, "And here we are!" our troupe burst out laughing. Wildly happy for them, we gladly toasted their triumph with their Champagne.

And they, as patrons of the arts – you don't travel two

thousand miles to San Francisco to take in a show unless you are experienced, moneyed patrons of the arts – were delighted to be hanging out with the group they were fated to be seeing that evening. For the while of a good long laugh, plus the downing of a magnum of French bubbles, the ten of us enjoyed a kinship of spirits who in our different ways had trusted providence to the angels.

Some years after my stint with Standing Room Only, I subbed on bass for Seth Evans in the San Francisco show, Beach Blanket Babylon. At the 1995 Grace Cathedral memorial for Steve Silver, Beach Blanket's founder and director, I ran into an old SRO alumna, Lisa.

A number of actresses passed through SRO's ranks. Some became Jack's girlfriends, and some of them became fiancées. The fiancées either married Jack, or failing that, quit. Lisa was one of these – girlfriend, fiancé, wife – I'm not sure which. Let's just say that she was an actress in Standing Room Only who became romantically involved with Jack.

At the time of Steve Silver's memorial, Jack Brooks had been deceased for a while, but in talking with Lisa about him I wanted to tread carefully. There had been rivalries between the ladies in Jack's life. He likely left a trail of unhappy women that was as long as his trail of divorcees. After reminiscing about SRO's old times and dancing around the edges a while, I finally had nothing left but to pop the question.

"Lisa, the guys in the band never figured out what it was about Jack that made him so attractive to the ladies. What did you see in Jack?"

Lisa closed her eyes and swirled the smoke of Jack's memory around her head. She took a slow breath, opened her eyes.

She smiled softly at me and said, "Jack made me feel … "

Lisa settled back in her chair, savored her moment.

" … like I was the only woman in the world."

I mumbled "Thank you," and shuffled away, bowled over by her answer, though I guess I shouldn't have been. Maybe every woman wants her man to make her feel she is the only woman in the world.

I wanted to ask her how Jack accomplished that. What did he do to make her feel that way? But by the time I had recovered my senses, Lisa had disappeared.

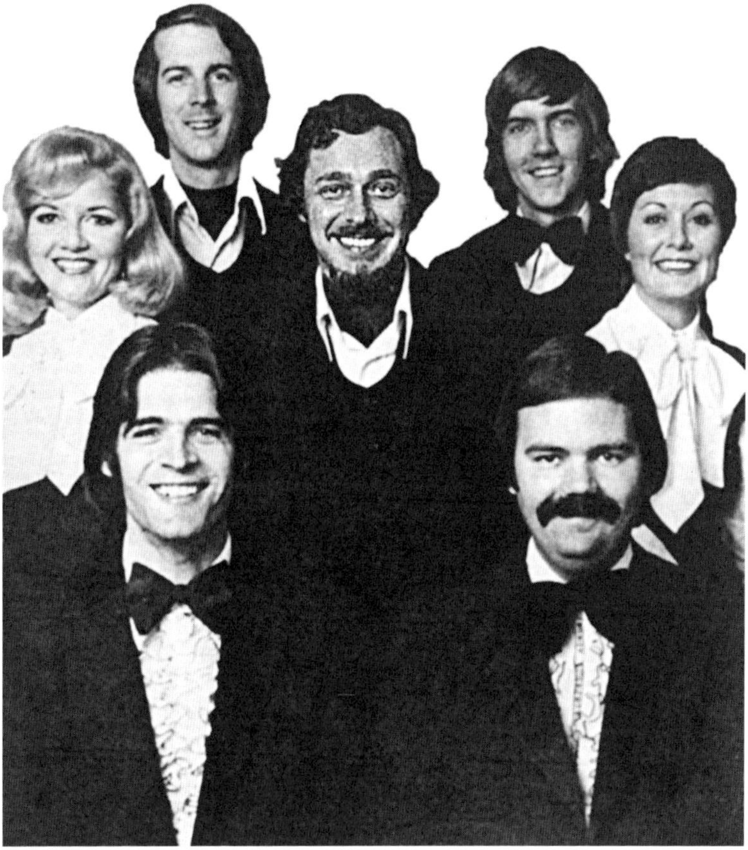

Standing Room Only · Jack Brooks (*center*)
(Clockwise from top:) Wayne Smith, Bob Hubley, Jamie Thomas, Marc Hinchman, the author, Pamela Deston
A publicity photo circa 1975 · anon

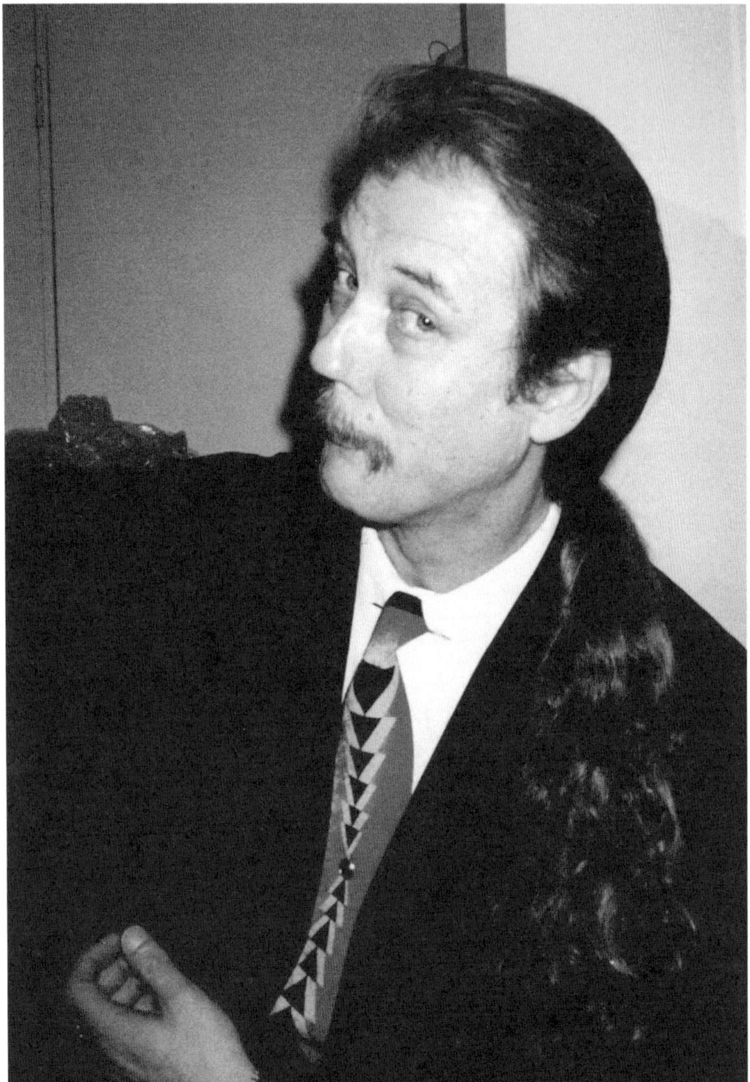

Tony Rice
McNear's Theater, Petaluma · February 21, 1999

Tee

I remember the first time I picked with guitarist Tony Rice. The David Grisman Quintet's first gig, on January 31st, 1976, was in Bolinas, California, where I was living. Tony was the DGQ's guitarist, Todd Phillips played second mandolin to David's first, Darol Anger fiddled, and Joe Carroll played string bass. Joe (may he rest in peace) was an excellent bassist – he recorded with Mose Allison, among others – but to my ears his roots were more in jazz than were the group's.

Listening to Joe, I thought: I can do that. So I tracked down Darol's phone number and hired him to play a square dance gig with me.

After the gig Darol said, "Hey man, I've gotta get you together with Dawg and us. I'll call you." ("Dawg" is David Grisman's nickname.)

A few months later the call came, and I drove over to the home that David and his girlfriend, Janis Bain, rented on the shoulder of Mt. Tamalpais. On a warm afternoon, Tony, Darol, Todd, David, and I went into a basement room that overlooked a Manzanita-lined valley leading down to the Pacific, got out our instruments, and commenced to play.

Well, there was a load of talent in that room, but you

could not overlook Tony's guitar pickin'. I had never heard a steel-string acoustic guitar played so hard and hot. Tony whipped the rhythm. He *was* the rhythm, and his rhythm was commanding, even as he stood stock-still and ramrod straight. David's rhythm on the mandolin is very strong and fun to play with, but Tony played a loud instrument and he played it forcefully.

When I looked closer at his right hand, I realized I'd never seen this kind of flat-picking by an acoustic guitarist. His right hand was doing something that jazz guitarist Howard Roberts called the "spin-drive" method. Tee held the pick between the upper side of his curled-in index finger and his thumb, like most folks. But most folks flat-pick just from the wrist and forearm. Tony moved his thumb, flat-pick and index finger as a unit. Squiggling this unit around furiously, like writing with pen on paper, Tee got all over the guitar, popping the strings with his tortoiseshell pick.

Another thing: Tony's right wrist seemed arched out more than most folks'. He didn't anchor his wrist on the guitar. It was away from the instrument, allowing him to put weight behind an attack when he went full bore. Tony was loud when the music called for it, but he had a full dynamic range on his guitar.

Playing with Tony was playing along with Tony, following him; rhythmically, he propelled the tune. His rhythms, interwoven, urgent, and precipitous, were far beyond the limits of bluegrass guitar as I had ever heard it. He finished his chorus with a flurry of right hand thrashing that left me breathless.

I stood there at the end of the tune, not knowing what to say or do. There was some shuffling of feet, some clearing of throats. Finally someone muttered something about the sanctity of poop.

Tee was awesome. He had rewritten bluegrass guitar.

Because Tony picks harder than anyone in the known universe – it must be physically wearing to play the guitar as hard as Tee does – his tone is unique.

So, Tee's first lesson on guitar is, "Attack the note."

Tee attacks the note. He jumps on it. He lashes out at it. He rips it. He whips it. No one attacks the notes like Tee.

His furious attack makes the guitar sing out, pushes the instrument to its vibrational limits. In this I believe Tony brings sounds out of the flattop Martin that have never been made before. He wails on chorded tone clusters, making the intervallic dissonances ring out so loudly against each other that the guitar roars with the clash of notes, overtones and difference tones, the clicking of the pick on the strings, and the slapping of the strings on the frets and the fingerboard.

Tony honors instrumental virtuosity, hand and finger dexterity. One day he said, "I can tell how well a man plays by how he opens his case." Tony was himself a systematic instrument-case opener. As I recall, each motion – placing the case on a surface, putting his hands on it, moving them in opposite directions to the latches – looked practiced.

One night we were riding in his car, coming up on his home on Sir Francis Drake Boulevard in Kentfield. I was sitting in the shotgun seat. Suddenly Tony said, "Get down!" I got down, not knowing what was up. He swerved into his driveway and killed the headlights. "Get down! Some guy hassled me at the last light and he's after me."

I know that when driving, stuff can happen that only the driver sees, only the driver knows about. Guys can be competitive in their cars, and conflicts flare up, sometimes to the ignorance of passengers. So I took Tony's word for it, and slouched all the way down in my seat, the back of my head jammed against the door's armrest. I looked up and saw Tony's hand holding a revolver, lit by the moonlight against a dark–blue-sky backdrop.

I was hoping the bad boy was going to cruise by; a shoot-out in Tony' driveway would have been tacky in this Marin County neighborhood. Fortunately, he did. Tee stashed the piece, we exited his car and trooped inside.

~

On May 3, 1977, the DGQ had a gig at the Bear's Lair at UC Berkeley. During the sound check, Tony was standing to the side of the small stage, guitar strapped on, about to light a cigarette. He held it to his mouth with his left hand, in the "V" of his middle and index fingers. He had the lighter *and* his flat-pick in his right hand.

At this moment, as he was about to light up, I said, "Tee, hit me a G, will ya?"

There was a heartbeat as Tony visualized it. Then, without looking, Tee flicked his right hand down at the guitar and popped a G-note as clean and clear as I've ever heard played.

The note filled the room. Then he raised his right hand and lit the stick.

What astonished me about this is what it says about Tee's relationship to his guitar. Here he was in non-playing mode, in cigarette-lighting mode. But he knew exactly where that guitar was and where the G-string was, and exactly how to move his body to hit that note hard and clean, without looking down. When it was strapped on, Tee was in a constant relationship with the guitar, no matter what he was doing.

It was also at this gig that I pulled a clumsy move. Tee's Martin was lying on the floor, stage right. I lifted my bass and moved it from one side of stage right to the other.

Please understand that a string bass is about as big as a person, a bulky, pear-shaped person. Over the years, a player learns how to pick this person up, move him, put him down. After a while you think you know how to move your bass without touching it to anything, … ever.

Well, I thought wrong. I picked up the bass, and as I floated it over Tee's Martin, I heard a tap. I didn't feel a hit – the bass has so much momentum – but I heard a tap. I looked down but didn't see anything. But Tony had seen the transaction go down. He walked over, looked, and showed me the blemish that my bass's endpin had just put in the finish on the top of his guitar, … that *I* had just etched on his guitar.

I was mortified.

It wasn't a ding. I didn't ding the instrument, I don't think, or I'd like not to think. It was a blemish the size of a dime on the finish of an already well-worn guitar. But I was heartbroken, and I apologized sincerely.

I recall that the bassist Buell Neidlinger was over at my digs one day. He accidentally put a blemish on my century-old Czech bass. Well, no one wants to injure another person's fine stringed instrument. Buell said, "I apologize. I always try to move an instrument carefully. I'll pay for whatever damage I've done."

He had done no damage that warranted repair. The next time my bass went in for its periodic restoration, a six-month odyssey that takes place once a decade or so, this bruise and all others were sanded and refinished.

But Buell's response was complete: I always try. I sometimes blow it. And I pay up when I do blow it.

So Tee, I apologize. I blew it. And if there was a bill, it's not too late to send it over.

On June 13, 1978, Tony and I drove down to Santa Cruz to pick up the first Tony Rice Model guitar from the Santa Cruz Guitar Company (SCGC), run by Richard Hoover and Bruce Ross. The instrument was based on the 1935 herringbone Martin D-28 that pioneering flat-picker, Clarence White, and later Tony, owned.

That D-28's most distinguishing feature was the oversize sound hole – the circular hole in the middle of the guitar's top. Clarence had enlarged this O-hole on his Martin, I guess, to "let more sound out." The SCGC Tony Rice Model had that enlarged sound hole as well.

And another thing: there's a pellet gunshot hole in the Clarence White Martin, somewhere below the 18th or 19th fret. Roland said that Clarence and dobroist LeRoy McNees (a.k.a. Mack) were at a cabin up at Big Bear Lake one night, hanging out, probably drinking beer. The guitar was standing up against a wall; a pellet gun was in Clarence's hand. He said, "I hate that guitar," took aim, and shot it.

When I asked Mack why Clarence might have said he hated the guitar, he laughed and said, "I know it was hard to play. That's probably why."

In any case, that gunshot hole was not replicated in the SCGC Tony Rice Model guitar.

Well, when we got back to Tee's home in Kentfield, Tony started playing the new instrument right away. And right away he heard something wrong.

"It don't sound right. It don't feel right," he kept saying. "Something's off."

It sounded fine to me.

Then he'd be playing it and he'd reach to fret some first fret notes with his left hand, and he'd say, "Something's the matter, the notes ain't there."

They sounded there to me.

So he took out a yardstick and measured the string length

from nut to bridge on the Clarence White Martin, and then he measured it on the Tony Rice model. The string length was 1/8th inch longer on the Santa Cruz than on the Martin. Tony could feel the 1/8th inch and the string tension that it added. He could hear the tonal difference.

That's when I knew that Tony had ears for days, and that the guitar was a part of him. The folks at the Santa Cruz Guitar Company made the changes Tee wanted, and kept some of their own modifications and innovations. The SCGC Tony Rice Model is, I understand, their bestselling dreadnought guitar.

Tony's famous Clarence White Martin was not being played for a spell, and there's a story behind that.

I visited Tee and his wife Pam in Florida, in April of 1991. He picked me up at the Tampa airport late one evening. We drove in the dark to their house in Crystal River, in the southern part of the state, on the Gulf Coast. Tony told me he lived right on the water, but when we pulled in I couldn't see a darned thing. They put me up in the guest bedroom. I was pooped from a day of flying and logged off instantly.

The next morning I was awakened by the sound of a diesel engine outside my window, maybe twenty feet away. I thought, OK, there's a trucker got his rig parked next door in the driveway. He'll pull out soon enough.

Sure enough, after he had warmed up, he did pull out, only it was not towards the highway. Near as I could tell, it was towards the water. Well, it was early, I was still dazed, … so who knows. I went back to sleep.

Two hours later I got up. Pam gave me a cup of coffee, and Tee took me around outside. We went out the living room door to a gently downward-sloping lawn. Twenty feet out, at the edge of the lawn, was a five-foot drop to water and Tony's runabout.

We walked to the rear of the house, and it was on the water too, maybe ten feet from the bay. Then I looked around to the back of the house, the side where I had been sleeping, where the trucker had his rig parked. It was on the water too, fifteen feet away. It wasn't a diesel truck that had been parked there; it was an industrial towboat. It was just pulling back in as we walked around.

Tee's house was on a small peninsula, a slim rise rimmed by water on three and a half sides. Only the driveway connected it to land. At that moment of low tide the waterline was maybe ten feet below the floor level of Tony's one-story house. As we got into Tee's runabout to jam out to the Gulf of Mexico – he drove at full-throttle just like he picked at full throttle – I turned to him and asked, "Aren't you concerned about flooding here?"

Tony said, "No way, Wild Bill. It would take a once-in-a-century flood to come up to the house."

Two years later, in the dawn of March 13, 1993, the "Storm of the Century" swamped Crystal River as it swept from Cuba to Canada. In Florida, record low barometric pressures produced a squall line ahead of a cold front that in turn produced a serial derecho – a straight-line windstorm – with wind gusts of over 100 MPH. Supercells within the derecho spawned eleven tornados in the state, three of them right there in Crystal River. The ensuing record storm surge (twelve feet at nearby Pine Island) flooded the Florida Gulf Coast so quickly that many folks awoke to water washing into their homes.

At five in the morning the fire department came to Tony's neighborhood and ordered everyone to evacuate: no belongings, no nothin'. You get out *now.* Tee and Pam split immediately, empty-handed except for their dog Pokie.

Three hours later, Tony paid sixty dollars to a guy in a motorboat to go over to his house and fish out the Martin. The man said the water in the living room was neck-high when he went in. He found the guitar after a few minutes, right where Tony had said it would be. It was floating face up in the water.

Tee says he got some advice from the Martin Guitar folks in Nazareth, Pennsylvania. They volunteered their assistance, but he opted for the services of Cincinnati luthier, Harry Sparks. Harry came to Florida and advised Tee on how to dry the instrument out, get it back into playing condition. Tony said it was two years after the '93 Superstorm, a.k.a. the Storm Without a Name, before the dreadnought started sounding like it used to.

~

Tony has the Clarence White Martin back home in North Carolina now. He's playing it, taking it on the road.

I'm glad you're with that instrument again, Tony. You two share a soul. I'd love to have a look at it some time. I'm hoping that ol' blem I own got washed away by the flood.

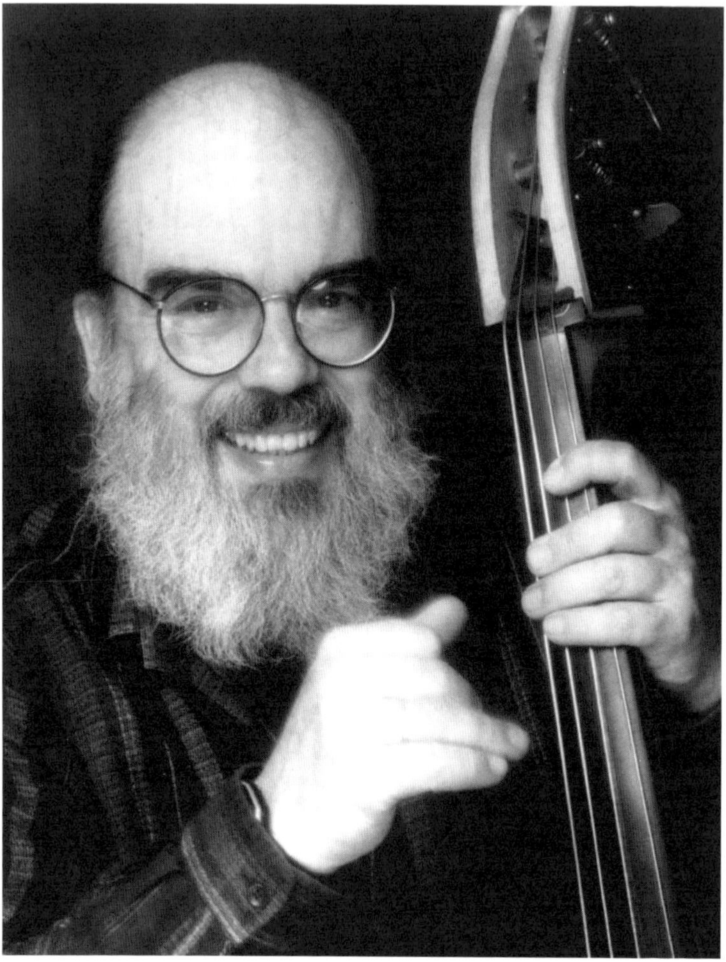

Buell Neidlinger
in a May 1998 publicity photo
By E.K. Waller

I Love the Bass

There is a secret that bass players know. We don't talk about it, because talking about it, … well, talking about it might only dilute it. So you won't hear me jawboning about the bass much, because I love the bass.

The string bass is a beautiful instrument to behold. I see the way little kids look at a string bass for the first time – drop-jawed, wide-eyed – and I remember how it looked to me the first time I saw one at Pete Carbone's violin shop down the street from us in Greenwich Village: massive, mysterious, powerful. An awesome sight.

The string bass *is* a mighty instrument.

The strings press hundreds of pounds of pressure into the bridge and the top of the instrument. So the top of a string bass must be strong to support this. But it must also be supple. It must flex underneath those strings, loose-limbed and Buddha-bellied, resonant of the low and slow vibrations.

There are essentially two ways to carve a string bass that is both strong and supple. The first is to build a bass with a thin top – the sounding board of the instrument – so it will be limber in its youth, for ten to fifty years let's says. After that, the thin top starts slowly caving in to the pressure of the strings, and ultimately collapses.

The other method is to build a bass with a thicker top, unlimber in its youth. Then you play that bass and wait a long time. Wait until the bass, like a well-aged wine, opens up. Wait a hundred years or more.

Buell Neidlinger, one of my bass teachers, told me something about this, about the age of a string bass. But first, a few words about him.

When he was very young, Buell proved to be a prodigy on the cello. His playing was so distinguished that the music patroness, Elizabeth Sprague Coolidge, loaned him a Guarneri cello to play while he was still a teenager. Some say that a Guarnerius is as good as, or even better than, a Stradivarius.

When Buell moved over to the string bass at age fourteen, he proved equally talented. In his twenties and beyond, after discovering jazz, he played with Coleman Hawkins, Zoot Sims, Lester Young, Tony Bennet, Billie Holiday, and for almost a decade with jazz pianist Cecil Taylor in Cecil's classic Greenwich Village years.

He has played and/or soloed with the Boston Symphony Orchestra, Houston Symphony, Berkshire Music Center Orchestra, Stokowski's American Symphony, the Los Angeles Chamber Orchestra, and with chamber ensembles such as the Guarneri String Quartet, Budapest String Quartet and Amadeus String Quartet.

So Buell plays both sides of the music fence. Symphony orchestra players refer to them as "legit" and "commercial." (Ouch!) There are very few folks who do that with authority. Only Edgar Meyer comes to mind as a double bassist with these dual credentials.

Buell and I met in the 1970s when he was living in Los Angeles. He was playing string bass in the L.A. recording scene on sound tracks and music albums. Buell was the guy they called when bowed bass was needed. He has bowed the bass with Barbara Streisand, Frank Sinatra, Elvis Costello, Frank Zappa, the Beach Boys, and Earth, Wind & Fire. I understand he played bass on a movie soundtrack standing next to jazz bassist Ray Brown. Ray played all the pizz, (plucked) parts, and Buell played all the *arco* (bowed) parts.

What Buell can do with the bow is ear bending. He has total control of the nuanced stroking of the bass with the bow. The bass takes a lot of energy to get vibrating. But it also requires as much finesse as playing a violin. Buell has mastered this athletic duality. Deep, smooth, visceral sounds bloom from his bass. Buell is an artist with the bow. All in the L.A. music business readily acknowledge his *arco* greatness.

His bass sound is sonorous with the bow, but with *pizzicato* as well. Buell can pizz a note on the bass, and the note will grow in volume, actually become louder for the first moments of its sounding … and then start to fade. Buell is a bass inspiration.

When I came to him for my first lesson on *pizzicato,* Buell said, "So, you want to learn how to pizz the bass? Oh, there are so many ways to pizz the bass."

What followed was a tour-de-force demonstration of right-hand *pizzicato* techniques, from one-, two-, and three-fingered pizz'ing, to something he called "Polish pizz." Favored by bassist Serge Koussevitsky, this technique produces a bell-like sound that only Buell can execute.

One afternoon he was bowing his William Forster bass, an instrument that dates from the 1700s and, he commented, was possibly played at the premier of Handel's *Messiah.* Buell said, "It's gotten to the point where I don't want to play a bass anymore unless it's around 300 years old."

Well, I liked that, because until then I don't think I had ever seen a 300 year-old bass. OK, maybe in pictures, or at the symphony through opera glasses. But touched one, …

played one? Probably not. This gave me a new view of Buell, of the breadth of his experience in playing and handling many basses of many ages and pedigrees.

So as I was saying, I love the bass. And I love *my* bass, an old friend whom I found at age seventeen. When I hold it in my arms, rest it against my belly and pop the E-string, the bass wHOOUUUUUUMMMMMMMZs vibrations deep into my gut. My body shudders in the wave, and my stomach and chest are blasted by a sound tsunami, the lowest expression of all music, the *cojones,* the mocha almond fudge, knee-deep-in-the-deep-muddy, beat-beating Governor of the groove and Atlas of the celestial music world.

Friends, playing the string bass simply feels terrific.

So I encourage you to go out tomorrow, buy yourself a double bass and start playing it.

You'll love it. You'll discover what the word "thrill" means. And then of course, you'll be in on the secret.

I caught up with Buell in February of 2013. Having retired from the L.A. music scene, he is living in Northwest Washington State. Buell wrote:

"I sold my last bass last summer, the one whose scroll appears in your pic [facing page 101]. I was in the biz for 60 years and when my last bass left I shed no tears, not one. I have one good bass bow left; it has never played 'col legno' [striking the strings with the wood of the bow]. I play cello now, and do solo gigs in coffee shops under the name 'Billy the Celloist.' Billy's new CD, "Cello Cafe," is out on Vivace Records. Billy plays a solo cello rendition of 'Ripple' on it that's a solid sender!"

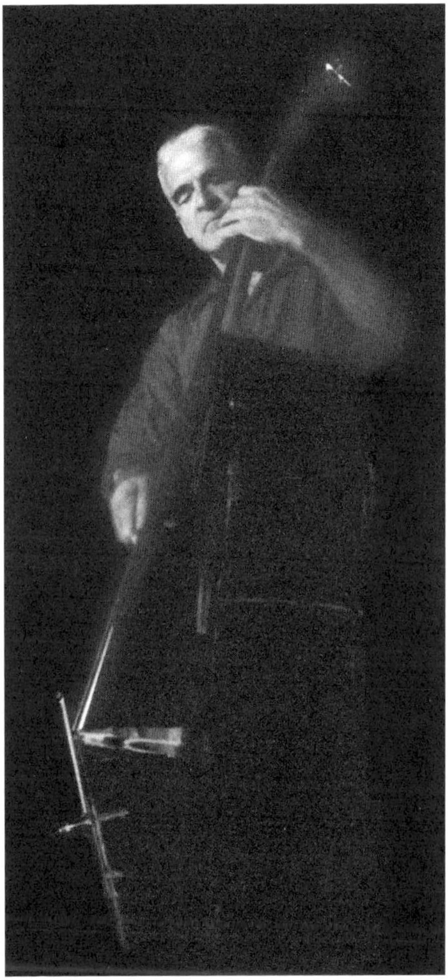

The author's 1875 Czech bass
Rancho Nicasio · March 23, 2007
Infrared photo by Linda Emme

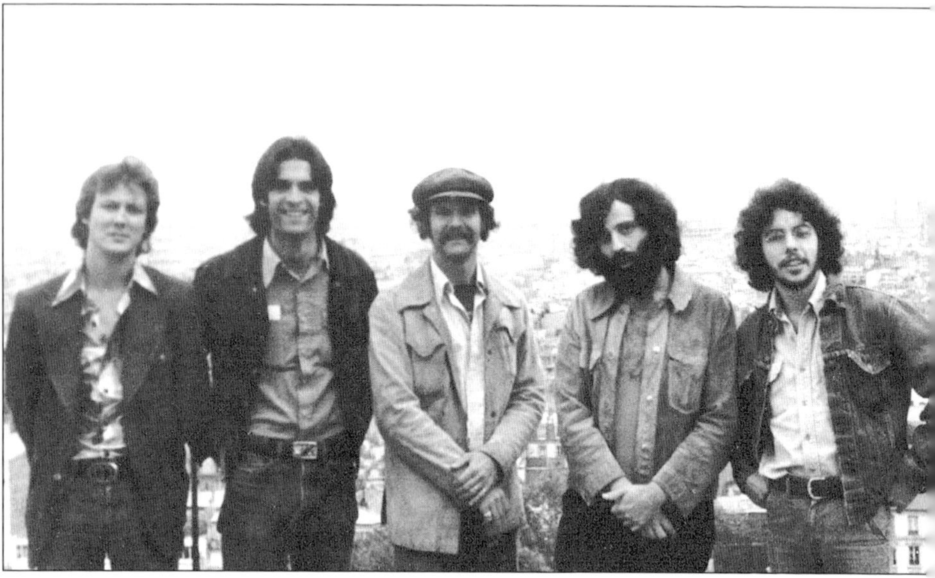

Bill Keith's Bicentennial Bluegrass Band · Sacré Coeur, Paris
Tony Rice, l'auteur, Bill Keith, David Grisman, Darol Anger
By Patrick Ciocca

Paris Remembers

My wife, Noni, and I toured the Normandy region of France in June of 1984, as all of Normandy – actually, all of France – was celebrating the 40th anniversary of her Allied liberation from the Nazis.

I've loved France since I first visited there as a teenager, and I've always had a mysterious attraction to this period of her history. So I was delighted that we arrived at a number of French towns and cities as their celebrations were peaking. Each had suffered a unique wartime experience, and each remembered with a commemoration that paid homage to it, with many who had survived the war in attendance.

The occupation of Paris was unique in how viciously the Nazis treated the Parisians. If someone from the French underground were to assassinate a German soldier on the streets of Paris, the Nazis would gather around that point immediately, round up the next dozen Parisians they found – men, women, young, old, it didn't matter – line them up against a wall, and mow them down.

So it is their very *moment* of liberation from this gruesome occupation that Parisians deliriously commemorate. The week we were there the French government projected period documentaries on blank building walls throughout

Paris. They all showed footage of the American troops – us Yanks – marching into The City in 1944 while the Parisians mobbed them, threw flowers at them, threw themselves at them, in joy and thanks.

But for us two Yanks, in 1984, Paris had forgotten. We were shortchanged and treated rudely, many times. This Parisian chill is well known to American tourists. It seems to come with the wine.

~

Bill Keith, the brilliant 5-string banjo man, hired a few of us in the DGQ to tour Europe with him in a group he called the Bicentennial Bluegrass Band. Tony Rice, the guitarist in this ensemble, dubbed it the "Keith Unit," in honor of our leader. Bill Keith, by the way, created a style of melodic banjo picking so distinctive that it is named after him: "Keith Picking." On this tour, Darol Anger played fiddle, David Grisman, mandolin, and me, string bass.

Tony of course picked the flattop guitar. That is, he played his 1935 Herringbone Martin D-28 with a flat-pick. These days most flat-picks are made of celluloid. At their cheapest, music stores buy them by the gross, stamp them with their logos, and give them away to their customers.

But Tony uses tortoiseshell picks. The French call them *"des vraies médiators en écaille,"* true shell picks, and they are the choice of discerning flat-pickers who love the unique tone they produce, and who can afford them.

You see, tortoiseshell picks are made from the shell of the Hawksbill turtle, which is an endangered species. The sale of "tortoise" is banned in most countries and the world supply has dried up as prices have spiraled. Tortoise fans actively seek out what is left of the world stash. It's an underground matter and sales are usually transacted in cash.

Tee and Dawg dogged tortoise wherever we toured. In Paris we asked all our friends and local musicians for leads. One of them suggested that a certain gypsy band at a local carnival had good possibilities.

It was a traveling carnival and it took us two days to catch up with them at a flea market in a working class suburb. A genuine-looking, walleyed, oud player led the band. (An oud is an Arabian lute.) Sure enough, he used a flat-pick: an orange day-glow plastic job stamped with a "Paris Musique" logo.

The guitarist, who sported a Jimmy Hendrix knee bandana and a three-day old shave, used white, oversized, plastic picks that he hand-cut from tourist credit cards. He swore to me that he pick-pocketed them for that purpose alone.

The day following this disappointment, a French friend, Mary-Paul, directed us to an address in a shabby, residential *arrondissement*. Bill and I joined Tony and David in this day's plectrum quest, though the two of us, who played banjo and bass respectively, had no direct interest in flat-picks. It seemed like it might be a fun thing to do.

There was no sign on the street indicating a music store might be down this dark alley. We felt our way down the alley's stone wall till we came to a door. I pushed it open. In the out draft I could smell horsehide glue, varnish, and rosin dust. We walked into a dark space that felt small.

Someone snapped on a light. It was the *propriétaire*, a gentleman who looked in his late sixties. The bare bulb revealed over twenty mandolins, lutes, and guitars lining the walls, most of prewar vintage. The mandolins, the specialty of the shop, were all of the Italian, bowl-backed shape. "Tater bugs," we call them down South, for the way they look.

This joint was authentic. Bill Keith and I were our French-speaking spokesmen:

"Monsieur, s'il vous plaît. Avez-vous des vraies médiators en écailles?" I was so pleased I had taken French in high school.

"Non. Absolument pas!"

Well, we all understood that.

But behind him was a wall of small wooden drawers, and on the end of each he'd pasted the item that was inside. At least a dozen drawers had variously colored plastic picks, but we noticed that two of them had plectra that were definitely tortoise.

"Monsieur, s'il vous plaît. Qu'est-ce que vous avez là?" Bill asked, pointing at the two drawers.

"Oh yes. Those are true shell picks, but not for you," he said, but in French, of course.

Not for us? "*Pourquoi*?" Bill asked. How come?

"They are all too soft for your needs," was the gist of his response.

If he was right, the gentleman had a good point. Tony has encyclopedic knowledge of tortoiseshell picks, and one day he gave us a talk on the subject as we drove to a gig in Keith's orange Mercedes minibus.

Tee told us that tortoiseshell picks are made from an organic substance, so each one has a different feel. The feel of the pick derives from the quality of the shell it is cut from, as well as the size and thickness of cut. A plectrum may be too thin or soft for an individual player (as the gentleman was suggesting), or too large or firm. A good tortoiseshell pick should be evenly brown to dark brown, without any ripples, pie-baldness, or light-colored veins that show where the pick will break if it is stressed.

And here Tony pulled a tortoiseshell pick from his pocket, bent it on a yellow vein that ran through it, and snapped it in half.

So you don't buy tortoiseshell picks by the gross. You audition them by hand, one at a time.

"May we take a look at them anyway?" I asked the gentleman.

"Mais certainement!" he replied.

With a flourish he whipped out the two drawers and presented them to us at the counter.

We all gasped.

It was the largest stash of tortoise I have seen in my natural life. We were looking at hundreds of glistening, solid-brown plectra, worth thousands. Many of them *were* too soft for our needs, but many were going to be just right.

The auditioning process began while Keith and I chatted with the old man, a mandolinist himself. He seemed interested to hear we were a touring string band, and asked where we had been performing. Bill told him about the festivals we had played in Gerte, Courville, and at Nyon, on beautiful Lake Geneva.

Then I asked him how much he wanted for the picks.

"You choose which ones you want, count them up, and I will make you a price. But first, tell me one thing. What country are you from?"

"What did he say, Bill?" Tony asked.

"He asked what country we're from."

Tony said, "Bill, you tellum w'ur 'Muricans!"

As the old man heard this, a facial tic rippled his cheek. I was sure the price had just tripled for the rich 'Muricans and gave up hope on the project.

So I took a walk, bought a half-dozen postcards, found a neighborhood bistro and wrote home over a sandwich and a beer. Then I found a post office, bought some stamps, mailed the cards and returned to the shop.

They were still sorting out picks.

Finally, they had chosen a hundred plectra. They were fully, gleefully prepared to plunk down what could have amounted to their tour wages in exchange for this find.

A moment of truth had arrived. I turned to the old man:

"Quel est le prix, monsieur?" I asked him what the price was.

"Combien d'écailles avez-vous?" He wanted to know how many picks we had.

"Cent," I said. A hundred.

He paused. *"Pour vous?"* For you?

"Oui, monsieur." Yes, for us.

He looked right at me. *"Pour vous 'Muricans?"*

"For you Americans?" he wanted to know.

Now I could hear it coming. This was going to be one million Francs, two cartons of no-filter Marlboros, and three pair of Levi's, extra wide.

"Oui, monsieur, pour nous Americans," I answered. Yes, for us Americans.

"Pour vous 'Muricans, … … c'est gratuit."

My jaw dropped.

Tony looked over at me. "Bill, what did he say?"

"He said that for us Americans it's gratis. It's free!"

"Free? Well Bill, ask him why."

So I asked the gentleman, *"Merci, monsieur. Mais pourquoi?"*

And he told us. He said, "Because in 1944, you 'Muricans, you liberated Paris. But you never charged us anything."

~

Some Paris-bound pickers made their way down the alley to the gentleman's shop a few years later. Finding the old man still there, they asked him if he had any tortoiseshell picks.

"I sold them to some crazy 'Muricans years ago," he said. "I have a few left. But they are all too soft for your needs."

"My greatest lesson from Mimi, who has been in my psyche for fifty-six years: I had never seen her the way other people saw her. I'd seen her always as my little sister, and I discovered she was so much more. She was everything more. ... It was the scale of Mimi's stature and her greatness that I had never seen. It was a gift that Mimi gave us that she was around long enough for me to tell her, 'Mimi, I didn't get it, and I do now.' "

—Joan Baez
eulogizing her sister, Mimi Fariña

Bread & Roses
~ Mimi Fariña

I first heard of her when I was in college. A folkie friend came back from a Boston summer saying that Joan Baez had a younger sister. She was more beautiful than Joan, played guitar better, and sang more sweetly. Her name was Mimi.

If true, these were impressive credentials. Joan was gorgeous, an ethereal singer, and a solid guitarist. More beautiful than Joan and a better picker and singer to boot was a combination that was difficult yet pleasing to imagine.

Mimi had married Richard Fariña when she was eighteen. Richard was a novelist, songwriter, and singer who accompanied himself on the dulcimer, a fretted, three-stringed instrument. He wrote a novel he titled, *Been Down So Long It Looks Like Up To Me.* They were living near Carmel when it was published and went together to Richard's first book signing on April 30, 1966. When the event was over, Richard asked an acquaintance for a ride on his motorcycle. He handed Mimi his wallet and boarded the pillion seat.

Somewhere along the highway the motorcycle took a bad turn and went off the road. Richard died at the scene, his head against a stone.

Back at a friend's home, waiting with others for Richard's return, Mimi heard sirens and felt something was wrong. They drove down the highway to the crash site where police met them. An officer told them that the driver of the motorcycle had lived but not his passenger. They couldn't identify the victim because he didn't have a wallet. Mimi was holding the wallet in her hand. It was her twenty-first birthday.

~

In 1974, Mimi started a nonprofit organization in Mill Valley that she called Bread & Roses. B&R brings free live music to people in Bay Area institutions. They have over a thousand volunteer artists who perform at convalescent homes, hospitals, AIDS facilities, homeless and senior centers, psychiatric, rehabilitation and detention facilities, and shelters for runaway kids and homeless people. With over 500 institutional shows a year, they bring entertainment, as Father Guido Sarducci quipped, "everywhere that Jello is served."

Mimi named the organization she founded after the poem, "Bread and Roses," by James Oppenheim. It is said that he wrote it in 1912 after witnessing a textile strike in Lawrence, Massachusetts. The women picketers carried signs that sloganized "We want Bread and Roses too." Mimi set the poem to music in 1976 and recorded it with her sister Joan.

As we go marching, marching
In the beauty of the day,
A million darkened kitchens,
A thousand mill lofts gray,
Are touched with all the radiance
That a sudden sun discloses,
For the people hear us singing:
Bread and Roses! Bread and Roses!

As we go marching, marching,
We battle too for men,
For they are women's children,
And we mother them again.
Our lives shall not be sweated
From birth until life closes.
Hearts starve as well as bodies;
Give us bread, but give us roses!

As we go marching, marching,
Unnumbered women dead,
Go crying through our singing
Their ancient call for bread.
Small art and love and beauty
Their drudging spirits knew.
Yes, it is bread we fight for,
But we fight for roses, too!

As we go marching, marching,
We bring the greater days.
The rising of the women means
The rising of the race.
No more the drudge and idler
Ten that toil where one reposes,
But a sharing of life's glories:
Bread and roses! Bread and roses!

Our lives shall not be sweated
From birth until life closes;
Hearts starve as well as bodies;
Bread and roses!
Bread and roses!

In August of 1978, I visited the Bread & Roses Mill Valley office, a month before they presented their second music festival at Berkeley's Greek Theater. I volunteered to be the house string bassist for whomever might ask for my services. They mulled it over and finally said Sure. I played their '78 and '79 festivals, and had the good fortune to accompany David Bromberg, Gibson & Camp, Tim Hardin, Ramblin' Jack Elliott, Steve Goodman, John McEuen, Tom Paxton, The Persuasions, Peter, Paul & Mary, Jeff Hanna, Paul Siebel, Jethro Burns, Odetta, Pete Seeger, and others.

In October 1978, I started playing behind Mimi, joining her and Lowell Levinger, a.k.a. "Banana," who played banjo, guitar and piano. We mostly played venues in northern California, often in the South Bay and Santa Cruz.

At one of these gigs, Banana and I were standing with the promoter in the parking lot after the show. The guy lit up a fat one and, as Mimi walked by us to the car, he said, "Mimi, you want to join us?"

Her reply set me laughing: "Oh. The boys are getting the girls high!"

A friend and I wrote a song based on that truism for all times.

We opened for Gordon Lightfoot on a tour of Alaska and Hawaii that winter. The tour started in Anchorage. We were slated to fly out to Waikiki that night, right after the gig.

On November 5 we were on stage at the West High Auditorium in Anchorage. It was colder than, well, than Alaska, and Mimi, Banana and I had performed our first two tunes.

Mimi, into her between-tune patter, said, "Tonight, after playing here for you, we're getting on a plane and flying to Hawaii for our next show." Here she thumbed her nose at the crowd and chanted, "Nyah, nyaha, nyah, nyah."

Inside I was thinking, Holy Toledo, what a risk! These are Alaskans. They love Alaska; they must love the cold. This could backfire on her. We could get booed off the stage.

But no, the room burst into laughter and then applause.

Mimi had pulled off a delightful coup. I appreciate spontaneity in a leader on stage. It can be risky, but when it works you put the entire room on your side. Mimi had the crowd in her hands the rest of the evening.

Mimi and I co-wrote a song in 1979 that she called "Feeling Left Behind." We played together for a while longer, but after a time, Mimi gave up performing to focus her energies on managing Bread & Roses.

We both lived in Mill Valley, so we ran into each other around town occasionally and stopped to chat. When I had my first storytelling gig at Sweetwater, Mimi showed up beforehand and gave me a long-stem rose and a note of best wishes. It knocked me out. That was very thoughtful of her.

In November 1999, Mimi was diagnosed with lung cancer. The news was a shock to all who knew her. She started chemo and radiation treatments that led to hair loss. I went to the show that Bread & Roses mounted at the San Francisco War Memorial Opera House on March 20, 2000, celebrating their 25th anniversary. It was a magnificent evening culminating in Pete Seeger singing for the packed house. Mimi was a delightful, entertaining MC, and her patter included some kidding about losing hair. I sent her a letter a few days later:

Dear Mimi -

I just wanted to say congratulations on a wonderful show Monday evening. It was a great concert with some of my favorite entertainers, including your sister, Jackson Browne, Kris Kristofferson, Boz Scaggs, Robin Williams, and Pete. You were an excellent mistress of ceremonies, and you looked gorgeous. It was Boz who said "Twenty-five more years," but I believe Bread & Roses will go on for as long as there are prisons and old folks' homes that need entertainment: that is, forever.

I was in Oklahoma City recently, playing their storytelling festival. I mentioned Bread & Roses in the tale I told about playing with Peter, Paul & Mary. After the show, someone in the audience approached me and said that they had started a similar nonprofit in OKC, based on B&R. Of course you know that your organization has inspired and spawned many others. But there it was, looking me right in the face. So, congratulations on Bread & Roses. Congratulations on all its offshoots. But most of all, congratulations and thank you for all the happiness you have brought to everyone in every institution that you have served.

I was more than blown away to hear of your health problems. When we ran into each other recently, you looked great, with hair and all. I think I even mentioned how wonderful you looked. I could not believe my ears. This must have come up suddenly.

But the Big C is no longer the life-defying illness it once was. I believe that the people who beat it are people with purpose, with stamina, and who have a strong support group. Mimi, you have all of these in spades. Please know that you will beat this, that you will live on, healthfully, and that you are by far too high-energy not to survive this battle. Keep your faith, and those of us who know you will keep it with you. May you be blessed with a full recovery.

Best wishes,
Bill Amatneek

A few months later she sent me a note. It was the first correspondence I had received from her, and I hung onto it. I have since learned that her notes are treasured by the stars and cons alike who have received them. She wrote:

Bill,

Thank you so much for the healing card you sent me. I opened it with joy, with a song in my heart. To be surrounded by friends like you with feelings of love is indeed a blessng. It affects me deeply.

With love to you and for you,

Mimi

P.S. You wrote such a lovely letter. It was more than a card and I appreciate it so. I'm fighting the good fight – be well and take care.

It was the last I heard from her. Mimi passed on July 18, 2001. There was a memorial service for her at San Francisco's Grace Cathedral on August 7. It was a fitting remembrance of and tribute to her life, and a wake-up for me.

Mimi was eulogized by a number of folks, none more touchingly than her mother, known as "Big Joan," or more insightfully than her sister, Joan. I think with deaths such as Mimi's – those that are a while in coming – that people have time to adjust. Sudden deaths throw people; the memorials that follow witness the wailing that can accompany abrupt departures, or sometimes just stunned silence. But the eulogizers at Mimi's memorial were remarkably dry-eyed in their memories of Mimi and insights into her life.

Grace Cathedral is resonant and vibration-filled. Between speakers there was time to reflect, so I closed my eyes and tried to come to terms with my relationship with Mimi. What did I have to learn from it?

Mimi had created a few folk "hits" in her day – some with Joan, some with Richard, some with Tom Jans later on, and some on her own. Her best-known song, written by Richard and Pauline Marden, and recorded by Mimi and Richard, is called "Pack Up Your Sorrows." The melody of the chorus and the song's sentiment are charming and memorable. Although other folks recorded this piece subsequently, Mimi's rendition is the one most people remember.

She penned another tune called "In the Quiet Morning," an elegy for Janis Joplin that to my ears demonstrates deft song writing skills. Both of these tunes are recognizable to anyone who was around the folk music movement when they were released. There were other tunes that Mimi wrote, co-wrote or recorded that became well known in the folk music community.

Mimi had a story that was being told by the time she was a teenager. Her story had gained the stature of legend by the time her husband, Richard, died. Just the tale that I heard about her from my college friend – that she was younger, prettier, played better and sang sweeter than Joan – was legend material.

Mimi came from a family whose politics were progressive, I believe it is fair to say. It was there she likely learned that a human being has two obligations. The first is to help your fellow man, especially the less rich, the less educated, the exploited, the newer to these American shores, … that is, the less well off. The second is to leave this world a better place than when you entered.

Mimi took these lessons to heart. She dedicated her life to these tenets with Bread & Roses. B&R has done many thousands of gigs for people who were uplifted by the experience. In that, Mimi helped humankind immeasurably *and* left this world a better place.

Listening to everyone who eulogized her – Reverend Alan Jones, John Burton, Lana Severn, Cassandra Flipper, Paul Liberatore, her sister and her mother – I heard that it was Bread & Roses, and not Mimi's music, that would define her life. I realized how hard she had worked on it, how it would outshine and outlast her considerable music contributions.

Bread & Roses' institutional performers give their services gratis. In this selfless expression of giving, you give all you have and receive nothing in return. Well, nothing but love and appreciation. This was what made performing for B&R the meaningful experience it was for everyone, including me.

Hearing all this at Grace Cathedral, I started to question my level of participation in social causes. I had done benefits for a number of non-profit groups while I was a teenager, playing banjo and singing, just as I played bass for Bread & Roses decades later.

One summer, while I was in high school, I took a paid internship at a government-run research center. In the fall, when I'd gone back to school, a certain three-letter government investigation agency sent me a letter. They had heard about these benefit shows that I had played and wanted me to tell them about these events. On the basis of what I said, the research center either would or wouldn't hire me again.

A lawyer friend advised me on how to answer the letter, but said that no matter how I responded, I'd never work for the center again.

This stung.

I still try to play every benefit that calls me, and for B&R have played their institutional shows, concerts, and festivals. But sitting there in Grace Cathedral that day, listening to what Mimi had done with Bread & Roses, I had to ask myself: what had I been doing to make this world better, to help mankind?

There was only one activity I could possibly point to, and that was playing music, telling stories. I hope it is fair to say that most everywhere I have performed, most everyone has walked out feeling better than when they walked in.

But helped the world? Benefited mankind? I left Grace Cathedral feeling I hadn't done much about that recently.

~

Playing bass for Bread & Roses music festivals was a rich experience, Mimi, and the story about accompanying Peter, Paul & Mary has become an audience favorite. Touring Hawaii, opening for Gordon Lightfoot, and driving home from our Santa Cruz gigs at two in the morning were all delicious times.

It was a pleasure making music with you, hearing you sing, and just hanging out in your band. Thank you for all these, Mimi, but also for the lesson you gave while we sat in Grace that afternoon. I am trying to do better with that.

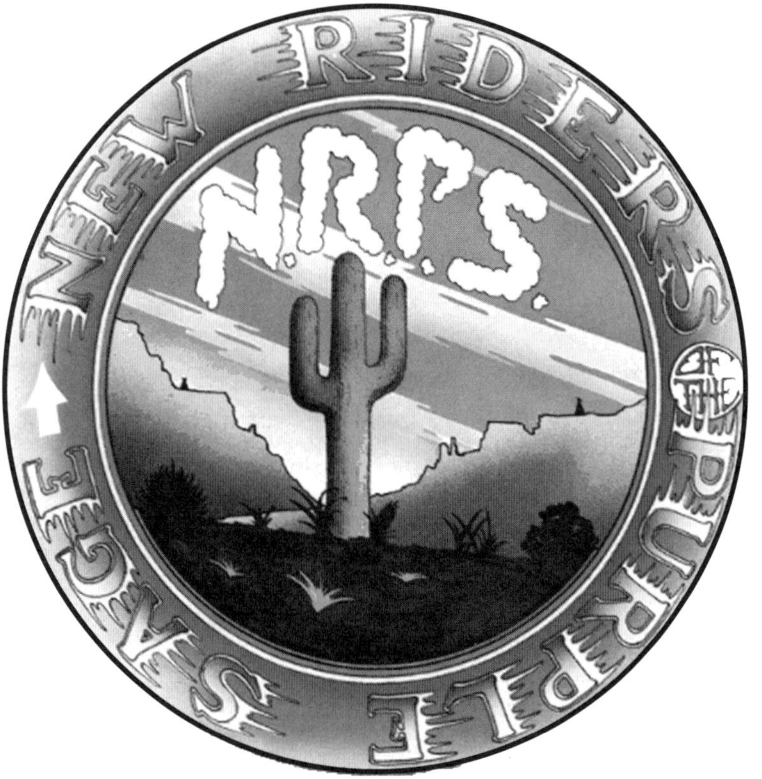

New Riders of the Purple Sage logo
By Michael Ferguson and Alton Kelley

New Rider on the Purple Sage

I'd been told that the single women who follow acoustic music groups tend to be a tad more ... cerebral ... than those who follow rock bands. So I was pleased to receive a call one afternoon from the country rock group, New Riders of the Purple Sage, asking me to play electric bass with them on a tour of the Midwest. The New Riders were related to the Grateful Dead, so Jerry Garcia would sometimes fall by and sit in. They also attracted their share of outlaw bikers and what some folks might call groupies. I accepted their offer with delight and dusted off my Fender bass. A genuine rock tour would be a first for me.

We arrive at the sound check for our first gig and I walk on stage to set up the Fender. Out in the room, a half-dozen ladies are dancing to taped music. Except for the bartender and the soundman, there isn't a guy in the house, so I figure they're here alone.

As we walk on stage, the pace of their dancing picks up and what had been freeform hippie dancing becomes more focused; they all dance facing the stage now. We haven't plugged in yet, but it's like we're already playing.

The ladies' eyes, mostly closed before we entered, are now wide open, checking us out. We act like nothing is coming down, but we are well aware that we are being watched.

As Patrick, our drummer, starts his sound check, the soundman kills the taped music. The gals stop dancing and scatter to the tables and the bar. None sit together. The bar ladies don't acknowledge each other. None of them drink alcohol; it's all Shirley Temples and diet sodas. They sip their drinks slowly and watch us.

When the five of us have finished our individual sound checks, we play a tune together. This brings the ladies back on the dance floor and they boogie full tilt to our music. They come closer to the stage now and their bodies move with language that any musician can read.

We return to the club for our show that evening and go down the back alley to avoid the crowd out front. Two guys from an infamous biker gang are waiting for us outside the back door. One of them has fists like wide-screen TV's and the other looks like his big brother, only meaner.

John Dawson, our lead singer, greets them with a cheery, "Howdy guys. What's happenin' ?"

"Hey John, is Garcia going to be coming by tonight to play with you guys?" the smaller but somehow more menacing one asks.

We're in Chicago, Jerry lives two thousand miles away and is playing with the Dead this evening in San Francisco, I happen to know.

But John says, "Hey man, he might fall by tonight. Ya never know. But tell me somethin', where are your hogs, man? Ya got 'em parked out front?"

"Out front? Hell no. We parked 'em inside."

"Inside? The club lets you park your Harleys inside?"

"No. The club don't let us park 'em inside. We just park

'em inside," and they rush back in to tell their friends that Garcia might be showing up that evening.

I turn to John. "Hey man. Do you always lie to guys who can kill you? I mean, telling them Jerry might fall by …"

John shrugs it off. "They'll have forgotten by the end of the second pitcher."

Inside the club, the room is full. When our first set comes, I walk on stage, plug in, and look out at the dance floor. It's jammed with people now, and it looks like most of the sound-check ladies are back. They're still alone but dressed, as Chuck Berry sang, in tight dresses and lipstick.

The first set, a solid two hours, hears the crowd pounding the floorboards. The band has pumped the room and we exit the stage to the smell of three hundred sweating bodies.

During the break, most of the band members head for the dressing room. But I break for the bar, post myself on the only empty stool, and order a Coke-squeeze. By the time the doctor sets it up, one of the ladies who had been at the sound check is standing next to me.

One of the nice aspects of playing out – playing out in public – is the rapport female audience members establish with guys in the band. They've seen you play on stage and they feel they know you enough to approach you and start a conversation. I like that. As a sometimes shy guy, I don't meet women easily. As a performing player, meeting women is simple: you just hang out.

She says, "I noticed you playing on stage. You have a nice face."

Please understand that most music fans, when they approach you after a show, will compliment the band or say something about your playing, like, "You had a good groove going, dude." The closest I've come to hearing a body part complimented was when a fan said to a fiddler, "Good left ring-finger, man; great independence."

Well, string players work on freeing the ring-finger from the pinkie- and middle-finger lock, so I understood. But when a woman tells a musician, "You have a nice face," she's not making a statement about his music. I think it's a shade more personal.

"Why thank you very much. And how did you like the music?" I'm genuinely curious.

"That was nice too," she says coolly.

"My name's Bill."

"Yes I know, Bill. My name's Claire."

After the last set, Claire is hanging around the stage, so I invite her back to my motel room for a bite to eat. It's 2:00 AM, I have no food, there is no room service.

She knows this, and she says, "Sure!"

With an able-bodied woman on my arm, relief is not the word here. I feel like I'm leading a charmed, rock 'n' roll life.

Claire and I arrive at my room, I slip the Do Not Disturb sign on the doorknob, and we settle in for our duet.

There comes a point in an evening such as this when it becomes understood between a man and a woman that they are going to be close. An interlude arrives with it, during which people reveal things about themselves, explain themselves to each other.

Claire says, "I'm a freshman at the University of Chicago. Haven't declared a major yet. I love music and I love to dance, but I don't play an instrument. So I don't think music will be my major. Maybe English."

And then, after we've shared our first kiss, she says, "I've never done this before, ya know. I'm not a groupie or anything." She says it in an accusatory way, as though I've called her on it.

"That's good, Claire, I didn't think you were. I've never done this before either."

I'm not sure what it is I haven't done before that I'm about to do now, but it feels like the right thing to say, and Claire seems glad to hear it.

When you've been alarm-clocked at 7:00 AM, traveled all day in a compact car, eaten deep-fat-fried food for lunch and dinner, and then put out a large amount of sweating energy playing loud rock for four hours, sustained social activity at 3:00 AM is something that can elude you, much as you wish it would not. So our time together is not so record-breaking. I don't mention it to the guys, and I don't imagine Claire writes home about it either.

She leaves at dawn. We've been together three hours. She has an English Literature class at eight and doesn't want to be late.

I never learn her last name. I never hear from her again.

At 6:30 AM, the phone rings. It's Richie, one of our two roadies, with a wake-up call. This is another day of driving – some three hundred miles due west and south – a fast-food lunch on the road, short naps in the car, a sound check at six, dinner at a greasy spoon, and the first set at nine.

When our last set is over, I go over to the bar for a soda. This time, one of our guitarists tags along.

"What's up, man?" I ask him.

"I saw that sign on your door, man. You got lucky last night. I'm just sticking with you to see if some of it rubs off on me."

"Sure. But I'm tellin' you, I didn't do nothing. I just sat at the bar and hung out."

"OK, Bill. I'll just sit with you and hang out too."

In a short while, two young ladies come over and ask us for our autographs. The detail of bringing pen and paper to this signing has escaped them though, so we settle on a pencil stub and two drink napkins that the bartender brings us.

I end up talking with Debbie. She is a sophomore in college, an art history major. I ask Debbie if she'd like to come with me back to my room – no pretense of food this time – and after a demure heartbeat, she says "Yes."

The moment of we-know-what-we're-doing-here seems to arrive sooner, as do the true confessions.

Debbie says, "I feel kinda funny being here. I want you to know I've never done this before. I'm no groupie or anything like that."

Her words are so similar to Claire's that I almost laugh out loud.

"Uh, ... well, that's good, Debbie. I didn't think you were. And I want you to know I've never done this before either."

I feel badly about the white lie. Whatever it is I'm saying I haven't done before, I *have* done before, and just last night.

Debbie leaves at dawn. I don't get her last name, and I never hear from her again.

By the third night, the entire band – David, Patrick, John, Buddy, Allen, and the roadies, Richie and Bernie – follows me to the bar after the second set.

"We're sticking with you, Bill. You've got the touch," one of them says.

"I'm telling you guys, I don't do anything. I just park myself on the stool and wait."

"Yeah, Bill. Whatever you say. But our buddy here got lucky last night and he *never* does."

So the eight of us are sitting at the bar, eight big guys hogging one end of the bar. If the bar were a boat, it would be sinking. The room is emptying, there are no females in sight, and I figure my chances are between zip and zero.

But no, eight ladies who had been sitting at a table around the corner from the bar, incredibly, like out of a movie, come over and start chatting. It feels like boy-girl heaven. For a moment I consider switching to electric bass permanently.

One of them sidles over to me. "Hi, my name's Patty," she says. "I really enjoyed your playing, Bill. You've got great hands."

Another body parts person, I imagine.

But here she takes my left hand and spreads it out on the bar, palm down, fingers splayed. She plants one of her hands by my thumb and the other by my pinkie. Then Patty holds her hands up in front of us, maintaining the length of my hand's span between her hands.

She smiles broadly. "Not bad, Bill. Not bad at all!"

We burst out laughing.

"What's this all about?" I ask her.

"I'm a nurse."

"A nurse?"

"Well, a student nurse. And in nursing school they taught us that there's a strong correlation between the size of a man's hand and the size of his ..."

She never finishes the sentence.

I believe that as we've driven southwest, deeper into the American heartland, the women have gotten faster. This is the most forward gal I have ever met. We turn and walk to my motel room, no questions asked.

The small talk isn't small, it's nonexistent. But when it comes to true confessions, I decide to take the lead:

"I want you to know I'm kind of new at this, Patty. I'm no rock star or anything. I've never done this before."

"That's OK," she says. "I'm kind of a groupie. I love music. And I just *adore* musicians."

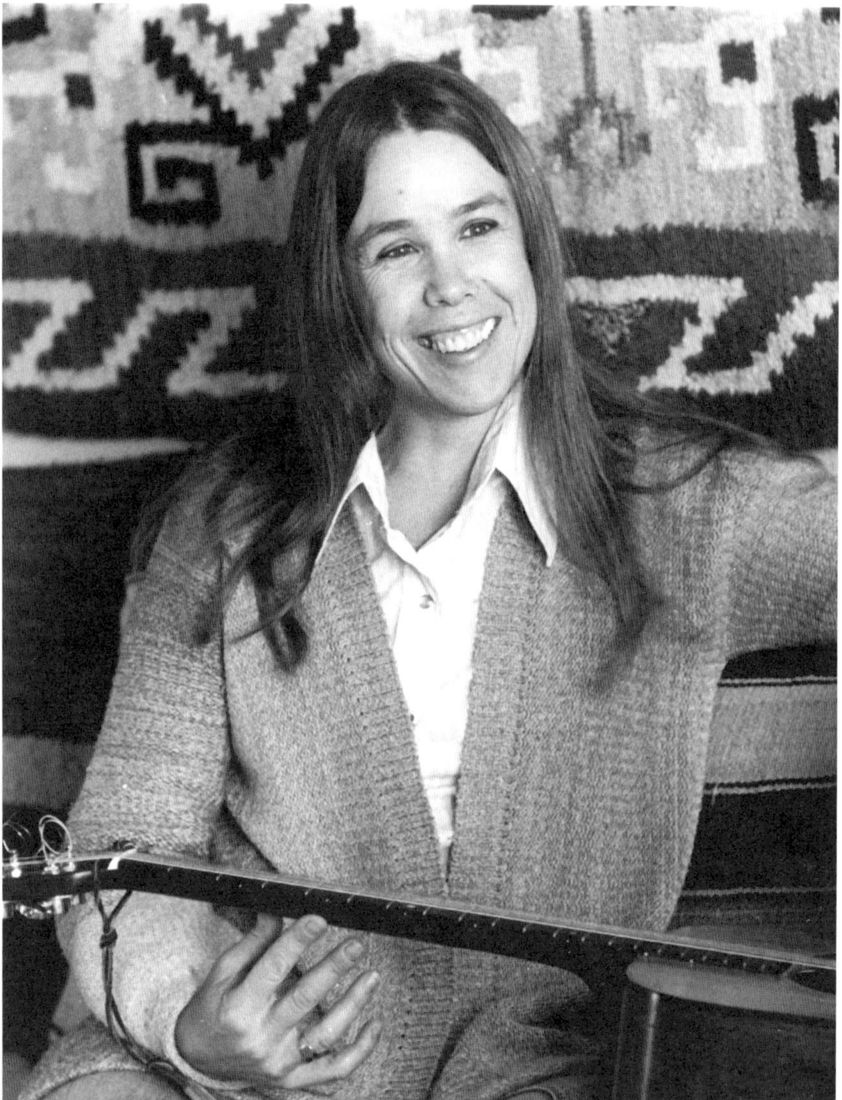

Kate Wolf
by Karl Leopold Metzenberg

A Maker of Songs ~ Kate Wolf

Nothing ruffled her serenity except the slow arrival of a recording session. Then she would get a little catch in her throat, a cough that she'd try to wash down with herbal tea. But it was just prerecording jitters, nothing unusual.

Other than that, Kate Wolf struck me as the most serene person I'd ever met. She was a Northern California singer-songwriter, and I had the pleasure of meeting Kate, getting to know her some, and playing on a couple of her albums in the late 1970s and early '80s.

Songwriters such as Kate are always asked, "Which comes first, the music or the lyrics?" With Kate, as far as I can tell, writing the lyrics came first; then she'd write the music. Spoken or recited, her lyrics sounded like poetry, and to me she always seemed to be a poet.

Her images are vivid. Her lyrics ride on the rhythm and lope on the line. Her rhymes tweak the ear, making her lyrics easy to remember. Folksinger Tom Paxton said, "With Kate, the message was always – always – love." Yes, Kate, both as a lyricist and as a human being, was always about love.

She called one afternoon in 1981 and said, "Bill, I have a lyric that needs music. Would you like to collaborate with me?" I said Of course, and she came over to my digs in Mill Valley. Kate said she was looking for a country sound. Then she read me her poem.

Gray-haired and flint-eyed, his sunburned face lined,
Grandpa was a man of few words.
He had a way of not wanting to say,
Any more than he thought could be heard.

The long years of living and day-to-day giving
Had carved a map on his face.
With little to lose, he'd learned how to choose,
And his choices were easy to trace.

Then the chorus came in:

He had the eyes of a painter,
The heart of a maker of songs, a maker of songs.
And his words fell like rain on the dry desert plain,
Precious and so quickly gone.

A melody crept up on me. It was in waltz time, with what I thought was a progressive country feel. The melody of the verse was fairly simple, and the progression was expressed with the basic I, IV, and V chords of American roots music. Together, I felt they let the verses' lyrics be heard clearly.

The music of the chorus was a dollop more complex and pushed the traditional country envelope. One of the chords was a half-diminished seventh chord – a minor seventh chord with a flatted 5th – something you don't hear all that often in country music. It added torque to the line, "And his words fell like rain," and twisted an otherwise fairly straightforward chord progression. To me, it was the pivotal chord in the music. The next stanzas read:

From a long line of teachers, and white Baptist preachers,
He was born with an Indian will.
His quiet dark eyes, reading the light
As he rode in the low Osage hills.

His school was the prairie, the sage, the wild berry,
The quail, the wide open sky,
The cottonwood thicket by the slow rolling river,
The Redbud and the hot cattle drive.

He had the eyes of a painter,
The heart of a maker of songs, a maker of songs.
And his words fell like rain on the dry desert plain,
Precious and so quickly gone.

She told me that the lyric was about her ex-husband's father. Grandpa, as the song called him, lived in Hogshooter, Oklahoma, and was the son of Baptist teachers and preachers on one side, and Cherokees on the other. He had blue, deep-blue eyes. Electric, she said.

Kate had an insight into him one afternoon. They were sitting in his kitchen, talking. She was about to go out for a ride, so she asked him what to watch for. He said that she should watch the light. That was when she knew he had the eyes of a painter.

There were days filled with thinking, nights with the drinking
For a lost love that raged like a storm.
But how his eyes smiled, when he'd talk to a child,
The rough hands so gentle and warm.

His strong arms were brown, where the long sleeves rolled down
On his faded blue cotton shirt.
When times got hard, he'd go out in the yard,
And cuss away some of his hurt.

He had the eyes of a painter,
The heart of a maker of songs, a maker of songs.
And his words fell like rain on the dry desert plain,
Precious and so quickly gone.

Kate called a week later to explain that the ex-husband, about whose father the song had been written, was himself a guitarist. But he couldn't play the half-diminished seventh chord. She wanted to know if I would change it.

I was surprised that she was asking for a change based on … *on the ex's not being able to play a chord!* The chord is easy to make, actually feels good in the left hand once you learn how to grab it. I told her I'd get back to her. But while I was licking my wounds, figuring out what to do next, Kate sat down and wrote her own music for the lyric.

An old friend, composer Gary Malkin, told me I had done wrong: "Always give the client what she wants."

Gary was right. But I'm happy that in the end it helped Kate come up with her own music. The song has been one of her audiences' favorites.

I didn't see Kate much past 1982. We talked on the phone once or twice, but her career was changing. She was on the road more, recording, writing, meeting new folks. Then, in the spring of 1986, she was diagnosed with leukemia. Within eight months the disease had called her home. She was forty-four when she died on December 10, 1986.

I remember how Kate could touch an audience. They loved what I loved: her centered calm, her beaming heart. She made them feel they were all in a living room and she was talking with them. She was accessible. She was adored.

It was more than her presence that won an audience. She wrote honestly beautiful songs that singers record to this day, songs that still touch people. There's an annual folk music festival held in her honor at a ranch in Laytonville, California: the Kate Wolf Memorial Music Festival. It draws a bigger crowd every year. Her spirit continues to influence even more of us.

All who were touched by Kate's music miss her love.

Now the garden's grown dusty, the hand axe lies rusty,
The door's banging hard in the wind.
Grandpa's store is closed down, like most of the town,
And it won't be open again.

And the big white car, sits out in the yard
Of the house he built solid and true.
But I see his eyes, burning tonight,
Like the stars in the sky he once knew.

He had the eyes of a painter,
The heart of a maker of songs, a maker of songs.
And his words fell like rain on the dry desert plain,
Precious and so quickly gone.

"Well you know my name, but ya still call me a guitar busker, a joint hanger, train hopper, tip canary or kittie-box man."

—Woody Guthrie

Under Paris Skies

The melody rolled off the fingers of the old man's right hand as his left oom-pah-pah'ed the chords of *"Sous le Ciel de Paris,"* a waltz he played with eyes closed on his piano accordion. The large instrument seemed so small in his lap, so light in his hands, you could imagine he had been born with it in his arms. He embellished the second verse with cascading triplets that swelled and faded, embracing the melody with his tenderness. I leaned back against the wall, closed my eyes, and let his dream wash over me.

The song's lyrics are about the lovers of Paris, and from his lyrical playing I could hear that the gentleman was one himself. But he had pitched his walk-by act in a breezy corridor of the Paris metro's *Porte des Lilas* station in the 19th *arrondissement.* The burned rubber of the trains' tires, whirling with diesel fumes sucked in from the streets, made it a difficult spot to linger in.

A busker – a street performer – usually drains his tip jar of all but a few coins. The message is, "Pickings are slim; please help!" His empty fedora, squatting on the concrete, said he was failing. I dropped a twenty-franc coin into it, mumbled *"Merci, monsieur,"* and picked up on the melody, humming it as Lynne Terry and I threaded our way to the train. Lynne was NPR's Paris correspondent, and I had joined her that day to interview a journalist whose book had just been published.

Some Parisian buskers, like this gentleman, are French-traditional accordionists who play the musette book. Musicians who migrated from France's Auvergne region to the 19th *arrondissement* in the 1800s started musette. Italian accordionists joined them, and the playing styles of the two cultures intermingled, creating a more sensual popular music and dance. Much of France's most lushly impressionistic music is from this era or influenced by it.

Younger buskers represent a more mixed bag. In Paris's subways I have heard a drunk belting "Feelings," classical guitar duos, rock and roll trios, and a legitimate string quartet wearing tuxedos.

On the metro platform, we found three musicians waiting for the next train. An unlikely combo of electric guitar, trumpet and high-hat cymbal, they piled into the center of the first car when the subway arrived. The guitarist set up his mini-amp, plugged in his instrument, and counted off the first tune, Vernon Duke's "April in Paris." They gave it a sloshed reading, playing woefully, probably because they were all woefully sloshed. The group tried one more with "Paris" in the title, Cole Porter's "I Love Paris" – maybe they thought we had forgotten what town we were in – and then the trumpeter, doubling as "hat man," set out to gather whatever coins he could from the riders.

In the summer of 1962, at age sixteen, I busked the streets of Paris playing "Old Joe Clark" on the 5-string, and coveted every *centime* that dropped into my open instrument case. My day's take told how well I ate that evening, whether I slept in a fleabag hotel with a squattoir down the hall, or under Paris skies. Being out in the elements all day – bombarded with noise and soot, blasted by winds and diesel fumes, shooed by the police and ignored by passersby – was exhausting, the cruelest gig. Because of this, I try to tip every busker I meet, regardless of his or her skills.

As the trumpeter walked by, I dropped ten francs into his hat.

"Thanks man," he said.

Disappointed to be so easily identified as an American, but unwilling to give up, I responded in my best French accent: *"De rien, mon pote,"* as in, "You're welcome, bud."

At the next stop the trio exited, and another busker entered. He was thirty, dark olive-complected, his left arm in a white plaster cast, apparently broken recently, though possibly the cast was a fake, a prop in his act. Tall, thin, hollow-faced – Christ-like hollow – his clothes were more greasy than dirty, his face and hands, sooted.

He boarded the car quickly as he had only seconds to perform his act before the train engines revved. He addressed his audience from behind the last booth. He spoke loudly enough to be heard at the far end, but not so loudly as to suggest good health. His tone was measured, his words memorized.

In French he said, "Ladies and Gentlemen. I am a homeless person who sleeps in the subways of Paris. I have broken my arm and cannot work. If you can spare a few coins for someone less fortunate than yourselves, I would appreciate your kindness. Thank you, messieurs-dames."

As if on cue, the hydraulic doors closed with a shriek and the subway whined down the track. His timing had been perfect, his voice mellifluous. He started to work his way through the car, pausing in front of each booth of four seats. As he approached us, Lynne dug into her purse for coins.

"Why are you giving to him?" I asked.

"It was a good sales pitch. He has a great voice. He could do voice-over work if he wanted. And he looks hungry enough."

That he did.

The young man thrust his bare hand a foot under our noses – unusual, a bare hand, not a cap. It was a strangely intimate move. We had to stare at it, read it's scratched story. Lynne and I pressed coins into his hand, and then looked up at him.

He nodded, *merci*'ed us, and moved on.

We exited the train, turned the corner to the first corridor, and there she was, propped up against the wall, sleeping. Her two-year-old daughter slept in her arms. They were like the concrete floor they rested on and the wall they were slumped against: gray with grime. The two slept though it was a noisy corridor and thousands walked by. They blended into the metro-scape so transparently, that at first I mistook them for discarded trash. It was the reflection of the overhead neon lights flashing in the woman's aluminum begging plate that startled me.

We were being swept along with the throng that had exited with us. It was a coming-home-from-work crowd, dog-tired, rushing towards rest.

The sight of this exhausted mother and daughter caused many people to drop change into her plate as they trudged by. But others saw her too late, and high-stepped to avoid walking on her as they passed. Then they pulled over, fished change from their pockets, and swam back against the stream to find her plate.

But as we dropped coins in front of her, a Parisian lectured us: "They are gypsies. She is not sleeping; she is faking it. And what child could sleep through that noise? The child has been drugged with a shot of wine to keep her asleep. When their day is done, they will leave the metro and her 'husband' will pick them up in his Mercedes."

Europeans have a different experience with Roma – gypsies – than do Americans. We see them in films that often romanticize their lives. Europeans know them from their daily experiences, and they don't like what they claim to sometimes see: vagabonds, trespassers, and worse.

Every busker we had seen that day was putting on an act. It could be that this motionless gypsy woman and child were acting as well. But their performance was a showstopper.

They would awaken to a mound of coins.

Jerry Loved to Pick

Mandolinist David Grisman, someone I've enjoyed playing music with many times over the years, called me one afternoon. It seems that David had spotted a rare old banjo – this was a pre-World War II, gold-plated, Weymann 5-string banjo – and he had brought it home for his old friend, Jerry Garcia. Jerry, of course, was an electric guitarist and the leader of the primordial jam band, the Grateful Dead. But originally Garcia was a bluegrass banjo picker, and his very first instrument was a Weymann 5-string that he no longer owned.

Well, the moment Jerry laid eyes on the Weymann David had brought him, he fell in love with it. He strapped it on, picked a few notes, turned to David and said, "Call up a bass player. Let's do some bluegrass pickin'!"

So, David was calling me that afternoon to see if I could come over *now* to pick some bluegrass with him and Jerry Garcia.

Well, … I had heard of Jerry Garcia.

So, I cancelled the rest of my life, tossed the bass in the back of the car, and was over at David's before he had hung up on our phone call.

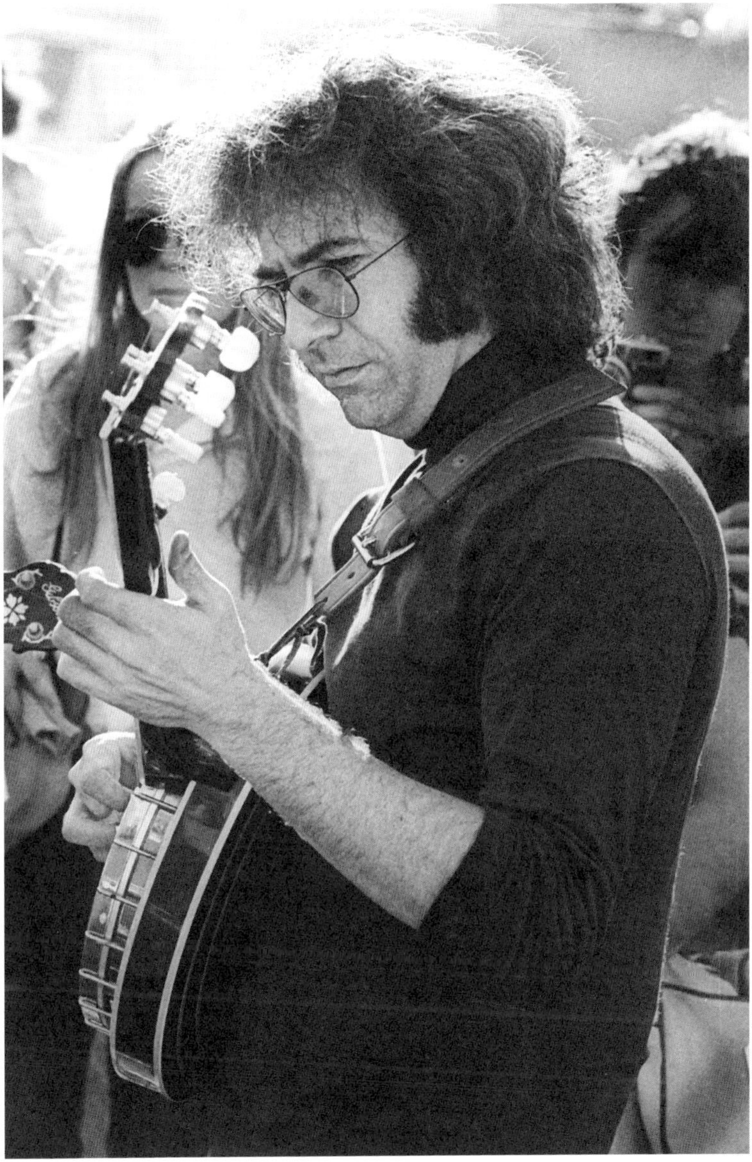

Jerry Garcia · April 28, 1974
By Jon Sievert

I walk into the living room and there, larger than life, is Jerry Garcia. First thing I notice about Jerry is, he's got a wall-to-wall smile that lights up the room. It sits behind a massive salt-and-pepper beard and a mane of salt-and-pepper hair.

He's wearing a plain black T-shirt – no Grateful Dead logo – plain Levi's, plain black high-tops. He's got this gorgeous Weymann strapped around him.

We reach out to shake hands. "Hi, my name's Bill."

"Hi man, I'm Jerry."

Ya see. I *knew* it was Jerry.

Jerry starts showing me the Weymann. He points out the mother-of-pearl inlay on the fingerboard, the engraving on the gold hoop. He flips it over and shows me the wavy grain of the pearwood resonator. He loves this banjo.

At this moment, David finally hangs up on our phone call and strolls into the living room. He gets out his Martin. Jerry's got the Weymann strapped on. As I unsheathe my bass they decide on the bluegrass classic, "Roll In My Sweet Baby's Arms."

Garcia kicks off the tune on the banjo. As soon as he starts playing, his face lights up into an even bigger smile, and I see this:

That Jerry is living the hippie vision of the '60s, which was, after all, the vision of love.

That Jerry gives his love through playing music.

And that Jerry *loves* to pick.

Then Garcia sings the first verse.

Ain't gonna work on the railroad.

And Jerry never did.

Ain't gonna work on the farm.

That neither.

Gonna lay around the shack,
Til the mail train comes back,
And roll in my sweet baby's arms.

Now that, I guess, Jerry did. Then David and I harmonize on the chorus:

Roll in my sweet baby's arms,
Roll in my sweet baby's arms,
Lay around the shack,
Til the mail train comes back,
And roll in my sweet baby's arms.

Above the clucking of the banjo, the boom of the Dreadnought and the heartbeat of the bass, a familiar voice sings plaintively. It is Jerry Garcia's voice, in its own way and to its own generation, an American classic, as recognizable as Sinatra's.

~

It was around this time, the early '90s, that Jerry was helping out on an album by the bluegrass guitarist and singer, Red Allen. Garcia had played on a few tracks and his name was on the cover.

The next time I bumped into Jerry was on April 5, 1993. By then the album had already done well for Red. It was the first recording he had ever made that had recouped its expenses and gone on to pay him royalties. This was due to the fine pickin' and singin' on the album, but also, most certainly, to Jerry's appearance on some of the tracks, which must have brought Dead Heads into the record stores.

I ran into Jerry as he was walking out of the 7-Eleven on Miller Avenue in Mill Valley. He had a soda in one hand and three packs of Pall-Malls in the other.

I had to tell him that Red Allen had passed away just two days before.

"What did he die of?" Garcia asked.

"Well, Jerry, Red had been a longtime cigarette smoker. He, uh, ... he died of lung cancer."

Jerry looked down sheepishly at the cigarettes he was holding. Then he looked up at me and said, "All the old-timers are goin'."

The last time I ran into Jerry was at San Francisco's Davies Symphony Hall, back in the greenroom. This was following a 1992 concert by the master of jazz violin, Stéphane Grappelli.

Stéphane has since passed on, but the velvet of his sound has never been surpassed. If there is a song that the word "gossamer" sings, it is of the lightness of Stéphane Grappelli's tone on the violin.

Well, Stéphane was in the greenroom receiving company. I had already gone through the line and congratulated him on a magnificent show. At this moment Grappelli was sitting on a green sofa, chatting with none other than the master of classical violin, Isaac Stern.

For some reason, there are many stories about Isaac Stern. With all respect to the revered maestro – may he rest in peace – here are two.

The first took place in Dallas, at the 1989 opening of the Meyerson Symphony Center, the new home of the Dallas Symphony Orchestra. Stern was the featured soloist at the Center's first concert, a free performance for Dallas's citizens in honor of their longstanding support of their hometown orchestra. I think the powers-that-were at the Center would have preferred to hire Texas native-son Bob Wills, the undiluted King of Western Swing. But Wills had passed away in 1975, so they settled for the next best thing, Isaac Stern, to open the Center for them.

It was a grand event, executed as only Dallasites know how, which is at full bore. Oil barons and cattle punchers arrived in their rented tuxedos, and their wives in their best gowns.

Stern was driven to the front door in a stretch limo, this being Texas, probably stretchier than any other. He stepped out of the vehicle wearing tailcoat and formal trousers, and trotted up the steps, his cased Stradivarius tucked under his arm. He arrived at the front door to be greeted by a security guard. The guard eyeballed Stern and, seeing through the formal ware, took him for a picker, albeit a well-dressed one.

"Sorry bud, all musicians gotta enter through the back door."

"My dear sir, you don't understand. I am Isaac Stern, the featured soloist with the Dallas Symphony Orchestra this evening."

"Look bud, I don't care if you're Bob Wills, you're going in the back door."

A pause for a laugh … and now the second story.

In another time and space, Stern was receiving company in the Green Room of Carnegie Hall following a concert he had given there. A matronly woman, dressed head to toe in ermine and pearls, breezed over to him and said:

"Mr. Stern, your concert tonight was marvelous, simply marvelous. You know, tomorrow afternoon I am giving a garden party for the *crème de la crème* of New York society at my estate in the Hamptons. It would be delightful if you would come by with your fiddle and play a couple of tunes for us."

"Madam, I would love to bring my Stradivarius violin and perform some solos for you, however, in deference to my managers and agents, I'm afraid I would have to charge you 100,000 dollars."

"You want 100,000 dollars? That's no problem at all. However in that case, I'll have to insist that you enter through the servants' quarters, and that you not mingle with my guests when you're done playing."

To which Stern replied, "That's fine, madam. In that case my fee will be 50,000 dollars."

A pause to think about that, hopefully a smile, … and then, where were we?

Ah yes, in the Green Room of San Francisco's Davies Symphony Hall, with Stéphane Grappelli.

At this moment David Grisman and Jerry Garcia entered the room. David had known Stéphane for some time, so he brought Jerry over to Grappelli and introduced these two music giants by saying:

"Stéphane, I'd like you to meet an old friend of mine. This is Jerry Garcia."

Stéphane smiled, said *"Enchanté!"* reached up, and shook Jerry's hand. But clearly there was no recognition on his face as to who this Jerry Garcia might be.

David saw this, so he continued in a slightly louder voice, "Stéphane, Jerry is the leader of the rock group, the Grateful Dead."

Stéphane replied, *"Ah oui. Mais certainement!* Very pleased to meet you," reached up again and more enthusiastically shook Garcia's hand, though again you could see in his face that he had no idea who the Grateful Dead was either.

But Grappelli was no dummy. He sensed that he was being introduced to someone important, and that he should say *something.* So Stéphane Grappelli, who was eighty-four years old, looked up at Jerry Garcia and blurted out:

"Myself, I am just grateful to be alive!"

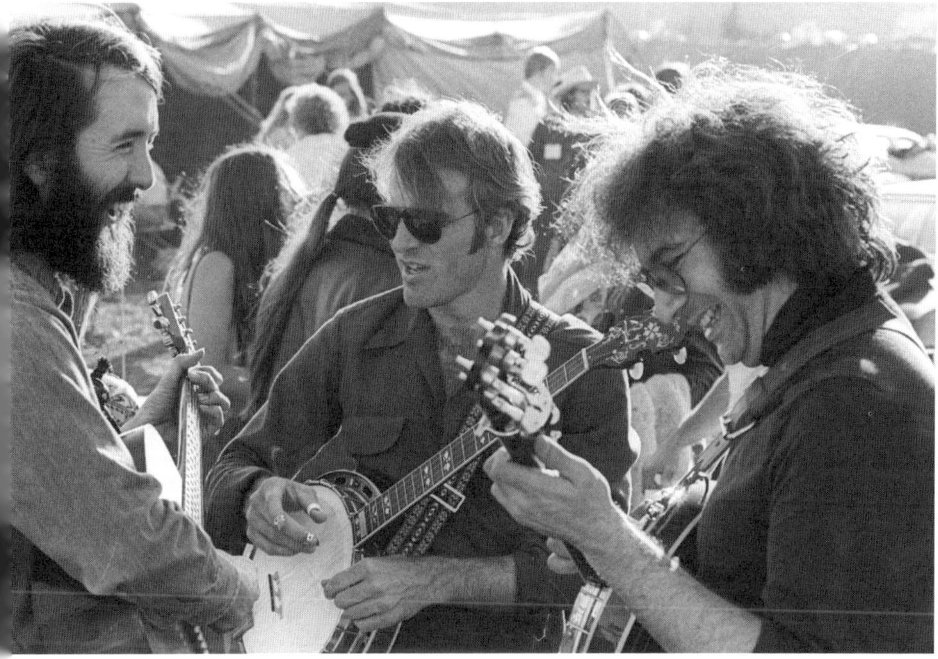

Steve Martin cracks wise
John McEuen and Jerry Garcia crack up
Golden State Bluegrass Festival · April 28, 1974
By Jon Sievert

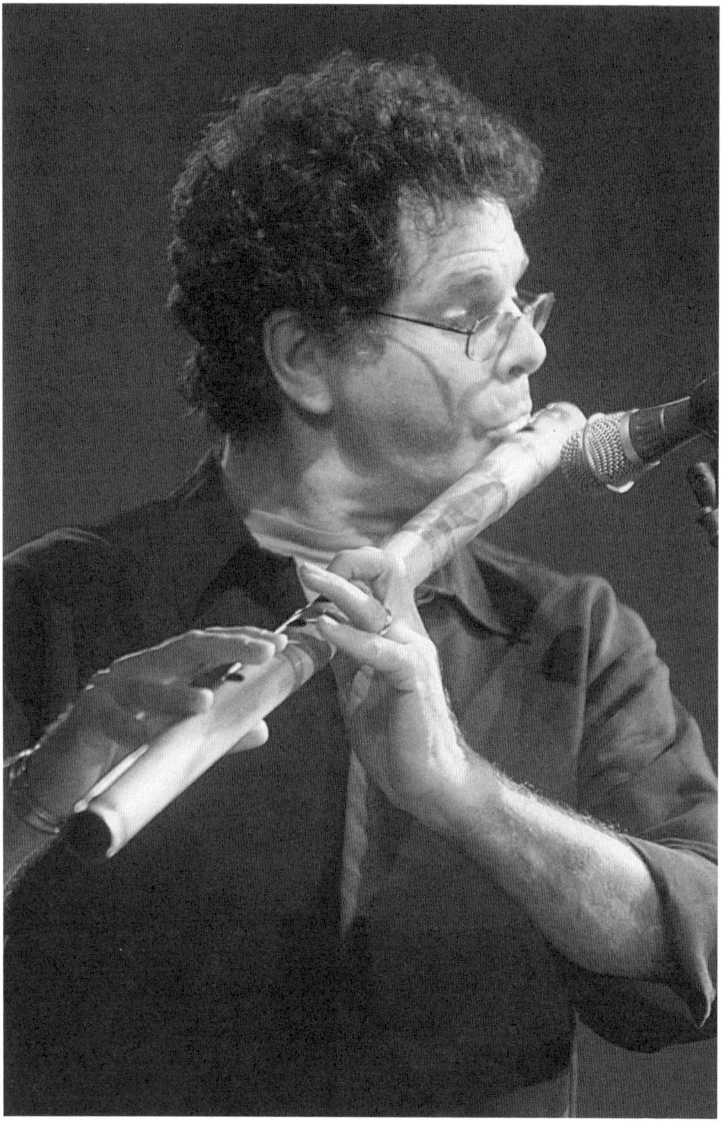

Steve Gorn
Guanajuato, Mexico · October 16, 2008
By Danilo Amilcar

Swimming the Oceans

"Baba would tune his sarode one final time and then, with the first stroke ... everything else blurred into nothingness."
—Lajo Gupta
Ali Akbar Khan's daughter

Steve Gorn, an old college friend, was visiting me in Mill Valley in February of 1991. We had played in a band together at Penn State, modestly called the Jazz Spokesmen. Steve led the group, composed for it, and played sax and silver flute. After graduating, he fell in love with the bansuri flute and moved to India to study the instrument and immerse himself in the culture.

He was staying at my home for a few days while on a North California tour playing Indian classical music. One of his solo flute concerts was at the Ali Akbar College of Music in San Rafael, founded by Ali Akbar Khan. Khansahib, as he is called, is a master of the Indian sarode, a 25-string, un-fretted, plucked instrument. He plays with spellbinding intensity, lyricism, and spiritual depth, and it was the renowned violinist Yehudi Menuhin who called him, "possibly the greatest musician in the world."

But perhaps more important, Khansahib is a master teacher of Indian music. One of his long-time disciples, David Trasoff, said of him: "Being his student was like being in the presence of a supernova of pure musical thought and awareness. Whatever you could show him you had learned, he was prepared in turn to show you how much further you could go, seemingly without limit. His dedication to teaching music, and his commitment to a goal of transplanting his music tradition into an international tradition, was unprecedented."

I drove Steve to the February 14 concert at the college, a blissful evening of Indian classical music. Afterward, while Steve was in the greenroom packing up his instruments, Khansahib phoned and invited him over to his home for a reception. Since I was driving, I got to tag along.

I'd had a standoff with my dad on the phone that day, so as we drove, Steve and I started talking about fathers and sons. I asked him how he had related to his father, a professional pianist who had passed away four years before.

"My father was not supportive of my jazz saxophone playing," Steve said. "He had called it 'primitive.' And as for my Indian flute playing, he simply couldn't hear it.

"But when he died, I wanted to honor his life. With the help of some of his old cronies, I held a memorial service at home and invited a hundred of my father's friends and relatives. The plan was for anyone who felt the spirit to stand up and say something about my dad.

"I spoke first, and when I was halfway through I made a casual, maybe slightly sarcastic remark about my dad's nonsupport of my music.

"Immediately a friend of my father's stood up and said, 'You're wrong Steve. Your father was very proud of your music. He always told me when you had a record coming out or when you were playing a big concert. Once we were together in a restaurant, the radio started played your Indian music … and your father went wild. He stopped everyone who passed our booth and said: "Ya hear that? That's my boy Steve playing!" ' "

Steve turned to me and said, "I felt this was a message to me from my father. Maybe he had been listening all along."

We drove a mile in silence, and then Steve continued, "But have you heard about the relationship Khansahib had with his dad?"

Steve told me that Ali Akbar Khan learned his music from his father, Baba Allauddin Khan, who was revered in his time as an *acharya*, the most knowledgeable master in his field. As a boy, Khansahib would awaken, dress in the dark, and put in a four-hour practice session before breakfast. Then he would take a long lesson from his father, a second practice, lunch, and then a quick nap. A third practice session followed, and finally a lesson from his father that went deep into the night.

Ali Akbar Khan followed this eighteen-hour a day regimen, within the environment of a formal Indian court, until he left home to marry. Then he took lessons from his father every time he visited home, until Khansahib was fifty and his father was in his hundreds.

That's a lot of instructional time with dad in any man's culture, and it made me wonder about the relationship of this famous father and famous son – what it must have been like.

Khansahib's San Anselmo cottage looked warm and homey as Steve and I pulled up. His number one American student, James Pomerantz, opened the door. Standing behind him were Ali Akbar's wife, Mary Khan, and then Khansahib himself. We removed our shoes and they led us through the house to a softly lit sitting room. Various religious symbols lined the walls: there were Buddhas, crosses, altars, and pictures of Hindu and Moslem saints.

Khansahib asked us about drinks, and since he was drinking Scotch, Steve and I went for the same. We took seats in a circle and Jim brought us the round. Steve had first met Khansahib twenty years ago, so they had much to talk about.

But finally there was a lull. Though I was sitting across from Ali Akbar in the circle, the circle was small. I leaned forward, put my elbows to my knees, and I was *this* close to his face. He was so vital, that even then I couldn't read his age, so I asked him: "Khansahib, may I ask, how old are you?"

"I am sixty-nine."

"And what religion are you?"

Mary and Jim laughed. Khansahib smiled, and gestured to the assorted religious icons: "I'm all religions, as you may see."

"Khansahib, you have had a long and productive career. At age sixty-nine, what are your music goals?"

Incredulous, Jim asked Mary, "What did he say?"

"He asked him what his music goals are," Mary replied. "*This* I want to hear!"

Khansahib said, "Oh yes. I have definite music goals. I want to swim the oceans of the world. I want to swim in all the music oceans."

"What kind of music is your favorite?"

"Oh, Indian music, most certainly, and Western classical music, Bach and Beethoven. But to me, Indian classical music has heart. So much music I hear, like this rock and roll, has no heart."

We all smiled at that.

"Khansahib," I said, "you have learned a lot of music in your life."

"Yes."

"Much of that music you learned from your father."

"Yes. I learned much from my father."

"Over a long period of time."

"Yes, a very long time. And after my father died, I continued receiving music lessons from him."

"Then could you please tell me this, Khansahib: All his life the son listens to the father telling him what to do. After a while the son wants to say, 'OK Dad. Enough already. I heard it!' And yet you had to take instruction from your father as both a son *and* a music student for a very long time. Please tell me this, Khansahib, how did you deal with that?"

Khansahib's dark-brown eyes lit up. The master sat up tall in his chair and he grinned widely with the wisdom I sought. *This* question he was going to enjoy answering.

"That's easy!" Khansahib said. "I hated my father. Yes, I learned much music from him. But I hated my father, sometimes. I hated … that he made me practice. I practiced so much, I had no chance to play. So I was fifty before I started loving music. When I started loving music, I started loving my father."

June 19, 2009

News has come today from Alam Khan, Ali Akbar Khan's son, that Khansahib passed away yesterday morning, at the age of eighty-seven. Shortly after, more details arrived from David Trasoff, and from another of Khansahib's protégés, George Ruckert.

On the eve of his death, June 17, 2009, Ali Akbar Khan was in the sitting room of his home, surrounded by family and students. Eyes closed, chin on chest, half-comatose, but sensing people around him, he said, "Lesson? Come for lesson?"

"No, Khansahib. No lesson. We are here to be with you," was their response.

"Lesson. Bring the harmonium," he said, turning to Alam.

The request astonished everyone. Khansahib was rapidly succumbing to kidney failure. His family wanted him to rest. But Khansahib insisted, so Alam retrieved the instrument, one that is used as a drone in Indian music. The master asked one of his youngest disciples, Gaayatri Kaundinya, who had been taking vocal lessons from him since she was five, to play Sa, the root on the Indian scale, on the harmonium.

As the lone note settled on the hushed room, Khansahib began to quietly teach "Rag Durga," an evening raga named for the Goddess of feminine energy.

Khansahib said, "Sing Sa."

The students intoned Sa, accompanied by gushing tears.

"Sing Re," said Khanshib.

The students sang Re, as tears continued flowing.

And so, one by one, slowly, he dictated the ascending and descending notes of Rag Durga. Khansahib taught while all in the room sang and wept.

At the rag's conclusion, he said, "End with sa-dha-sa."

The students sang sa-dha-sa.

"No, not like that. Sing sadha-sa."

They sang the sadha-sa with the first two notes in quicker succession.

"Again," he said.

They repeated it.

Then silence.

In the centuries-old tradition of Indian music, one of passing knowledge from guru to disciple, Khansahib was, like his father before him, a dedicated teacher. Even on death's threshold, semi-conscious and unable to lift his head, he passed along his knowledge with his last breaths.

Ali Akbar Kahn taught Indian music to disciples who in turn teach it to their students across the globe. The effect of his teaching and his power as a teacher will be felt for generations.

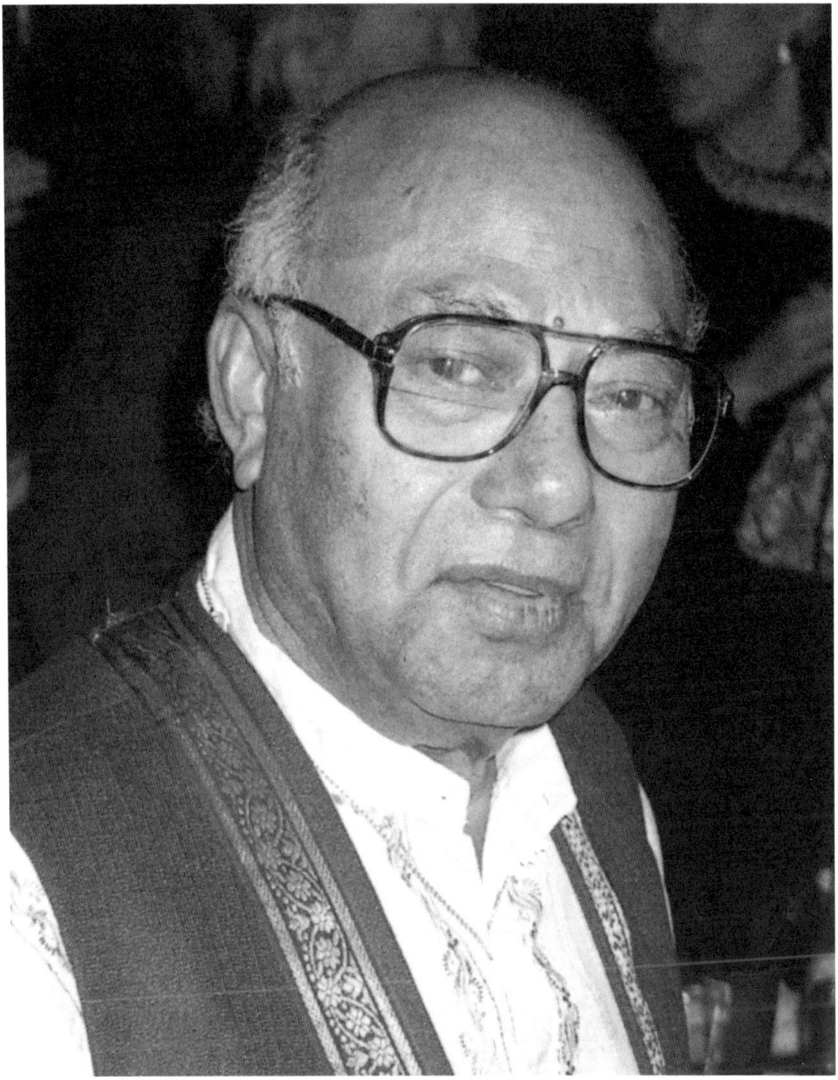

Ali Akbar Khan

Bay Area Grammy Awards, San Francisco · February 15, 1998

"If the button-down, scrubbed-looking Kingston Trio are the undergraduates of big-time U.S. folk-singing, The Limeliters are the faculty."

—Lou Gottlieb

Open Heart ~ Lou Gottlieb

Khansahib said that he continued receiving music lessons from his father after his father had died. I wondered what he meant by that, but didn't ask. It seemed too personal.

At a packed San Francisco State big band concert in 1981, I found myself sitting next to a guy who looked mid-fifties. Tall forehead, dark eyes, thick brows. We started chatting and found we were not only fellow lovers of big band but fellow string bassists as well. Soon it became clear that he was there for more than the music. He also had a romantic interest in the band's girl singer, a fetching blond soprano some thirty-five years his junior.

He introduced himself as Lou Gottlieb. After the show he introduced me to his singer friend, and the three of us drove to his home on Scott Street in San Francisco where we hung out in the parlor.

Lou Gottlieb was the organizer, driving force, front man, spiritual rock, string bassist, bass vocalist, and musical director of The Limeliters. This folk music trio was wildly successful in the early '60s, and included Alex Hassilev (playing banjo and singing baritone) and Glenn Yarbrough (playing guitar and singing tenor). Their 1961 LP featured two big hits for them, "There's a Meeting' Here Tonight," and Have Some "Madeira My Dear." The album rode the Billboard charts for seventy-four weeks.

Lou's brilliant vocal arrangements spotlighted Glenn's crystalline high notes, while Alex filled in the high baritone line and provided intricate guitar and banjo accompaniments. The three brought the art of American folk group vocals, some have said, to its highest form. They projected a "Stout Hearted Men" stage persona, like eating haunches of roast beef with bare hands and sly smiles. The original group ended in 1963 when Glenn Yarbrough left for a solo career.

Lou had a Ph.D. in musicology and loved playing the piano, especially Bach. A genuine Bösendorfer grand sat unpretentiously in his parlor. Hand-made in Austria and profoundly expensive, they are rarely seen, even in major symphony halls. The tone of a Bösendorfer is called "floating." Every pianist who has played a "Bosie," as they are called, would love to own one. Jazz pianist George Shearing, whose ears were elephantine, played one. (It was said that Shearing could make an out-of-tune piano sound in tune.) Oscar Peterson's piano was a Bösendorfer Imperial, one that his roadies, legend has it, hauled from gig to gig.

While I was admiring Lou's Bosie, out of the blue he asked, "Bill, have you ever thought about the words to 'Oh Danny Boy'?"

Since the 1960s I have thought a lot about Bob Dylan's lyrics. I mean, who is the joker? Who is the thief? But offhand I had not reflected on the lyrics to "Oh Danny Boy."

"No, Lou. I haven't thought about 'Oh Danny Boy' all that much."

"Well, what are the words?"

"Let's see, 'Oh Danny boy, the pi … '."

"Wait. Wait right there. What does that mean?"

" 'Oh Danny boy?' What does 'Oh Danny boy' mean? … Gee, Lou. I don't know."

"Well, think about it."

I thought about it, hard. I still didn't know.

"Well," he said, "who would call another man, 'boy?' "

"OK. I got it. A father might call his son, 'boy.' "

"Exactly! So, who is singing the song, and to whom?"

"A father is singing the song to his son."

"Right. What's the next line?"

"The pipes, the pipes are calling."

"OK. What does that mean?"

I was trying not to look too stupid, and failing badly. "Uh, I dunno, Lou."

"Well, how many pipes do you know?"

"Only one, I guess: the pipes of war."

"Perfect. So what's happening here?"

"The father is telling the son that the pipes of war are calling. There's a wartime draft of some sort going on."

"OK! Good. What's the next line?"

"From glen to glen, and down the mountain side."

"And what does that mean?"

"Well, it could mean that it's a big war, a large call-up, from the glens to the mountains."

"Well, maybe. The words could mean that. But when the British wanted to conscript Irish lads to fight their wars, they didn't dare go into the towns themselves. So they sent their bagpipers to the hills surrounding the towns. There they'd skirl the pipes of war, and the Irish lads would know that they had to go fight. What's the next line?"

"The summer's gone and all the roses falling."

"And what does that mean?"

"Well, it could mean that it's autumn. Or it could mean that the father is in the autumn of his life."

"Good! What's next?"

" 'Tis you, 'tis you must go and I must bide."

"And that means..."

"That the father is too old to fight. The son must go to war."

"Sure. What's next?"

"But come you back when summer's in the meadow, or when the valley's hushed and white with snow."

"Which means?"

"Well, it could mean 'Come back next summer or the following winter.' "

"It could be that. And the next line...?"

"It's I'll be there in sunshine or in shadow..."

"And that?"

"Well, it means the father will be waiting for his son in summer or in winter."

"Or what else?"

"Well, I guess 'shadow' could be an allusion to the father's death. He'll be waiting for his son even if he's died."

"That's right. And the last line?"

" 'Oh Danny boy, oh Danny boy, I love you so.' Well, that line speaks for itself."

I was impressed that Lou had wrung so much from the lyrics. Just what he had gleaned from the first three words, "Oh Danny boy," was impressive. I have listened to the song differently since then.

Lou didn't talk about himself all that much. He mentioned The Limeliters only once. He said it was just the three guys and a roadie, the halls were filled and the money was great. It was an easy gig. And he said that the guys in the original group, Alex and Glenn, were his best men friends.

Lou never mentioned that he was the founder of California's first and best-known open-land commune, called Morning Star Ranch, legendary among students of 1960's-era California history. It was a different time, the '60s. If you didn't live through it, if you were born into the Greed Era, you may find this hard to believe, so hang on for the ride.

In the 1960s, many young people believed that if you were hungry, you should have food, and moreover, the food should be free. If you needed clothes, you should have them, and they should be free. Across the country, groups such as San Francisco's Diggers sprung up to fill these needs with free food banks and clothing bins.

Lou Gottlieb believed that if you wanted to live on the land, you should be able to do so – and that too should be free. He owned thirty acres in western Sonoma County on what had once been a religious retreat named *Morning Star,* another name for the Virgin Mary. Lou opened up his land to all who wanted to live there. He used a phrase to describe the ranch, one that reflected his intellectual side as well as his generosity. Morning Star, Lou said, was "Land access to which is denied no one."

Folks came from around the globe to live this experiment. They created a new community lifestyle that was tribal, yet independent and free. Many were artists, some, maybe most, were deeply spiritual, and some were deeply Christian. But the ranch also attracted its share of misfits, hard druggies and winos who had not understood the heart of communal living, who were just there to mooch.

In time, one powerful neighbor, and then the Sonoma County powers-that-were, grew to resent the presence of these young folks who were living contrary to the principles of the "Great Society," as Lyndon Johnson called it. These hippies were living free, doing their own stuff, and the District Attorney didn't like it. The county leveraged the building and health codes to literally bulldoze the place under. It's said that it cost Lou a million dollars to fight them over the course of five years, at a time when a million meant something.

Lou went back to The Limeliters in 1981, maybe to rejingle his pockets. It was around then that I met him. The

Limeliters at that time were Lou, Alex, and Red Grammer, who had replaced Glen Yarborough. In 1991, I met another Limeliter, Rick Dougherty, who took over the tenor chair vacated by Red Grammar and played in the group for five years with Lou.

Lou Gottlieb died July 11, 1996. At Lou's memorial, Rick summed up his band mate with these words: "Lou loved life as no one I have ever known. He was a compassionate teacher, a good friend. Lou believed that life itself was the greatest comedy, and he talked about how the true spirit of the universe was hysterical laughter at the great cosmic joke of life."

Meeting with Rick got me thinking about Lou. I started researching him, the Limeliters, Morning Star Ranch, and "Oh, Danny Boy."

I read up on the song, composed in 1810 by an Englishman, Fred Weatherly. Originally there were only two verses. Any third verse you've ever heard, and there are many, are not among the original lyrics. So the song has reached folk music status. It has changed as it has been handed down. This in spite its having been printed and recorded from its inception, acts which usually solidify the original in the public's ear.

I'd been practicing "Oh Danny Boy" as a string bass solo, and played it in front of Rick one day as he was telling me about Lou. Rick stopped in mid-sentence and said, "You're giving me goose bumps playing that on the bass. That's the song Lou used to play for sound-checking his string bass before a gig."

So "Oh Danny Boy" had deeper resonance for Lou than I had previously realized: as a song, as a lyric, as a bass part he played behind the tune, and as a melody he played as a bass solo. He had immersed himself in the song.

I researched Morning Star Ranch. One of the women

who figures in its history, Gina Sutton, took me on a tour of the place, still lived on and maintained by a caretaker. As we walked the grounds, she told me that all who knew Lou loved him. He was deeply generous, not frivolously, not "to a fault," she said, just generous.

Lou was also a seeker. Like Khansahib, he was interested in God in all forms: Vishnu, Shiva, Christ, Buddha.

Lou loved to talk and could converse with anyone. He spoke with his Hollywood friends as easily as with a king or a drunk.

Gina paused at a spot on a hillside and pointed to a spot where Lou, she, and another Morningstarian, Pam Millward, famously had a shared vision. They saw a figure, a female apparition floating above the ground. Lou said it was the Virgin Mary, the mother of Jesus.

I asked Gina about this.

She said, "Well, I'm Jewish, so I didn't see Mary. I just saw a woman."

Ramon Sender, a seminal Morning Star figure, told me of Lou's compassion for all, but also said that Lou loved to joke and could dominate a gathering with his off-the-wall humor. Lou was very bright and very funny, a rare and forceful combination. When Morning Star died, the Morningstarians lost their hope for a revolution of love and peace. The Ranch lives on in their hearts, and the open land movement lives on, Ramon said, in the encampments of the Occupy movement.

At Morning Star, Lou's generosity was there for *all* who wanted to come and receive it, pretty much without restriction.

On the Internet, I watched the videos of the Limeliters shot at performances through the years. Lou's personality shines, and his way with a room is masterful. He turns songs into performance pieces for frontman and audience. It is Lou making out with the room, joking, miming, singing, cracking wise, and always having great laughs.

I've been trying to put Lou in the middle of The Limeliters, Morning Star, and "Oh Danny Boy," trying to understand the part of him that ran through them all.

My dad was killed in an automobile accident in 2007. An electronics engineer, he went about tasks in his life systematically, often taking notes in his ever-ready black book, making data tables, plotting trends. As my mother's health declined over a three-year period, he recorded every drug she took – and there were many – and charted her reactions to them. He researched her prescriptions, and could correlate dosages with the effects and side effects they were having on her. He advised the prescribing doctors about what her drug levels should be, and they learned to trust his word. As an engineer – a meticulous one – he was a fellow scientist, and they understood and trusted his methodology and analyses.

I can be more intuitive and haphazard in my approaches to problem solving. But for this research on related subjects, it seemed that going about this methodically, a little like my dad would have, might serve my purposes. I started a file folder.

One evening, pursuing this project, I was on the web with four browser windows open. In one was the history of Morning Star, in the second, a biography of Lou. The third displayed a history of The Limeliters, and the fourth, a treatise on "Oh Danny Boy." They were neatly tiled next to each other on the screen. I noticed this tidiness and organization that were more like my dad than me, and enjoyed the kind of laugh that Lou gave to many.

I saw that it was Lou's open heart that ran through Morning Star Ranch, his Limeliters career, and his love of "Oh Danny Boy," a father's lament for his son. And I understood what Khansahib meant when he said he had taken lessons from his father after his father was gone.

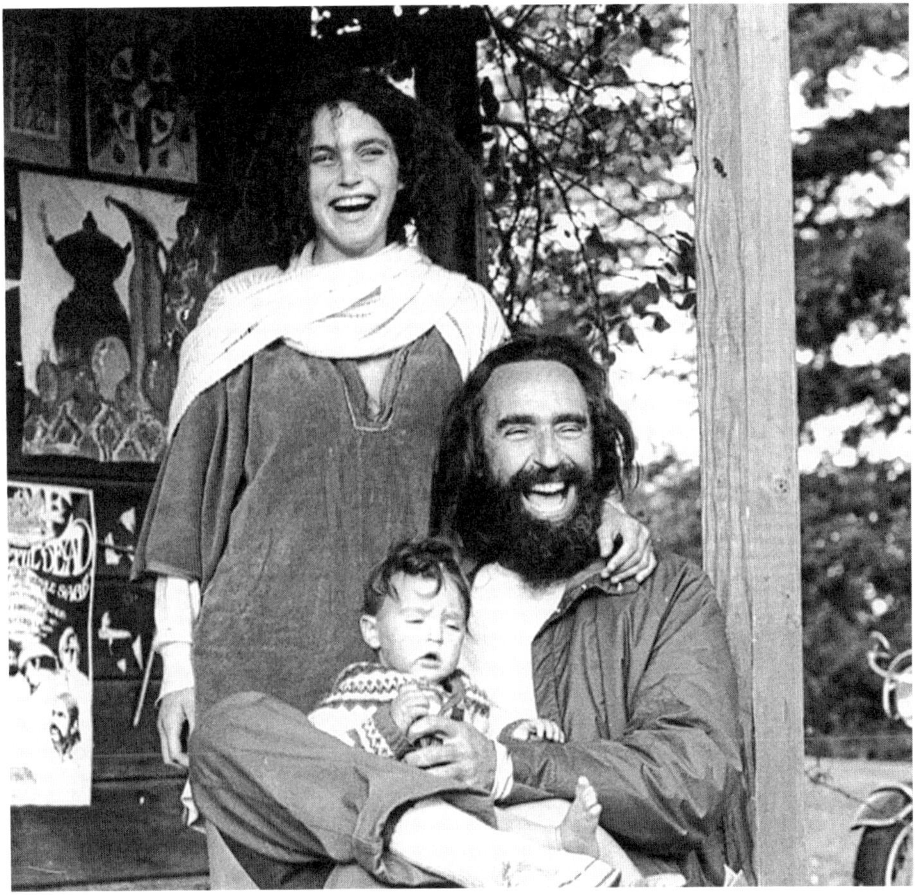

Lou Gottlieb with Rena Morningstar and their son, Vishnu
Morning Star Ranch, Occidental · 1970
By Gilles Boisvert

Catching Up with Mary

In 1982, I read that Peter, Paul and Mary were going to be playing the Concord Pavilion, an hour's drive from my home. So I sent Mary, through one of her agents, a manuscript of my story, "MARY, … Peter & Paul." Then I bought a ticket for the show, still a month away, and waited.

Finally, the big day of their big show arrived. I drove out to the Concord Pavilion, and watched Peter, Paul & Mary preside over another heart-warming love-fest. When the show was over I went to the stage door and knocked. A burly guard opened it. He was not going to let me in. But after a few minutes of persistent persuasion he caved, and I scampered inside.

I found myself in a major backstage hangar of studios, refectories, rehearsal nooks, and greenrooms. I caught up with Mary when she had finished greeting her fans and signing albums, and the two of us settled down in a small dressing room.

"Mary, I wrote a story about the time I played bass with you guys at the Bread and Roses Festival. I tried to send it to you through your agent. Did you receive it?"

"A story about playing with us? Gee, I don't know. If you had a copy, all I'd have to do is read the first sentence or two, and I'd know whether I've seen it. Do you have a copy with you?"

I had three copies with me.

So I took one out of my coat pocket, opened it to the front page and handed it to her. The story's title was typeset like this:

MARY, . . . Peter & Paul

Mary looked at the title. Then she looked up at me and said, "Oh, I like it already!"

Brotherhood of the Stick

The liberation of France from the Nazis, a saga that began with the Allied invasion of the Normandy beaches on Debarkation Day, June 6, 1944, is a period of history that has called me since I read "Is Paris Burning?" as a kid. I traveled to Normandy for both the 40th and 50th anniversaries of D-Day. The fortieth was a wave of quieter ceremonies that rippled through the Norman countryside, riding in the wake of the original invasion front.

The 50th anniversary saw tens of thousands of vets from America, France, England, Scotland, Australia, Canada, and New Zealand, driving Normandy in vintage army jeeps, ambulances and trucks that they had brought over at personal expense. It was likely the world's largest block party.

On that 50th anniversary of D-Day, June 6, 1994, I was staying at the Normandy farmhouse of an old friend, Jean-François. We had heard that the landing beaches of Omaha, Utah, and Juneau would be jammed with world dignitaries, their guards, and the French police. So I headed off to one of the only other French towns that would be celebrating its liberation that day, Ranville.

Ranville had been a vital crossroad for the German army. Reinforcements traveling from Calais to Germany's front line in Normandy passed through this hamlet.

To cut this supply line, the Allies liberated Ranville on June 6, at just past midnight. An attack on neighboring Bénouville Bridge, spearheaded by three Horsa gliders, the 2nd Battalion Oxfordshire and Buckinghamshire Light Infantry and the Royal Engineers, succeeded in retaking the town.

Fifty years later, the veterans of Ranville returned to remember. I joined them to commemorate what some in the American press had been calling the last "good" war.

Having parked my rental car on the outskirts of this hamlet – Ranville's population is about fifteen hundred – I started out for the war cemetery by the church, three country blocks away. I caught up with a veteran who introduced himself as John Hammond and asked him what he had been doing on D-Day.

"I parachuted with the 6th Airlanding Brigade close by to Pegasus Bridge. The first commander with his three gliders, at about six minutes past midnight on June the 6th, landed at Pegasus Bridge. His three glider pilots were magnificent in the execution of the job. They dropped those gliders so close to the bridge that the soldiers in the gliders were able to take that bridge in *six minutes.* They cleared the explosives in *fifteen minutes.*

"They had to hold that bridge until the seaborne forces came in," Hammond said. "The first to arrive was Lord Lovat with his commandos, and they marched right across the bridge with their piper Bill Millin. It was a simply *magnificent* sight."

John Hammond had imaged it more vividly than the movie *The Longest Day.* In that film, Peter Lawford played the English aristocrat, Brigadier Lord Lovat, who, with his 6th Commandoes of the 1st Special Service Brigade, landed on Sword Beach at 8:40 AM. Lord Lovat's personal bagpiper, Private Bill Millin (played by Pipe Major Leslie de Laspee in the film) marched up and down Sword beach skirling Scottish airs – "Highland Laddie," and "Road to the Isles" among them – to rally the troops. Newspapers around the world ran a photo of him trudging the beach, playing the pipes under a dark hail of German shells. The sheer bollocks of this man, marching the sands in a kilt and skirling pipes while mortars exploded around him, was an inspiration to all the soldiers who witnessed it. It also earned Millin the nickname, "The Mad Piper."

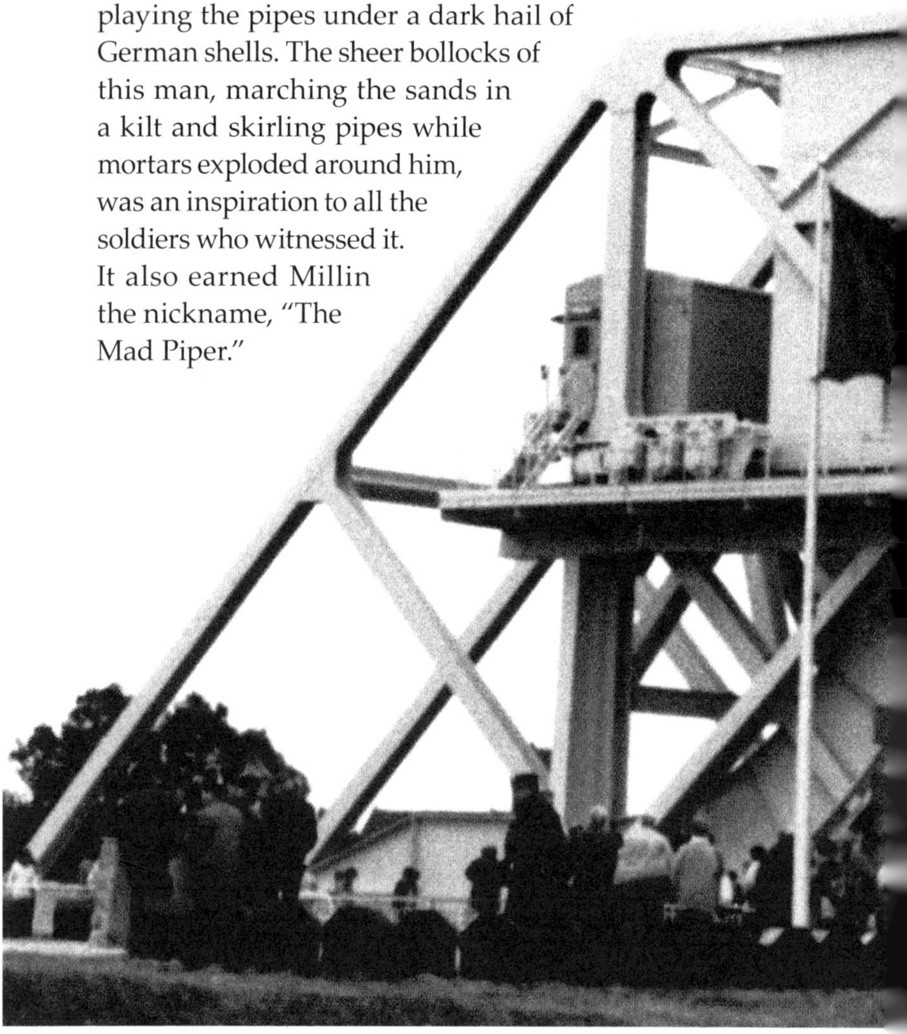

Pegasus Bridge, Bénouville, France

When the Brigade trooped inland and reached Bénouville Bridge, Lovat and Millin marched bolt upright across the bridge under withering German fire while Millin played "Blue Bonnets Over the Border," a Scottish war song from 1689.

Bill Millin's skirling at Sword Beach and Bénouville Bridge (later renamed Pegasus Bridge), though neither the first nor last time music was used to rally troops to battle, must rank as the most fearless pickin' by any picker under fire in any war.

I asked Hammond, "Is this the first time you've been back to Normandy?"

"No. I've been back three times, and the reason is this. I had a comrade, Charlie. We enlisted together and were together for four years. He looked after me; I looked after him. "

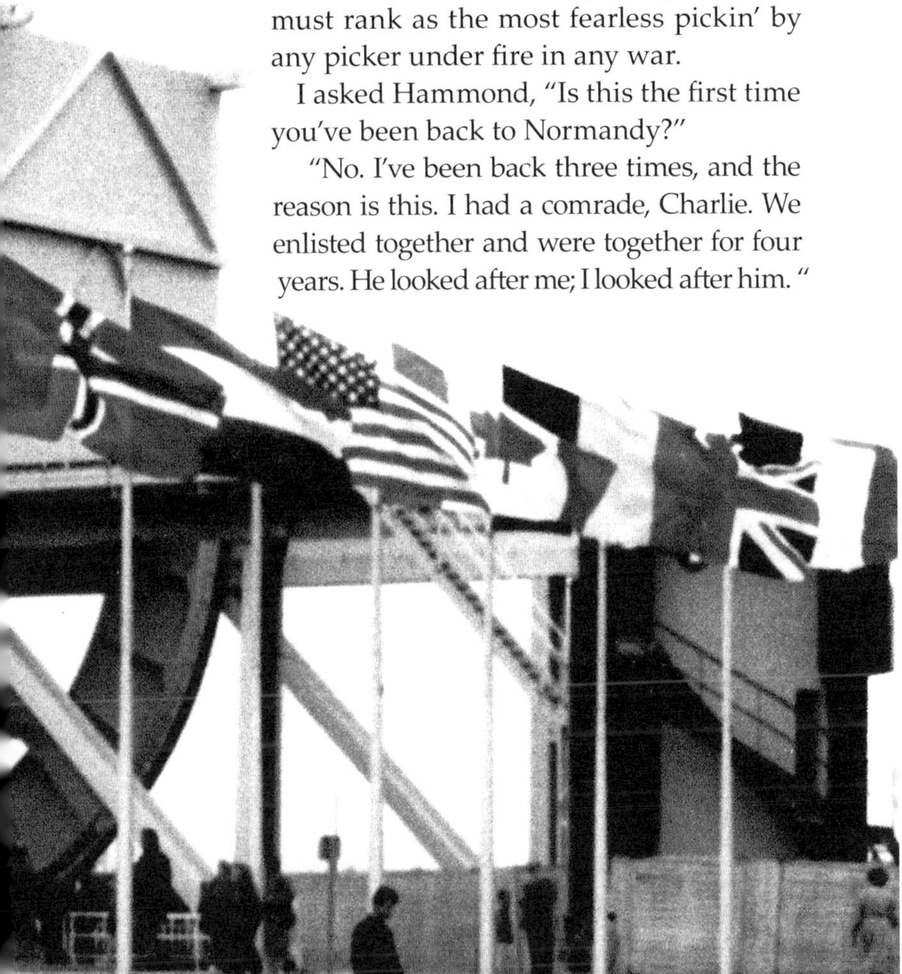

June 6, 1994

"Now when we were on leave, prior to the invasion, he had a bad feeling. And he said to my father, 'Pop, I don't think I'm going to make it this time. I don't think I'm coming back.'

"As a young man of twenty-four, a bit facetious I guess, I wouldn't accept what he was saying. And I said, ' Well if you're going to stay there, I'll come back and see you, Charlie.'

"And low and behold he didn't come back. He lies in Ranville church yard. And ... "

Here John Hammond cleared his throat; his eyes glassed.

"So I had to come back. I've come back a third time, and this time I went to his grave and I said, 'Charlie, I'm not coming back again. I'm getting too old, Charlie.' So that's why today I can go home in the knowledge that I've kept a promise. It's a nice feeling I'll have for the rest of my life."

"Has we learned anything from World War II?" I asked.

"No, no. The politicians haven't learned a bloody thing. They're as daft as ever. They still get us into wars, from World War II to Viet Nam to Bosnia. There's just no stopping the politicians from waging war. They're bloody cock-ups."

Hammond left to join the official ceremony in the Ranville War Cemetery at the town's center, which was closed to the general public. I stood on top of a stone mill wheel propped against *"L'Ancien Moulin de Ranville"* – Ranville's Old Mill – the location of a plaque in memory of the Belgian fighters of the Piron Brigade who fell in August 1944. This perch afforded a dandy overview of the cemetery, the church that dominated it, and the town.

Vets and young soldiers, wives and widows of veterans, artillery freaks, history buffs, French locals, and tourists – a large crowd of Yanks, Frogs, Brits, Jocks, Aussies, Kiwis, and Canucks – were all gathering. We were high-spirited and very much connected to a Normandy-wide feeling of excitement and anticipation on this historic day.

As the ceremony began, the town filled with easily ten-thousand people. Folks started passing me cameras to take shots of the officials who were gathering across the street.

A gentlemen with a wreath arrived at the mill. Joined by other flower bearers and by veterans of Britain's Parachute Regimental Association, they laid their wreathes at the foot of the tower under a plaque commemorating the war dead.

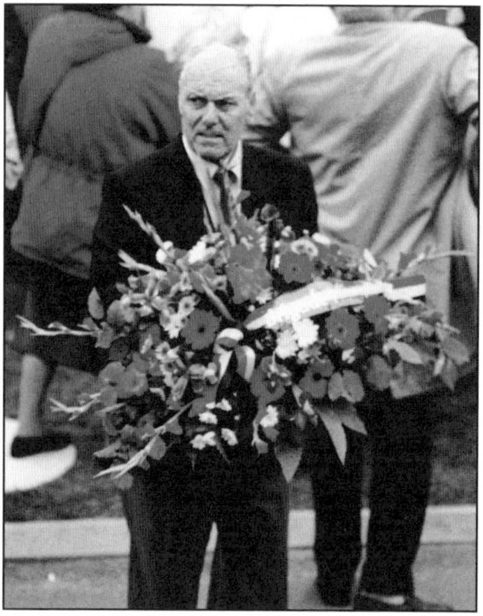

Britain's Parachute Regimental Association, Lincoln Branch, lays wreathes at Ranville's Old Mill beneath a plaque memorializing their fallen comrades of Belgium's Piron Brigade

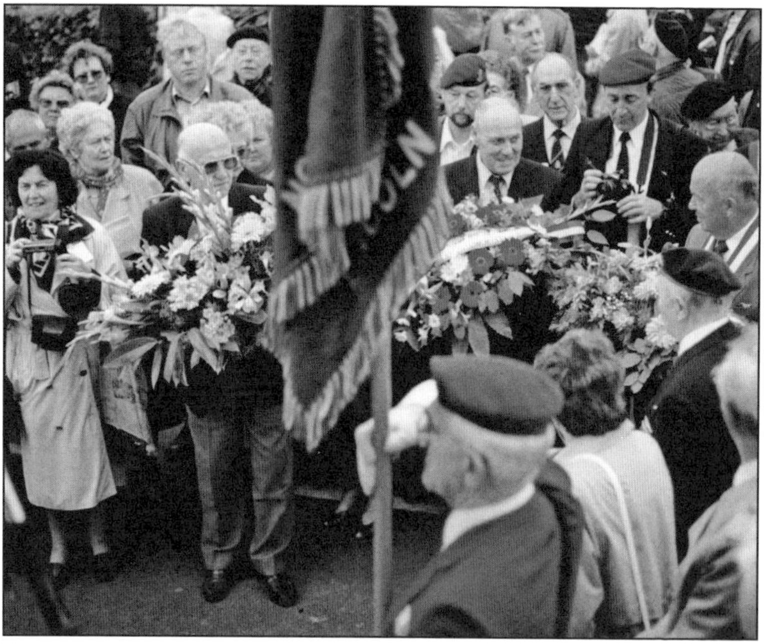

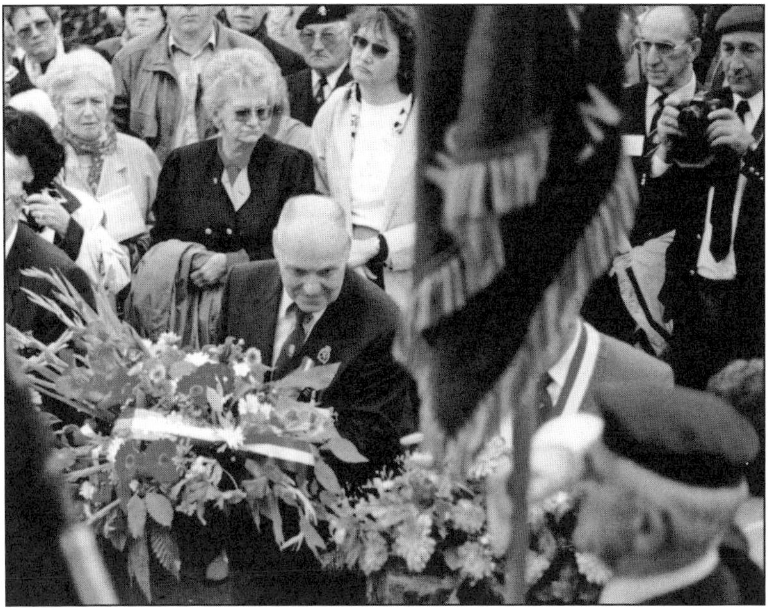

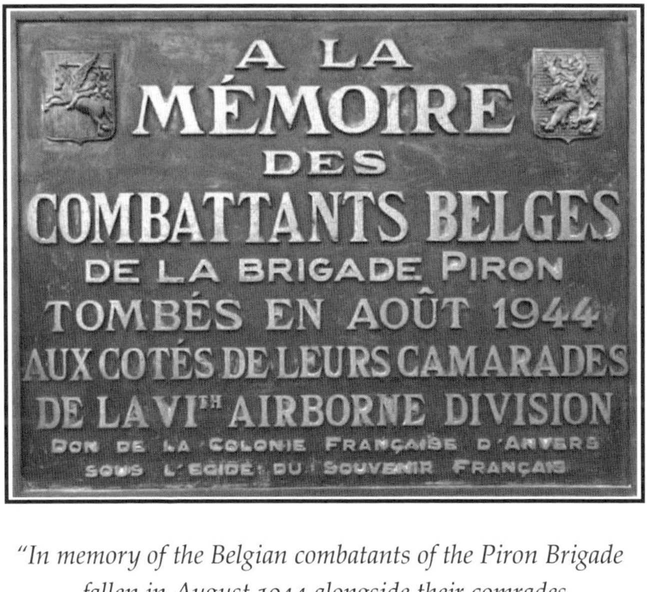

"In memory of the Belgian combatants of the Piron Brigade fallen in August 1944 alongside their comrades of the 6th Airborne Division"

The star of the show, England's Princess Margaret, arrived in a police convoy and took her place near the cross-topped obelisk at the center of the cemetery. I heard the buglers blow and the brass band trumpet, but when the Princess said her say, the sound system didn't carry a single word. In twenty minutes she had been swept away in the police convoy, and the official ceremony had ended.

Then the unofficial ceremonies began. The veterans and their guests walked to a large hall across the road where the town was hosting them to a champagne reception, an art at which the French are well versed.

I walked in, tossed back a bubbly, and found two veterans who were two drinks ahead of me, a good sign of openness to conversation, I've always thought. One of them, a Scotsman I reckoned, introduced himself as Alec.

"When you were down there fighting on D-Day and afterwards, what were you fighting for, Alec?"

"I was fighting for the stick, mon!" He seemed surprised by my question. "Everyone there was fighting for the stick."

"The stick? Alec, what is the stick?"

"Your jump buddies. The mates who jumped with you from the plane."

"And how many are in a stick?"

"Oh well, that depends doesn't it? Sometimes ten will be in your stick, sometimes twenty."

"You mean you weren't fighting for freedom, or for democracy, or … ?"

"Don't be *daft,* lad. No one fights for that. *No one.* Yer fighting to save your …" and here he pointed at his backside, "and your mates'. It's the brotherhood of the stick, lad."

I asked Alec and his friend if they had seen best friends fall.

"Yes. But there's nothing you can do about it. Ya don't even stop to kiss 'em good-bye. Ya just keep on moving forward towards your objective."

"Did you ever have to kill a man face to face?" I asked.

Alec's friend turned on his heel and walked away.

Alec said, "Maybe we had to, yes. But that's nothing we'll be wantin' to talk about," and he walked off too.

On the way back from my next trip to the bar, I found myself standing next to a pair of young British paratroopers. They were two of twelve hundred paratroopers, including veterans, who had parachuted over Ranville the day before, June 5, which had been designated "Airborne Day." They were about twenty-one, and cocky with youth and drink.

"Did you guys get to talk with any of these veterans yet?" I asked them.

"These blokes here? Of course we have. We parachuted with them yesterday."

By calling them "blokes" he had said much about his feelings and respect for his elder comrades-in-arms.

"Well, let me ask you this then, if I may. Who is the better man: these veterans, or you men?"

One of them came back after a beat: "I'd have to say they're the better man, really: they've jumped into battle. I mean, we've read about it, we've studied it, we've practiced it, but we've never actually jumped into battle. They've jumped into battle, and that makes them the better man."

I thought it was big of him to have said this in response to my question.

"Tell me something then," I continued. "I know what these vets say they were fighting for. But what do they teach you in class that you're fighting for? For democracy … freedom?"

"Listen to him talk," the other scoffed. "It's the stick, man."

"The brotherhood of the stick," the first one echoed. "And anyone who tells you no is a son of a liar."

They had a large laugh at my expense and headed off towards the party at Pegasus Bridge.

I returned to the cemetery when the grounds had been opened to the public. It was row on row of 2,563 white headstones marking the resting places of soldiers, most of them between 16 and 26 years old when they died.

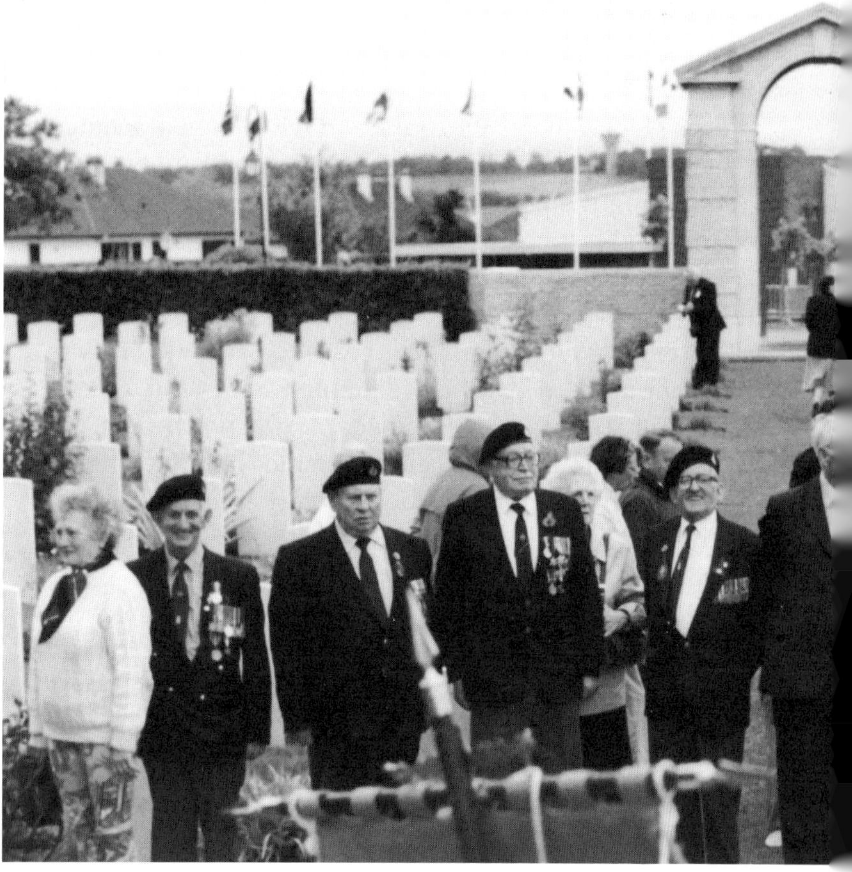

A dozen vets, some wives and war widows

Veterans from a British Royal Legion chapter arrived for their own ceremony. There were a dozen vets from various branches of the British armed services, some with wives, and a few war widows – maybe twenty seniors in all.

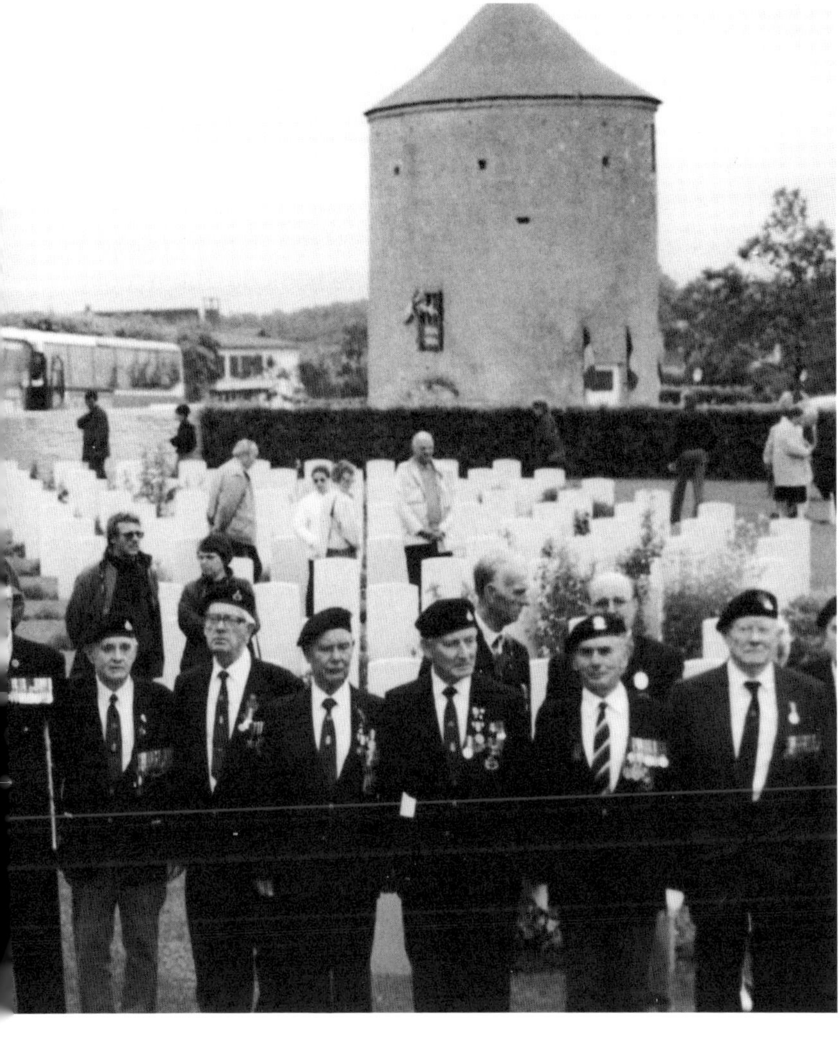

Ranville's Old Mill and memorial plaque, seen from the obelisk

They had brought a chaplain with them, a bugler, and a young captain.

Two veterans removed a pair of gold braid-wrapped regimental flags ("standards," the British call them) from leather carrying cases and began assembling them. The captain gently reminded the older men of each step. They threaded together the brass joints of the two-piece oak flagstaffs – the "pikes." Then they clipped the standards to the pikes and unfurled them, taking care not to let them touch the ground. Each veteran pulled on white leather gauntlets, strapped on a white leather colour belt, and mounted the pike in the belt's cup. They pointed the standards to the sky and stood at attention, wrists away, elbows out. The young captain stood rigidly; the veterans stood slouched by time and still as rocks.

The chaplain gave a blessing and then said:

"Today we wish to thank Thomas Joseph Adcock from Oxfordshire, England. The elders of the town can still remember you when you were a boy, Thomas, riding like the wind down the streets in your new red tricycle and them callin' after you, 'Slow down Tommy, slow down, you'll be hurtin' yourself.'

"They remember how you married your school sweetheart, Iris, who's with us here today. She says Hello to you, Thomas, and declares with all her heart how much she still loves and misses you, and how your daughters, Katlin and

Anna, both infants when you went to war, now grown women with grown children of their own, love and miss their dad so, though they hardly ever knew you, lad.

The whole town remembers you today Thomas, and joins with those of us here in thanking you with all our hearts.

"Tommy, … you died so we could be here today. Thank you, Tommy, so very much."

And we who were there in deed because Tommy had died for us, we whispered, "Thank you, Tommy."

For each of the battalion's war-dead who lay beneath our feet, the chaplain told a story which brought the man to life. In this he had a gift.

Then the bugler blew "Last Post" as the bearers began a ceremony called "vailing the colours." Each tucked the foot of the pike under his right arm, and pointed the staff skyward. Then the bearers slowly lowered the pikes. They dipped them another notch, and then another until the lowest corner of the standards touched the ground.

I'd never seen a flag touching the ground, and I flinched as it happened.

They lowered the pikes again and with a flourish draped the standards over the ground, each pike's spear-pointed finial slicing the earth. The flag that the war dead had died for, that had draped their coffins, now touched the ground they lay in.

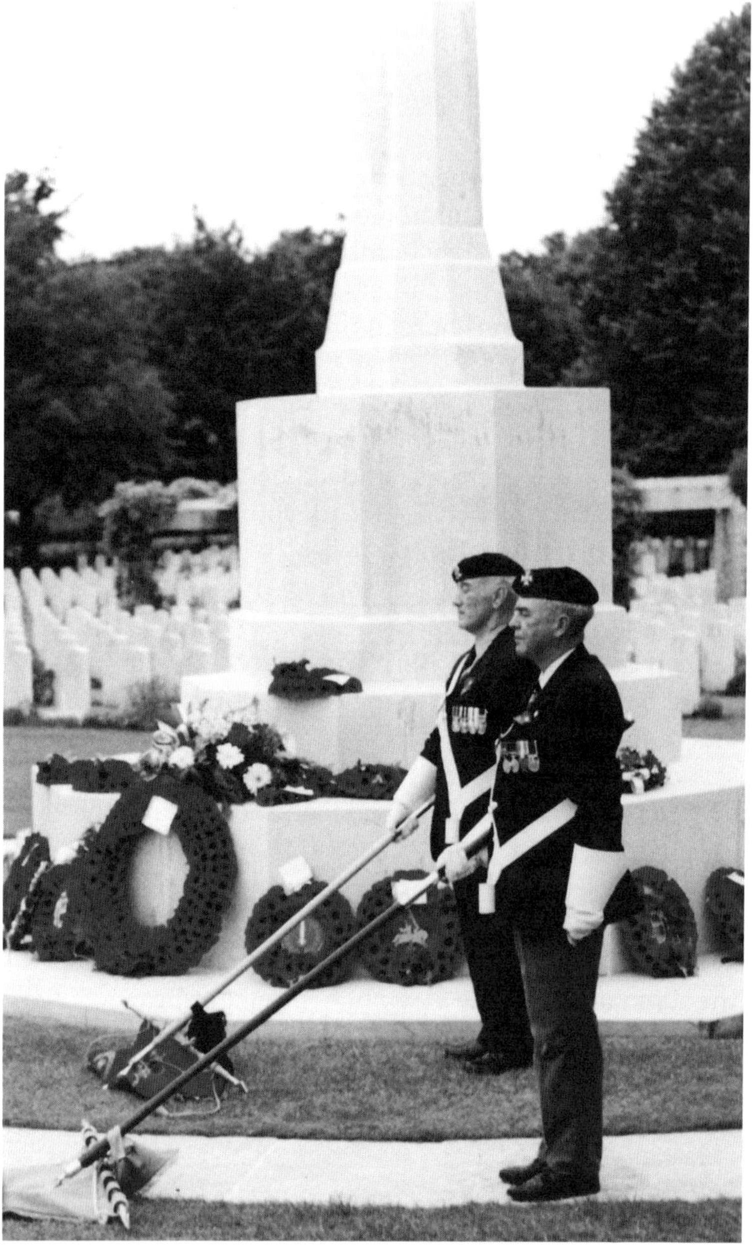

Vailing the colours

The chaplain read the names, the widows wept. Some of the vets teared up, though most had finished with that by then. The bearers stood like boulders, and the flags lay on the grass, their colours surrendered to the earth.

Each senior there had lost a comrade, friend or husband who lay buried beneath us. Their sadness flowed from them, through the bearers, the pikes and standards, into the earth below us, hallowing it.

For fifty years these veterans had kept the brotherhood of the stick alive in their hearts. They had stuck with their comrades, living and dead. This was their last fight for the stick.

The tableau of these brave souls, grey stalks huddled beside white headstones under a darkening day, is in my memory. I am grateful to have been there.

Back at the hall the crowd had thinned. Most had headed for the festivities at Pegasus Bridge, and Alec was looking at his watch. There was one last question I wanted to ask him.

"Alec, there are some people in America who call World War II the last 'good' war, . . . you know, 'Good' versus 'Evil' and all that. What do you say to that, Alec?"

Here he turned on me angrily, literally whirled around on me and said:

"Bloody hell, mon, World War II was no' a good war! No wars are good wars, and *no one* knows *that* like a *vet.* World War II was a *necessary* war; we *had* to drive the Germans out of Europe. But World War II was no' a good war.

"You'll be rememberin' that now, won't ya lad?"

Bill Millin piped the lament at Lord Lovat's funeral in 1995. In 2001 he presented the bagpipes he had played at Sword Beach to the museum in Dawlish, the English coastal town where he lived out his days, a legend alive, until his passing on August 17, 2010, at the age of eighty-eight.

Piper Bill Millin at Ranville's Old Mill

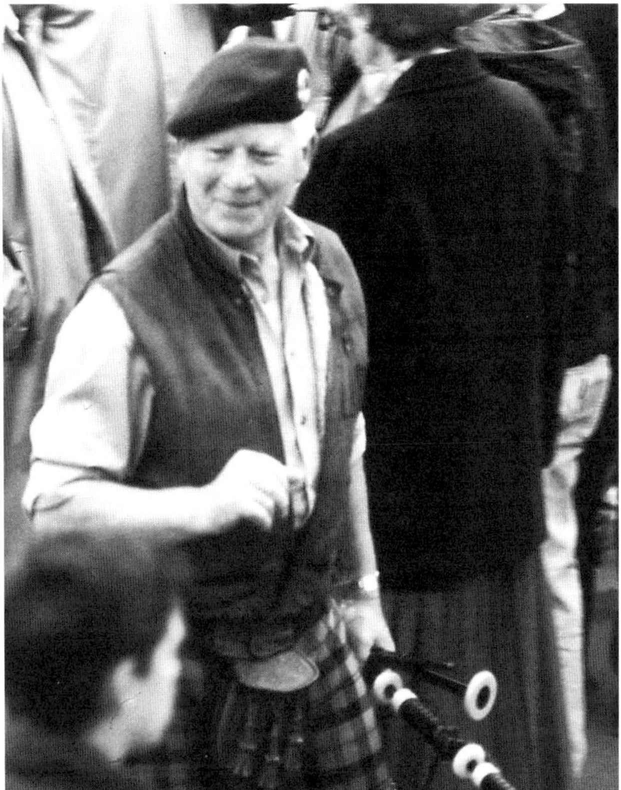

"I'm a farmer with a mandolin and a high tenor voice."

—Bill Monroe

Big Mon

Bill Monroe was the founding father of that richly American music called Bluegrass. It was on September 16 and 17, 1946, that Bill brought his band, the Blue Grass Boys, into the Columbia recording studios. They cut ten tunes that created and defined this music.

The recordings featured Monroe's furious mandolin playing – lightning fast, up the neck – and his high tenor singing that broke easily and often into a fluted falsetto.

They featured the monstrous playing of Earl Scruggs, a machine-gun style of 3-fingered, 5-string banjo-picking that he first recorded with Monroe, and that is named after him: "Scruggs Picking." Earl's banjo was bell-clear, driving, and essential to bluegrass. Your group may have Tee and Jim Hurst playing double guitars, Mark O'Connor, Stuart Duncan, and Bobby Hicks on triple fiddles, Jerry Douglas and Rob Ickes on dueling Dobros, Roland White, Frank Wakefield and Sam Bush on sequentially-numbered, Lloyd Loar-signed mandolins, with Buell and Edgar doubling on doghouse basses, but without someone pickin' some kind of Scruggs-style banjo, well sir, you ain't got a bluegrass band.

These 1946 recordings featured the voice and guitar of Lester Flatt, including his so-called "Lester Flatt G-run," a guitar lick that figures in about every bluegrass song subsequently recorded. Lester's guitar was urgent and goading. His lead singing varnished the sound of his duets with Monroe and created the template for smooth bluegrass tenor singing that is still used. Chubby Wise complemented the band on fiddle, adding a sawing, bluesy sound that fiddlers to this day try to emulate. Howard Watts, whose stage name was Cedric Rainwater, played string bass and sang bass and baritone. He drove the frantic 2-beat instrumentals and plucked 4-to-the-bar on tunes you'd expect to be 2-beat, leading the band from underneath.

These recordings were a quantum jump beyond whatever had been done previously in hillbilly music. This seminal band jumped from the tracks fully formed. They laid down the law for all bluegrass groups to come: acoustic string instruments flogged to their limits, breakneck tempos, screaming solos, high lonesome harmonies, a galloping rhythm section wheel-hossed by a honking string bass, a dollop of 4-part rural gospel, and many exceeding-the-speed-limit instrumentals. Essential American music.

Bill Monroe crossed over Jordan, as pickers say, on September 9, 1996, at the age of eighty-six. His last performance with the Blue Grass Boys was on March 15, 1996, at the Grand Ole Opry, ... the Friday Night Opry. It is not often we witness the passing of a bona fide music genre creator, and it reminds me of how young Bluegrass is, a half-century young almost to the day of Bill's passing.

Bluegrass has progressed since 1946, allowed more influences, and sharpened vocals and instrumental techniques while still maintaining deep allegiance to the ancient tones recorded in '46. The course that Bluegrass takes now that its father is gone, will be instructive to follow.

Besides these considerable music accomplishments, Bill Monroe was known as a man of few words.

I was playing bass behind Peter Rowan at the 1995 Wintergrass Festival in Tacoma, Washington. Peter had played with Bill Monroe's Blue Grass Boys in the mid-1960s, and his duet singing with the master was renowned for being tight as jaws. It was Saturday night. We were on the main stage. Peter was playing guitar and singing with his brothers Lorin and Chris, with the incomparable Jerry Douglas on Dobro. Peter had just started introducing the second tune of the set when the audience burst into applause. If you've seen him perform, you know Pete is a natural storyteller. His introduction to his tune "Panama Red" is a fantasy tale that sets the audience howling every time he tells it. But this introduction to this tune was not that spectacular in my opinion.

So I looked around to see why the room might be going nuts, and there was Bill Monroe, leaning on his walking cane, trooping out to join us. Bill was eighty-four at the time, and his face showed those years. But the light inside him burned as hot as any youngster's.

When Bill arrived at the center stage microphone, he and Peter, who was in his fifties, did a mock pushing match for the mike. With a Zen-placed elbow, Monroe about launched Rowan clean off the stage. When Peter got back to a side mike, he turned to the crowd and said, "That man's got strong chi," which Bill did.

Then the two sang a tune they're both identified with, "Walls of Time," as lonesome a bluegrass song as there is. Bill sang an angel part so high above Peter's lead, it was ghostly. It wasn't harmony. It was like an improvised counter-melody, a descant drifting skyward.

Finally they rendered a song that Bill wrote called "The Little Girl and the Dreadful Snake." There is an old story about Monroe and this song that over the years may have become enhanced by what is called the "folk process." The folk process is about the changes that a story or song undertakes as it passes orally from one person to another. So like I said, this legend may well have changed over the years, but this is the way I remember it.

At a university folk music festival some years back, there was a round-table discussion. The topic of this dialogue was "The Lyrics of Bill Monroe's 'The Little Girl and the Dreadful Snake'." On the panel were two Ph.D.s in Psychology (a Freudian and a Jungian), a professor of American folk musicology, and Bill Monroe. The Jungian shrink, Dr. Zleitag, kicked off the symposium by reciting the lyrics, which he had transcribed from an old Monroe recording:

Our darling wandered far away,
While she was out at play.
Lost in the woods she couldn't hear a sound.
She was our darling girl,
The sweetest thing in all the world.
We searched for her but she couldn't be found.

I heard the screams of our little girl far away,
"Hurry daddy, there's an awful dreadful snake."
I ran as fast as I could,
Through the dark and weary woods,
But I reached our darling girl too late.

Oh I began to sigh,
I knew that soon she'd have to die,
For the snake was worn and weak close by.
I held her close to my face,
She said, "Daddy, kill that snake.
It's getting dark, tell mommy good-bye."

To all parents I must say,
Don't let your children stray away.
They need your love to guide them along.
Oh God, I pray, we'll see our darling some day.
It seems we still can hear her voice around the house.

I heard the screams of our little girl far away,
"Hurry daddy, there's an awful dreadful snake."
I ran as fast as I could,
Through the dark and weary woods,
But I reached our darling girl too late.

Then the panelists – well, three of the panelists – tore into the song. The first to speak was the Freudian psychologist. Freudians are fixated on dreams and what they call "transference."

So this ol' Freud boy got to talkin', Viennese accent and all, about the girl wandering "var away. Yust like in a dream." He related how she was "lost in der voods," where the parents "couldn't hear ein sound ... yust like in a dream." And he spoke of the father hearing "der screams of our leetle girl var avay." "Var away," the professor repeated, "yust like in a dream. Mr. Monroe's entire sonk iz ein metaphor fur ein dream."

Then he pointed to the "glassic Freudian transverence" in the last verse: "Mr. Monroe has the girl transverrink her feelinks from the father – 'daddy, kill dat snake' – to the mother – 'dell mommy goodf-by' – as she lies dieink."

This was heady stuff, and the audience murmured in appreciation of this psychoanalytic profundity.

Then Dr. Zleitag, the Jungian, who was deeply into symbolism – aren't they all – said to the crowd:

"The little girl, ... the dreadful snake. Do we need Dr. Ruth to explain this to us?

"And the line that reads 'For the snake was worn and weak close by.' Do I need to draw you a diagram?"

The crowd tittered knowingly.

In actual fact, the lyric reads, "For the snake was warning me close by," and not, "For the snake was worn and weak close by."

It seems to me that the Jungian shrink had made a Freudian slip.

Then the folk musicologist polished this off with his analysis, contrasting this song to others by Bill:

"Most of Mr. Monroe's lyrics tell simple stories with little meaning beyond the first, literal level. 'The Little Girl and the Dreadful Snake,' on the other hand, is rife with complex layers of sub-text and symbolism unique to Mr. Monroe and this micro-ethnic genre."

The room "ah'ed" in solemn appreciation.

After well over an hour, the three Ph.D.'s had come to the end of their dissection of Monroe's song. It makes you wonder whether Ph.D. doesn't stand for "Piled high and Deep" after all.

Through this entire discussion, Big Mon – that's what Bill Monroe was called – Big Mon had kept silent.

Finally, one of the professors allowed that Monroe hadn't said a word. He turned to Bill, a little embarrassed, and said, "Well, Mr. Monroe, just what did motivate you, *do you think,* to write this song?" … as though Bill himself might not understand his own true reason.

Monroe stood up and walked over to a lectern at the side of the stage.

The room went deathly quiet.

He tipped back his white Stetson hat as he leaned into the mic, and then said:

"Neighbor down the road, … his daughter wandered off, got bit by a snake, … up and died. Me? … I thought I'd write a song about it."

And with that, Big Mon doffed his Stetson to the roaring crowd and walked off stage.

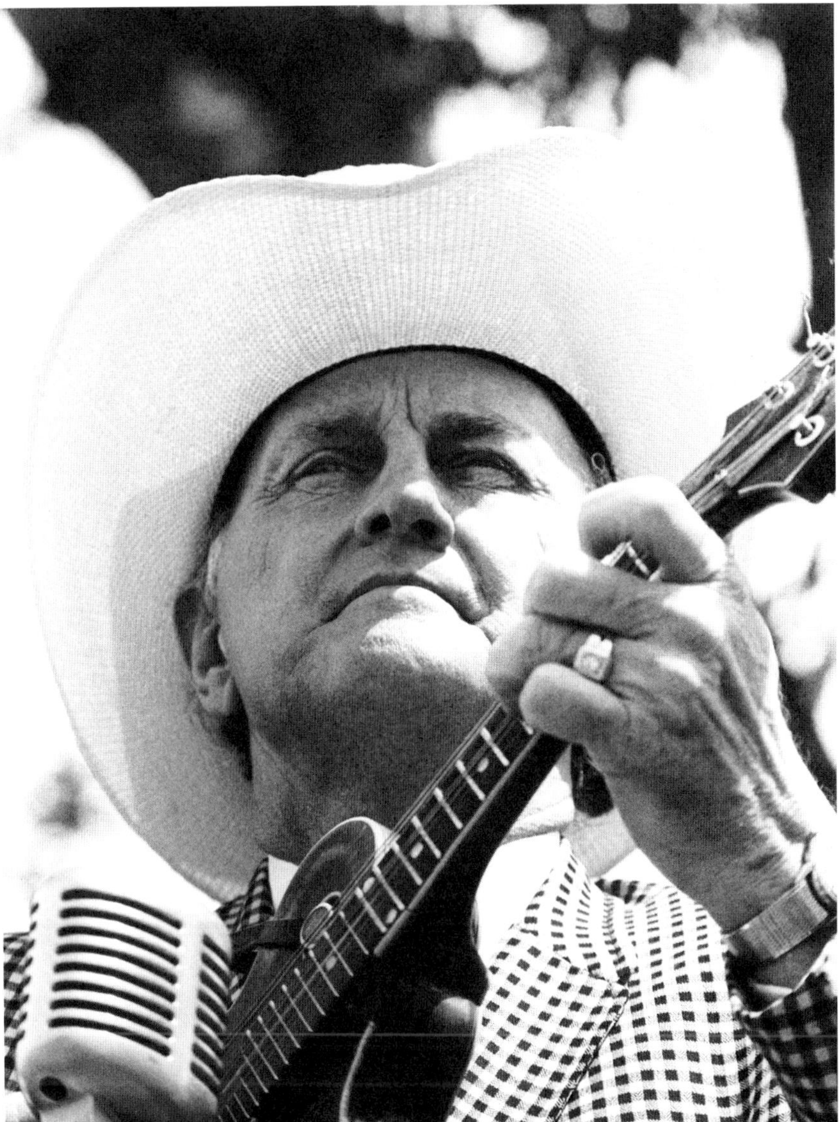

Bill Monroe
Berryville, Virginia · 1965
By Marshall Freedland

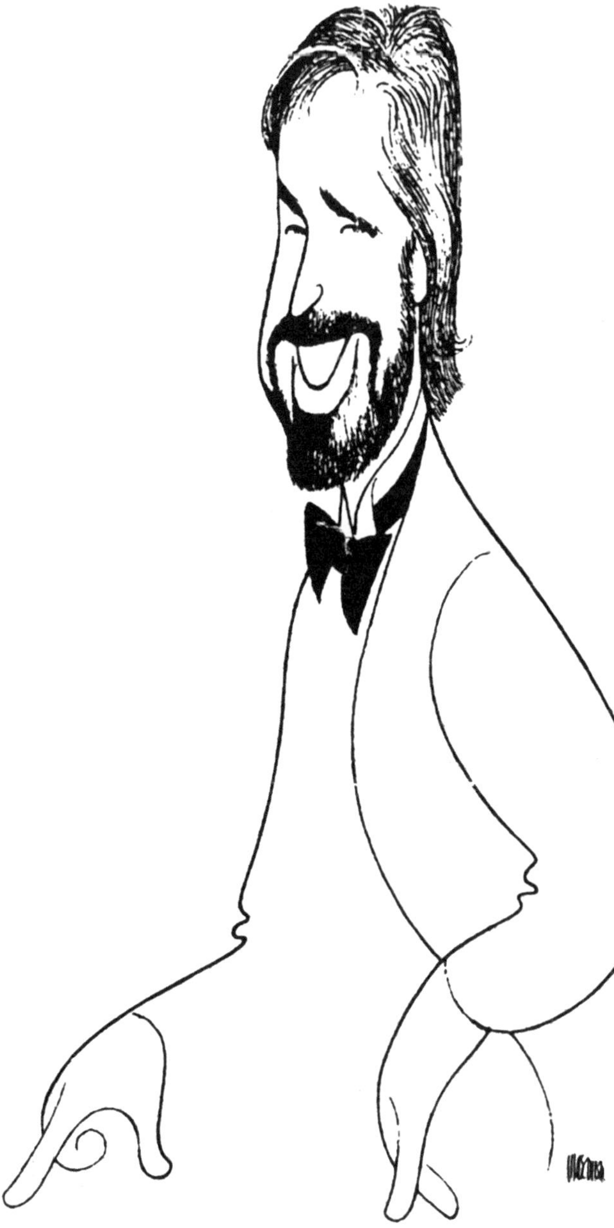

Steve Silver
By Al Hirshfeld

To Steve, With Hats off

"Musicians are out there," a friend told me when I was nineteen. "You dress different, hang out with fast women, keep late hours, ... do all that stuff straight people don't. Musicians are not like other people."

I resisted this at first. But by the time I was twenty-one, I got it.

June 15, 1995

Today, some musicians, actors, singers and dancers gathered at San Francisco's Grace Cathedral to bury Steve Silver. Steve's show, Beach Blanket Babylon, has been playing in North Beach since 1974, as long a run as we've had in the Bay Area. Most everyone who lives here, and virtually every tourist who has visited the City have most likely seen the show at least once.

Over the years, hundreds of performers have played in the ranks of "Beach Blanket," or "BBB" as it is called. I am proud to be a member of this extended family.

What is Beach Blanket Babylon?

BBB is a revue, a music show of song, dance and skits that satirizes popular American culture. It surfs on a plot about Snow White's search for love with all the wrong faces, a gallery of popular culture icons that changes with the times. The objects of BBB's barbs have included the Obamas, Michael Jackson, Dolly Parton, Elvis Presley, Lady Gaga, Sarah Palin, the Queen of England, the Governator, and Oprah, among scores of others.

Beach Blanket is performed by a cast of outrageously-hatted performers in extreme, full-body costumes, who sing a torrent of snatches from show and pop tunes – some lasting for as little as four beats – segued together. BBB is crammed with sly campy skits, song medleys, puns, and bits, all going by in a blur while the audience roars its eyes out.

And hats. I mentioned hats, right? The cast wears a parade of outlandish hats that gets bigger and more bizarre as the show progresses. Finally Val Diamond, who, along with Renée Lubin, was one of the stars of the show when I played it, finales with a hat of the San Francisco skyline that includes the Golden Gate Bridge, the Trans-America Pyramid, the Bay Bridge, and cable cars that light up, blink, and move. A hat as wide as the stage is wide and tall as the stage is tall. A hat so large that only the magic of the theatre could possibly support it.

I played bass in the Beach Blanket pit band, subbing for Seth Evans who held that chair for fifteen years. Since I sat in irregularly and infrequently, the bass book was tough for me. There were constantly changing time signatures, tempos and keys, many of them sustained for just a measure or two. I had to keep an eye on Michael Ashton, the musical director and pianist, who kept us together with exaggerated head and hand movements.

Playing a BBB show presents unusual cues for the pit musician. They come from the director, but also from the lead singer, a dancer, a punch line, or a bump of the ingénue's hip. Beach Blanket was a cue a second. If I let my concentration stray, or got caught up in some madness on stage, I was "off the page" … totally lost.

I remember the first night I took a seat in the audience to see BBB, in preparation for playing the show. As the performers made their entrances, I sensed something different was happening. This was not a cast of uniformly gorgeous girls and boys. (In the American theatre, performers in the troupe are called "boys" or "girls," apt names for them both.) One of the girls overflowed my arms when I hugged her. One of the boys was so homely looking, I thought he was a comic and this was his "duh" look.

Something different *was* happening. Steve's people were hyper-talented, wildly uninhibited actors who delivered unfettered performances. Steve picked his cast for their raw, unbridled energies, not stage beauty. This is fairly uncommon in the world of American theatre.

On evenings when I played the show, I would walk from the relatively tame world of San Francisco's North Beach into Club Fugazi, BBB's home on Green Street. I'd trudge up a long flight of stairs and enter the boys' dressing room and the backstage world of Beach Blanket Babylon. It was called the boys' dressing room, but it was also the greenroom and the costume shop, so the girls hung out there too. It functioned as the social room for the entire cast and crew.

Walking into this room was walking into Never-Never Land. Dancing ballerinas in tutus and prancing queens in leotards singing at the top of their lungs, strutting around the room, preening, posing, primping. Everyone rushing around – many in states of undress – acting, trilling, rapping, riffing, being cranky, brassy, bossy. Everyone psyching themselves up and hoisting their own egos, as actors must. And always a dozen attendant costume mistresses, wardrobe assistants, prop masters, stagehands, publicists, journalists, boyfriends, girlfriends, the band, stage-door Johnnies, and hangers-on, hanging on.

Bedlam.

Me, I'm just sitting in the corner of the room, shades on, trying to look as inconspicuous as a six-foot person can while wearing a tuxedo in the midst of many half-naked boys and girls. I'm trying to look blasé, trying to look like, Hey, I see this stuff all the time. Girls prancing around in their bras and panties, boys down to their dance belts – think industrial-strength thongs – girls chasing boys, boys chasing boys.

I'm a musician; I'm cool. This scene is boring.

So I pick up my bass and start playing scales and arpeggios, trying not to gawk fish-eyed at this three-ring circus exploding in front of me, impossible to out-blow, out-weird.

For once, at Beach Blanket Babylon, we musicians were the squares, the straight guys. Steve put us in that role every night we were there playing music. He made us see ourselves from another side, and it was a hoot.

All in Grace Cathedral learned showmanship from working in Beach Blanket Babylon. I learned from Steve by playing the show he created. I went on to the next gig knowing this:

The show *is* the thing, and there are no limits to the show. But nobody put on a show like Steve Silver.

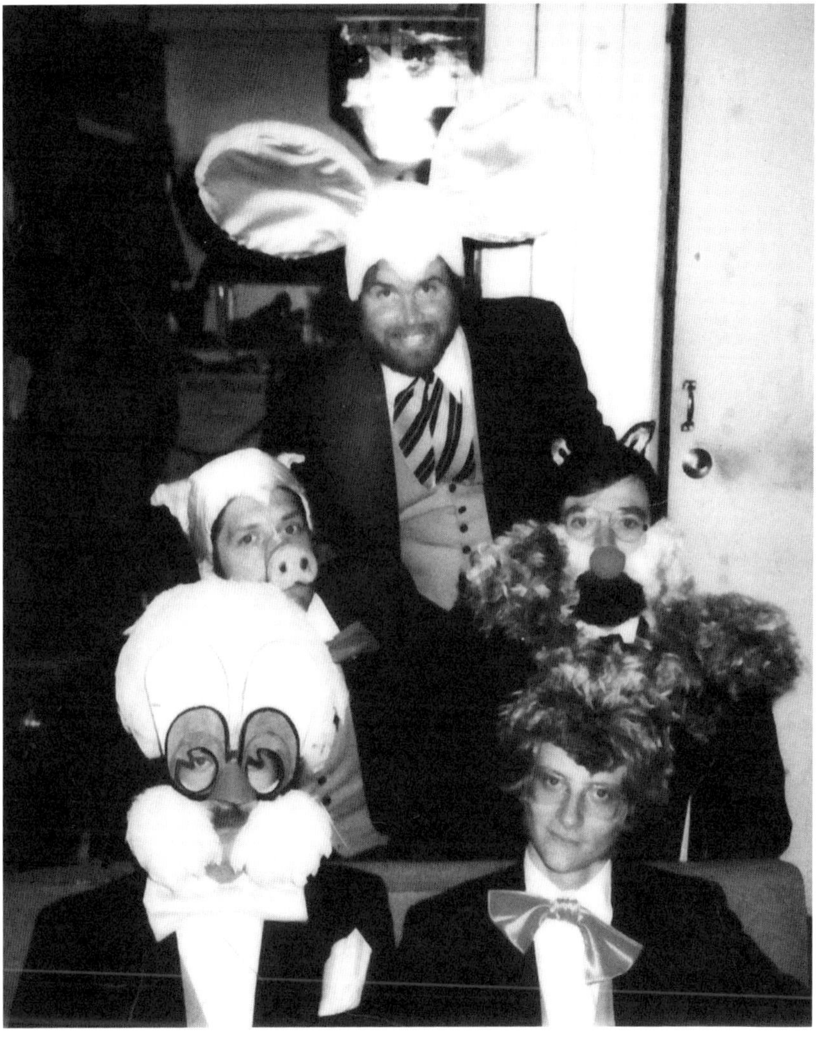

The Beach Blanket Babylon Band · circa 1979
(Clockwise from top:) Michael Ashton, Charlie Keagle, Bob Elkjer, Seth Evans, Victor La Gambina
Photo courtesy of Seth Evans — anon

JAZZ FUNERAL &
OFFICIAL DEDICATION OF MEMORIAL MARKER

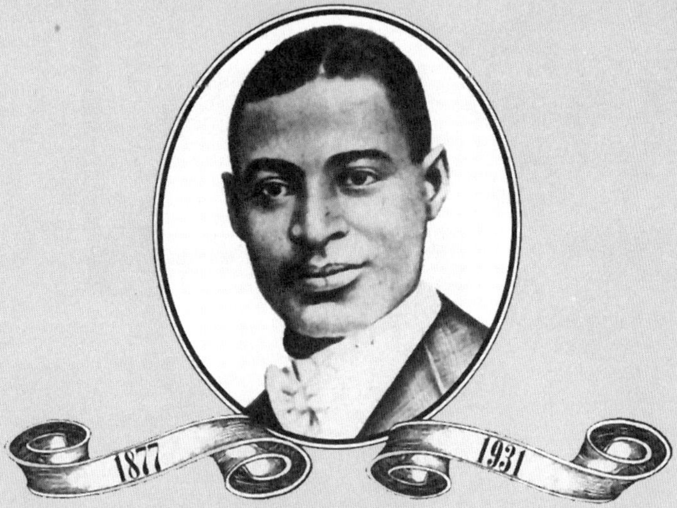

FOR
BUDDY BOLDEN

LEGENDARY JAZZ PIONEER

FRIDAY, SEPTEMBER 6, 1996

6 P.M.

Layin' Buddy Down

Strolling the streets of New Orleans's French Quarter in September 1996, my wife, Noni, and I saw a poster in the window of the Palm Court Jazz Cafe. It read:

JAZZ FUNERAL &
OFFICIAL DEDICATION OF MEMORIAL MARKER
FOR
BUDDY BOLDEN
1877 – 1931
LEGENDARY JAZZ PIONEER

The poster hadn't told us much about this Buddy Bolden. I vaguely remembered that he was an early New Orleans horn man, but beyond that, who was he? This got me too: why was the city of New Orleans staging a funeral in 1996 for someone who had died in 1931, sixty-five years earlier? So we decided to go to this jazz funeral, which was the following day, September 6, at the Delgado Community College, at 6:00 PM.

We arrived at quarter till, expecting maybe a hundred hard-core jazz fans. What we found was almost a thousand people, black and white together, cramming the college quadrangle, waiting to give the long-buried Buddy Bolden a N'Awlins funeral.

A New Orleans funeral procession has two parts, called lines: the first line and the second line. The mourners constitute the second line.

The first line, the marching jazz band that leads the parade, saw Dejan's Olympia Brass Band led by trumpeter Milton Batiste. Their two trumpeters, two trombonists, sousaphonist, sax man, bass drummer and snare drummer were fronted by the Grand Marshal.

The Grand Marshal, an African-American gentleman, was so strikingly tall that when I first saw him – I was sitting down – he appeared to be standing on stilts. He wore a coal-black tuxedo with a black top hat and black tux shirt. A rhinestone-encrusted, royal-burgundy satin sash was draped over his shoulder. A thick, black leather belt wrapped around his waist two times, and three multicolored parasols were hanging on it.

The man was stylin'.

At six o'clock the Grand Marshal nodded to the snare drummer, and the drummer started playing a street beat. Then the Marshal blew his whistle and the band tore into "When I Lay My Burden Down."

They marched out of the quadrangle and into the streets of New Orleans, the second line following them, second-lining to the music.

And what is "second-lining?" Well, there's a pigeon-toed strut, big on the hips and big on the butt. The women twirl brightly colored parasols over their heads while the men whip out handkerchiefs and wave them around, all in time to the music. That's second lining.

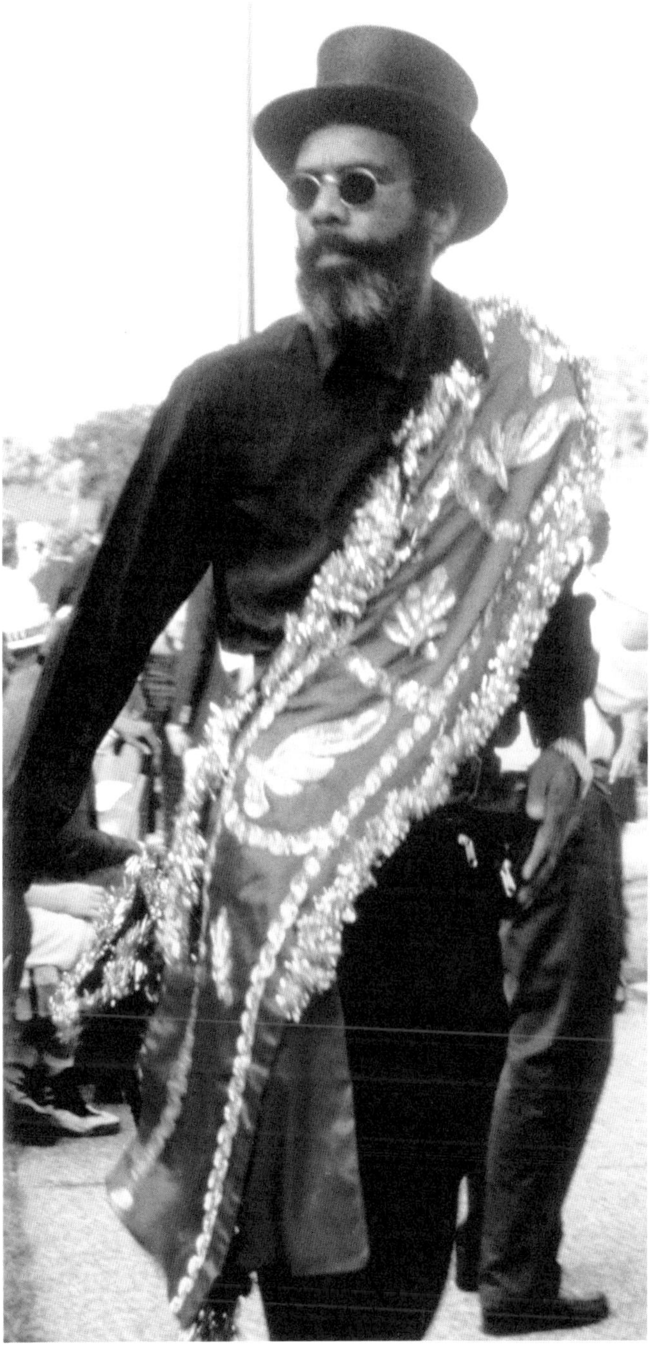

Richard "King" Matthews, Grand Marshal

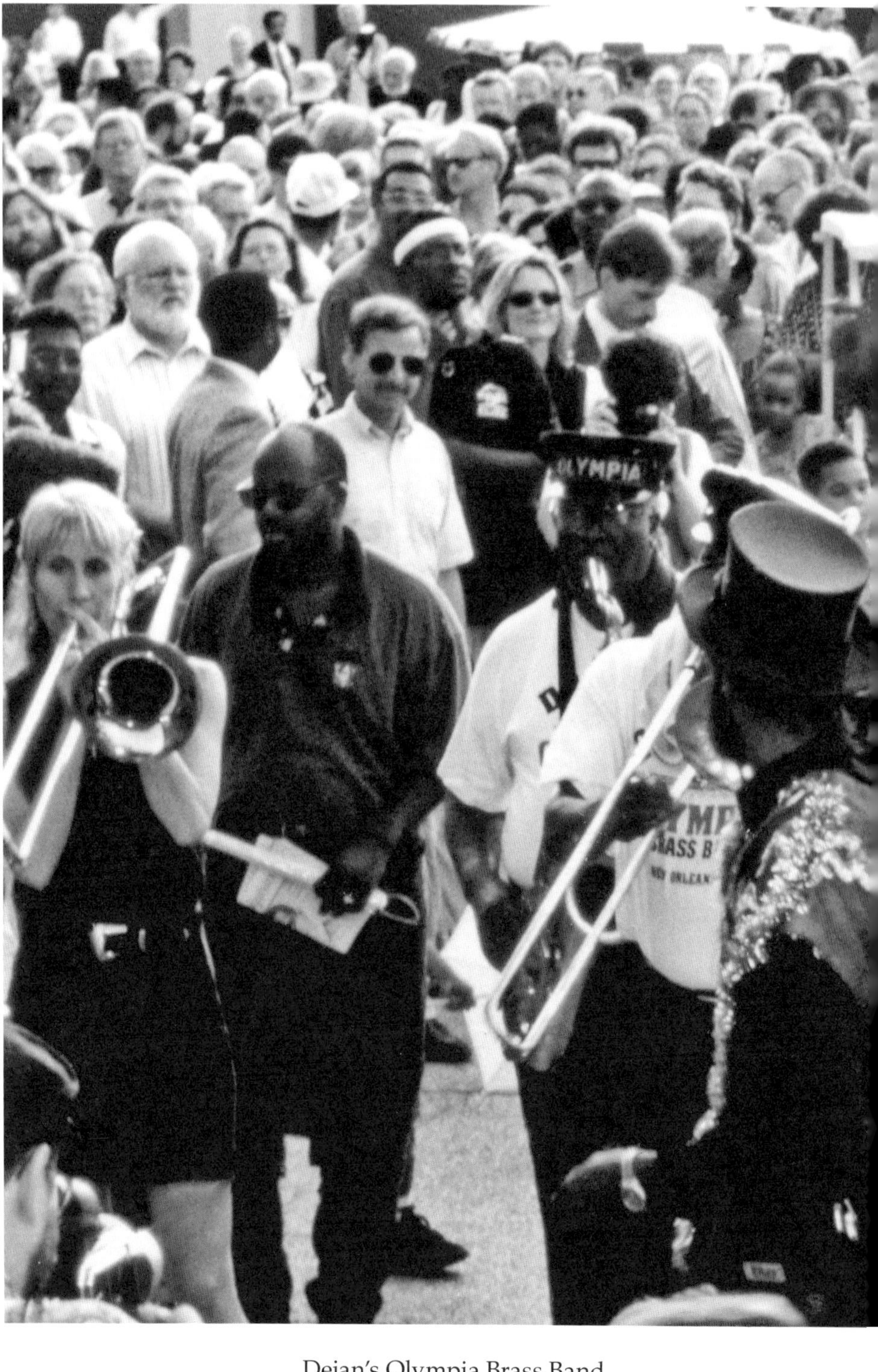

Dejan's Olympia Brass Band

Delgado Community College, New Orleans · September 6, 1996

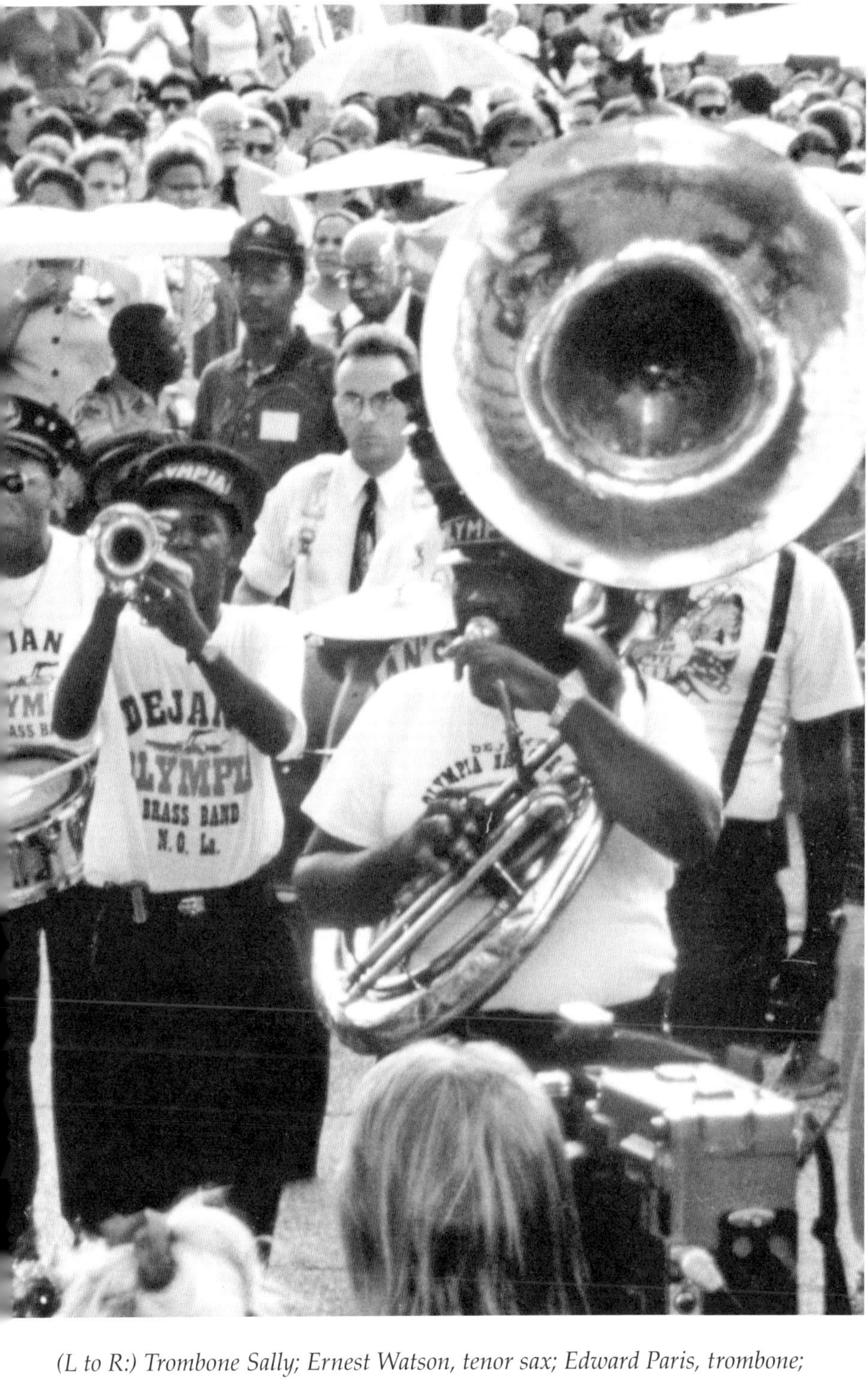

(L to R:) Trombone Sally; Ernest Watson, tenor sax; Edward Paris, trombone; Leroy Breaux, snare; Milton Batiste, trumpet; Nowell Glass, bass drum; Edgar Smith, sousaphone; Kenneth Terry, trumpet (in suspenders)

Then the band started singing:

> *Glory, glory hallelujah*
> *When I lay my burden down.*

And the second line joined in:

> *Glory, glory Hal-le-luuUUUuuu-jah*
> *When I lay my burden down.*

Everywhere we went, we stopped traffic. Cars pulled over. Folks got out to join us. People walking home with groceries in their arms put the groceries down on some neighbor's stoop and fell in. Within a quarter mile, a couple hundred more second-liners had joined us. Now we were well over a thousand people marching down the streets of New Orleans, strutting, butting, twirling, whirling, clapping, singing.

But I was thinking, Wait a minute. Funerals are supposed to be somber, sad affairs. This was no somber affair. This was a raucous street party, two blocks long.

Finally we arrived at the Holt Cemetery, a paupers' graveyard. It was in a sorry state and a shock to everyone. Most of the graves were unmarked swells of earth. A few had two tree branches placed as a cross lying over them. We marched a slow, respectful procession around the cemetery until we reached a wooden bandstand, just built, off to the side.

A headstone shrouded in a black cloth stood in the middle of the platform. As we gathered around, some people took the stage to speechify: the college's president; a New Orleans Councilwoman; Buddy's granddaughter and great granddaughter; and the Mayor of New Orleans, Marc Morial.

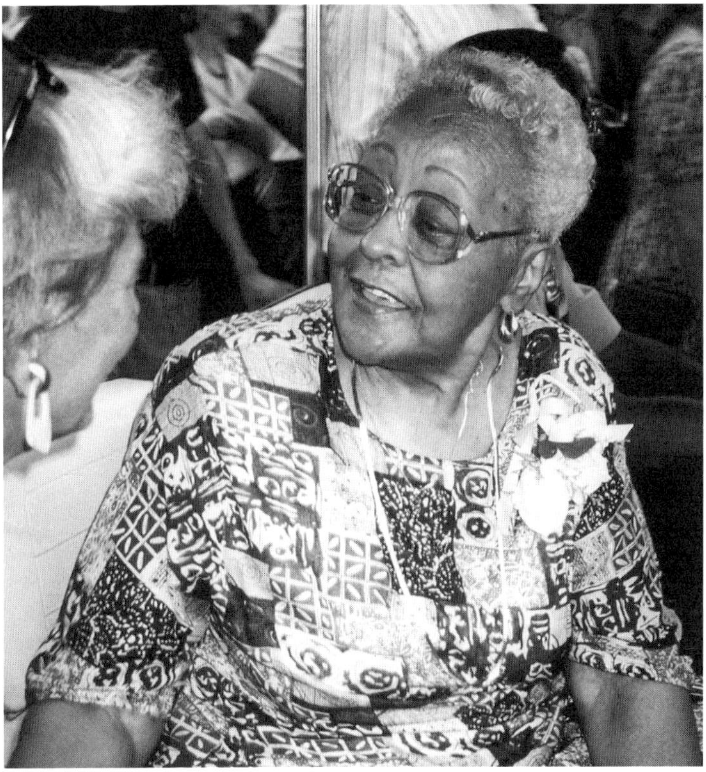

Gertrude Bolden Tucker · Buddy's granddaughter

But the most interesting person at the funeral was an old jazz professor who told me all about Buddy.

Those who had known him described Buddy as a handsome, light-skinned Negro. As a young man he took up the cornet, a cousin to the trumpet, and proved so talented with the instrument that by the time he was twenty-six, Buddy had become the first musician ever to be crowned "King" of N'Awlins. And to be called "King of New Orleans" means that you are the hottest horn player in town, the big noise from N'Awlins.

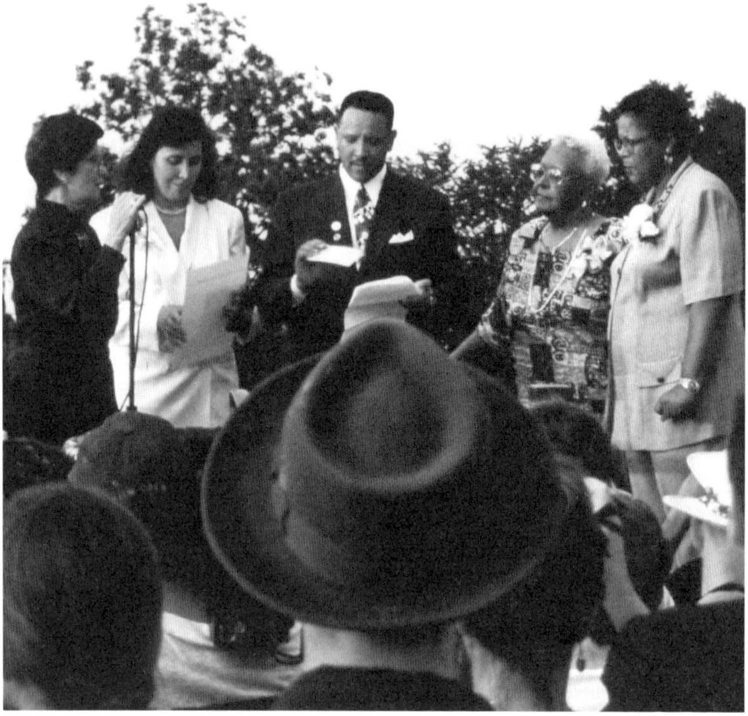

Delgado's President, Ione Elioff; Councilwoman, Suzanne Terrell; New Orleans Mayor, Mark Morial; Buddy's granddaughter and great granddaughter, Gertrude Bolden Tucker and Rita Camille Bell

But King Bolden had more "firsts" than that.

Buddy didn't just play the melody on his cornet.

He didn't just embellish the melody.

Buddy broke free of the melody and improvised over the tune. Moreover, he replaced the straight march-time feel of N'Awlins rhythm with a "big-four" figure that pushed the second 4th beat, giving dancers an accent they could shimmy to. And that, all together, is called "jazz."

Everyone who saw him said they'd never heard anyone play like that. Bolden was bold, sassy, loud, and inventive with both rhythm and melody. He was our first jazz player, first jazz personality, and he led the first jazz group in 1895.

Then the professor told some stories on Buddy.

One tale said that it was not unusual to see Bolden walking down Perdido Street with four women on his arms. Well, he was a dapper dresser and a ladies' man. Miles Davis styled his persona on Buddy.

But four women? Buddy, that was asking for trouble.

Another story said his cornet playing was so clear and loud that he could be heard for fourteen miles.

Fourteen miles? Well Buddy, if you could handle four women ....

Another story about him: When he was twenty-nine years old, Buddy was playing a Labor Day parade in New Orleans. It was a hot day, the band had taken a break, and Buddy, reputedly a hard drinker, had been drinking hard. They had just started up again when Buddy went stark, crazy, raving mad.

The police came, took him away and stood him in front of a magistrate. The magistrate threw Buddy in the East Louisiana State Hospital at Jackson, also known as the Jackson insane asylum. And in those days – this was 1907 – when you were placed in an insane asylum, the doors of your life locked behind you.

Buddy Bolden was never heard from again.

He could not give an interview – was incapable of it – and he was never recorded. Or, another story goes, he was recorded, on a lone Edison wax cylinder that has never been found. Most of what we know about Buddy Bolden we learned from his contemporaries, such as Jelly Roll Morton, who outlived him.

Buddy died on November 4, 1931, at age fifty-four. Some

say it was booze that drove Buddy insane. Some say it was women. Jelly said Bolden blew his brains out into the cornet.

The funeral home unceremoniously threw Buddy's bones into an unmarked grave at plot C-623 of the Holt Cemetery. Over the years as many as nine folks were buried on top of Bolden.

Then the cemetery's records were lost. Now they can't say exactly where Buddy's bones lie, but legend has it that he rests beneath the old Oak tree that dominates Section C of the cemetery.

"Today, September 6, 1996," the professor concluded, "is Buddy's 119th birthday. It's high time we were layin' Buddy down with the N'Awlins send-off he's always deserved."

At that moment they lifted the shroud from the headstone and we all crowded around to read what had been said about Buddy. On the tombstone they had engraved these words:

IN MEMORY OF
CHARLES JOSEPH "BUDDY" BOLDEN
SEPTEMBER 6, 1877 – NOVEMBER 4, 1931
IN AN UNMARKED GRAVE NEAR HERE RESTS
BUDDY BOLDEN
LEGENDARY CORNET PLAYER
NEW ORLEANS JAZZ PIONEER
AND FIRST "KING OF JAZZ"

I liked that. Someone had summed up Buddy in a dozen words. But beneath this was a one-sentence quote from Jelly Roll Morton. Jelly had recorded an old song about Buddy called "Funky Butt Blues," later renamed, "Buddy Bolden's Blues." It goes about like this:

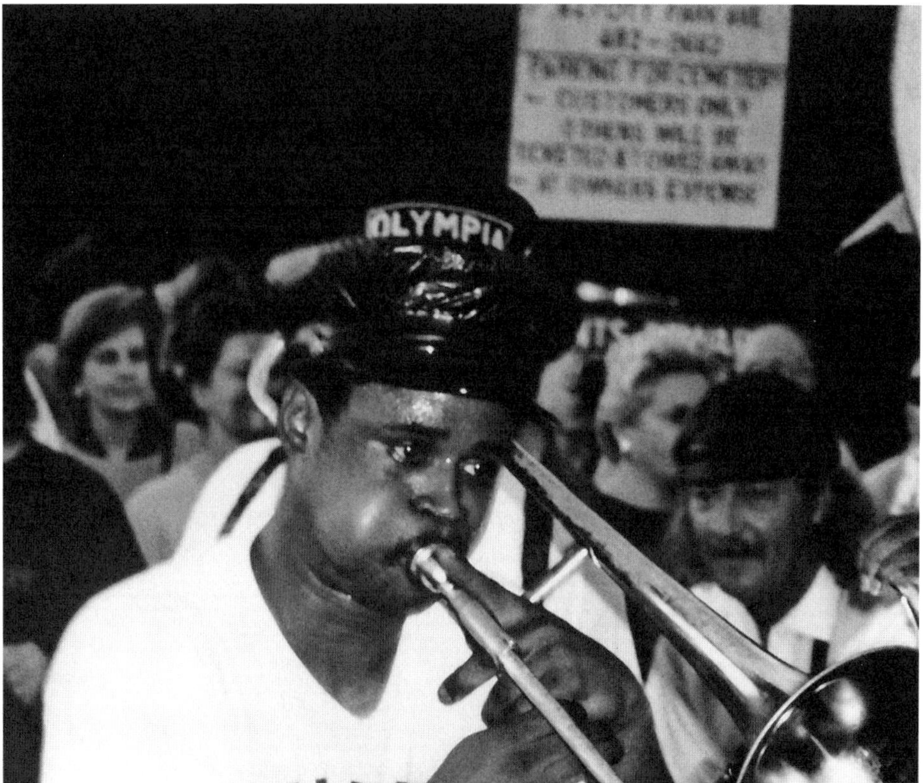

Edward Paris, trombone

I thought I heard Buddy Bolden shout,
Open up the window, let the bad air out,
Open up the window, let the bad air out,
That's what I heard him shout.

I thought I heard Buddy Bolden say,
Funky Butt, Funky Butt, take him away,
Funky Butt, Funky Butt, take him away,
That's what I heard him say.

I thought I heard Judge Fogarty say,
Give him 30 days in the market, take him away,
Give him a broom and take the prisoner away,
I thought I heard him say.

I thought I heard Frankie Dusen shout,
Give me our money or I'll beat it out,
Give me our money or I'll beat it out,
I thought I heard him shout.

In the music business it is sometimes said that when you sing a song about someone, it may just mean that you love that person. So I was glad to see that someone who had known and loved Buddy had summed him up in just a few words. And what Jelly Roll Morton had said about King Buddy Bolden was engraved at the bottom of the headstone:

"THE BLOWINGEST MAN SINCE GABRIEL"

Donald M. Marquis' exceptional biography, "In Search of Buddy Bolden: First Man of Jazz," was published by Louisiana State University Press in 1978. It is the factual story of the King.

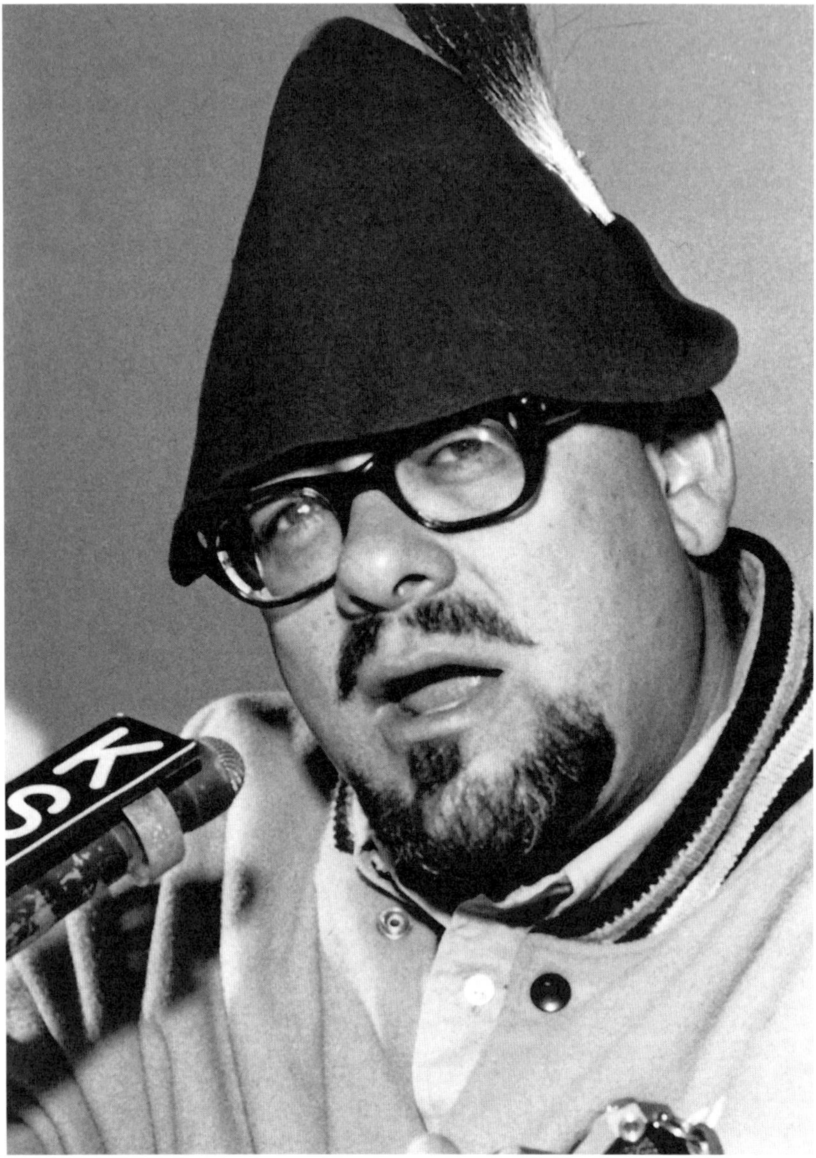

Jazzbeaux

San Francisco · circa 1963

Publicity photo courtesy of Patti Collins

anon

Jazzbeaux Got There

On the evening of September 30, 1997, Al "Jazzbeaux" Collins, jazz personality and creator of the outrageous radio show, the Purple Grotto, passed away at his Tam Valley home at the age of seventy-eight. He was a good friend of jazz. He was a good friend of mine.

I remember Jazzbeaux from the radio. He broadcast live from a state of mind he called the Purple Grotto, a stalactite- and stalagmite-daggered cavern, three stories below ground level, at 42nd Street and 3rd Avenue in midtown Manhattan.

Jazzbeaux described it so well, and in so few words, that he brought you into his purple haze. And from the Purple Grotto of his mind, Jazzbeaux cast his purple spell on ours.

He played jazz records, and Jazzbeaux had impeccable taste in music. Between cuts he'd play soft background music, usually by a piano trio like Nat King Cole's. He said, "That made my audience feel that somethin' was going on, somethin' was happenin' in the Grotto where I was talking."

And over this music background, he rapped at you in '50s bop-talk about whatever pleased him: about jazz, which he loved and spoke of insightfully, or about the cut he had just played. Most memorably, Jazzbeaux could be outrageous, bouncing between honking horns, banging purple gongs, shouting "I don't got to show you no stinking badges" (a favorite line of his), riffing on whatever – on mushroom steak – and taking live phone calls from jazz celebrities. He was Ruler of the Purple Mayhem.

Or he'd have the cats in to play live on his show, cats like Count Basie – Al's favorite jazz was big band and his favorite big band was Basie's. Cats like Louis Armstrong, Teddy Wilson, and even Art Tatum. Tatum, maybe the greatest jazz pianist who ever lived, played live on the Grotto for six months straight.

Or Jazzbeaux might tell one of Steve Allen's "Bop Fables" – the Little Red Riding Hood stories Steve rewrote into hipster vernacular.

He'd take phone calls from his listeners *off* the air, while he was playing a cut. If he found a caller that he was having a good time with, he'd take him on-air when the tune ended. He was a master of these interviews, and had off-the-wall discussions with his callers. The ones who gave him the biggest laughs would become mainstays on his show for years, checking in regularly to update Al on their stuff.

A pioneer in radio, Jazzbeaux invented the man-on-the-street interview in 1949. In his version, Al would lie down flat on his back at some downtown street corner – like he was gone – and when someone bent down to look at him, he would stick a mic in his face and start interviewing the guy.

Jazzbeaux had a rich life outside the Grotto as well, because he was at the center of a large jazz scene and knew everyone. All the cats hung with Jazzbeaux, and Jazzbeaux was one of the cats, a major player himself.

Miles Davis once called Jazzbeaux up – yeah, Jazzbeaux knew Miles – and Miles, knowing how Jazzbeaux dug a good car, asked Al to take a ride with him in his new Ferrari.

Sure Jazzbeaux went. He said it was a gasser.

Al was one of the few hosts of the Tonight Show, doing a stint following Steve Allen and preceding Jack Parr. In 1953 he released *Grimm Fairy Tales for Hip Kids,* a recording of Al reading Steve Allen's "Bop Fables" while Steve played piano. It sold three-quarters of a million copies. Al was so strong in the New York scene that MAD magazine caricatured him for a while.

Jazzbeaux was an independent. He never let management dictate a play list to him. He played what he wanted and he did what he wanted.

One evening, Count Basie came by with his entire band. They played live on the Purple Grotto for two-and-a-half hours straight. Jazzbeaux didn't air a single commercial the entire time.

The station manager was furious, and nearly fired him the next day.

"I wouldn't have cared," Al told me. "We had a blast!"

The Purple Grotto was a magical show born in a magical era of radio. Jazzbeaux took it with him for fifty-six years, from WNEW in New York, to San Francisco's KSFO, Los Angeles stations KMET, FKI and KGBS, and Pittsburgh's WTAE. He came back to the Bay Area in 1976 and was last on-air with the Purple Grotto at KCSM radio on September 20, ten days before he passed.

Early in the spring of 1997, Al and I drove to Carmel to dig Mose Allison. Mose was playing a concert at KRML radio, the local jazz station. The station had invited Al down to be their guest at the show and was offering to put him up at a fancy inn.

Al said, "Yeah, but you've gotta put up my driver too. I don't travel without my driver, ya know."

The station said, "Driver? … Uh, no problem, Al."

Fortunately, Al asked me to be the driver.

It was a beautiful day, the sun was shining on the Pacific, the early spring flowers were in bloom, and as we drove, I asked Al about his beginnings in radio.

"I looked around and I saw what the other guys were doing and I said, No, I don't want to do that. That's not funny, that's not refreshing. Let's talk about something that's fun. That's my whole philosophy. The more laughs I can get and the less serious I can get, the more I like it.

"I don't believe in settling the great questions. A lot of people want to know why we're here. I'm satisfied with just knowing that we are."

And then he said this, carefully:

"I just want to get so relaxed, so mellowed out, that no matter what happens on my show, no matter what any of my guests say or do, I will be totally in the groove with it and flow with it perfectly."

He looked out the window; the Pacific Ocean sparkled in his eyes. Then he looked back at me and said: "And I haven't got there yet."

I was surprised to hear Al say this – he was the king of laid-back – so later when we had arrived at the inn, I asked him, "Did I hear you right, Al, that you haven't got there yet?"

He looked over at me and said, "No. Not yet."

Al was a little Buddha on his way to enlightenment. And on that September evening, in the arms of his wife Patti, with a picture of Count Basie hanging over the bed, Jazzbeaux got there.

Hello Al. May your message of jazz and laughs liven up the heavenly scene forever.

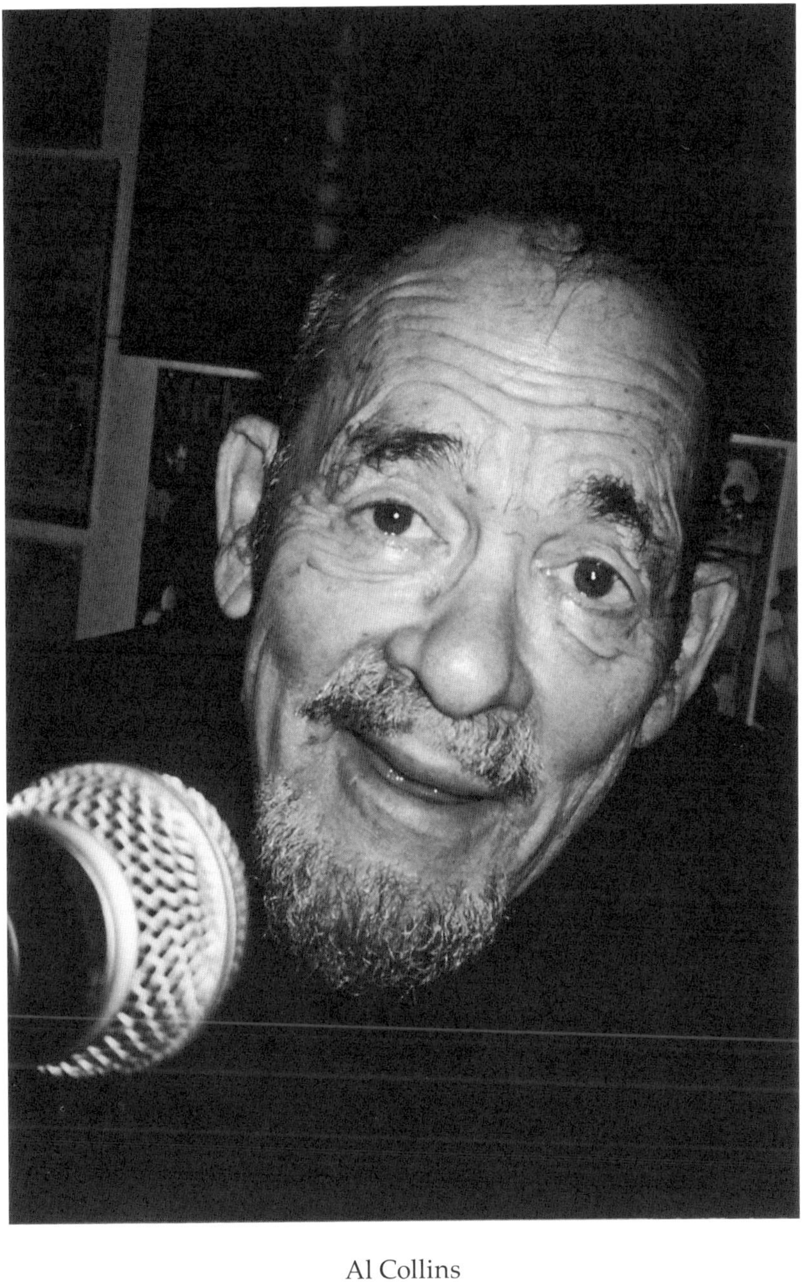

Al Collins
Mill Valley · circa 1995

Will Sudmeier
~ A Song from His Heart

May 3, 2001

Trombonist Jeff Barnard called me up last night. Jeff is one of the regulars in the J. H. Big Band, an 18-piece group I direct and play bass with. "You won't believe who'll be subbing with the band tomorrow evening!"

"Yeah? Who?"

"Will Sudmeier."

"Will who?"

"Sudmeier. Will Sudmeier. You don't know who he is?"

"I'm not sure. Would you refresh my memory?"

"Will is a legendary trombonist. He has played with the San Francisco, Oakland, and Marin Symphonies, the Art Linkletter band, the Tennessee Ernie Ford Show, and the ABC and CBS bands. What's more, he was the principal or lead trombone in *all* those groups."

"Wait a second. I bumped into his name on the Internet. Isn't Will the guy who created the "mwa-mwa" voices of the adults in the Peanuts television series?"

"Yeah, using his trombone and plunger mute."

"So, anyone who's seen Peanuts on TV, has probably heard Will play. Jeff, who'd he study with?"

"Will studied with Emory Remington, one of the 20th century's greatest trombone teachers, and he is recognized as a great teacher himself. He has also written, arranged, transcribed, or adapted hundreds of compositions for trombone. And he's a conductor. Last year, at the International Trombone Association Festival in San Francisco, Will, at age seventy, directed the San Francisco Bay Bones, an 80-piece trombone choir.

"Jeff, you're a fount of knowledge about the guy."

"I'm telling you, Will is *legendary*."

"So Jeff, what is a trombone choir?"

"A trombone choir is 12 to 40 or more trombonists, like the Bay Bones, a group Will co-founded and co-leads. He's reconstituting it in Santa Rosa, and every trombonist he approaches wants to be counted in. His writing, arranging and conducting changed the way trombone choirs work. He got them out of the old repertoire and into the new. A critic I read said that he had never heard a trombone choir play so loud, so soft, so long, or so beautifully as Will's."

"What a compliment. It's great that he'll be playing with us. That would be like Pavarotti sitting in with a community glee club. I'm looking forward to this."

"Good. But let me warn you, Bill, he can be a demanding guy. And he's punctual. Get there on time, OK?"

So I left early for tonight's rehearsal and arrived at 6:55 PM for our 7:30 start. Tim, the facilities manager, and an excellent trombonist in his own right, met me at the front door. "Hey Bill, did you know that Will Sudmeier is playing with us tonight? He got here ten minutes ago."

And there was Will, sitting alone on the bandstand, a brass mouthpiece in his lips, warming up, waiting for the downbeat, ... waiting for me. I welcomed him warmly, told him we were honored he was playing with us, and apologized for arriving late.

Twenty minutes later the rest of the group started straggling in. Just before the hit – the downbeat to the first tune – the gal who was subbing on tenor sax made an announcement that she was forming a new big band. Will bounded out of his chair, gave her his card and told her he was interested.

The first set began, and for the second tune I called an arrangement of Hoagy Carmichael's "Stardust," one that features a trombone solo. Will stood up and played a simple, curving melody that was graceful and mesmerizing; he glued our ears to it.

For the rest of the evening, everyone who played a solo played a simple, curving melody. Will had taught us a lesson without saying a word. Here's how you play a solo, he demonstrated: you let a song out of your heart.

The trombone is a much-maligned instrument, the undeserving butt of many jokes in the classical music world, just as the banjo is in the folk music community. But in Will's hands tonight it was an instrument of weeping beauty. His tone was compact, accurate, and honeyed. He played Tommy Dorsey's lead on "Marie" sweeter and more effortlessly than Dorsey. His tone set the band's tone for the evening.

After the rehearsal, a few of us went out for a bite to eat. Someone asked Will if he considered himself "retired." Will turned to his friend Dick, who is about sixty-five, and asked Dick if he was retired. Dick laughed and asked Martha, who will always be about thirty-nine, and she laughed too.

I said, "Will, you came to a Thursday night community big band rehearsal and arrived first. And you were the first to tell the lady recruiting musicians for her new band that you'd play with them. You play first chair with the Marin Symphony, you've lead the Bay Bones, you write, arrange, and conduct. Retired? No I don't think you've retired."

There was a heartbeat, and then Will said, "I'd like to die with a trombone in my mouth."

It had a chilling effect, his saying this. It meant that Will had been thinking about death. No one at the table was a spring bunny. We had all thought about it. Will had spoken it.

I told the story of how Walt Tolleson died. Walt was a society bandleader in San Francisco, very successful, and a guy who *loved* to play the trumpet.

In the end, Walt was vacationing with his wife in Honolulu. One evening, he stood on the lanai, faced the sunset, and played his pocket trumpet for an hour. Then he put his horn down and took a walk on the beach as the sun melted into the sea. Half way to the surf, Walt fell down in the sand and passed away.

"That would be the way to go," Will said.

December 6, 2001

When rehearsal began this evening, Martha told us that Will Sudmeier had died. He had played his steady gig in Healdsburg on Sunday afternoon. On Tuesday, Will was at his digs – a "Salvation Army high-rise" Martha called it – when a massive heart attack hit him. He called 911, but they arrived too late.

Will had said that he wanted to go with the trombone in his mouth. He came fairly close to his wish.

Jeff was playing 'bone particularly well tonight, so I complimented him at the end of the rehearsal.

"Thanks, man. I'm trying to make this evening a tribute to Will."

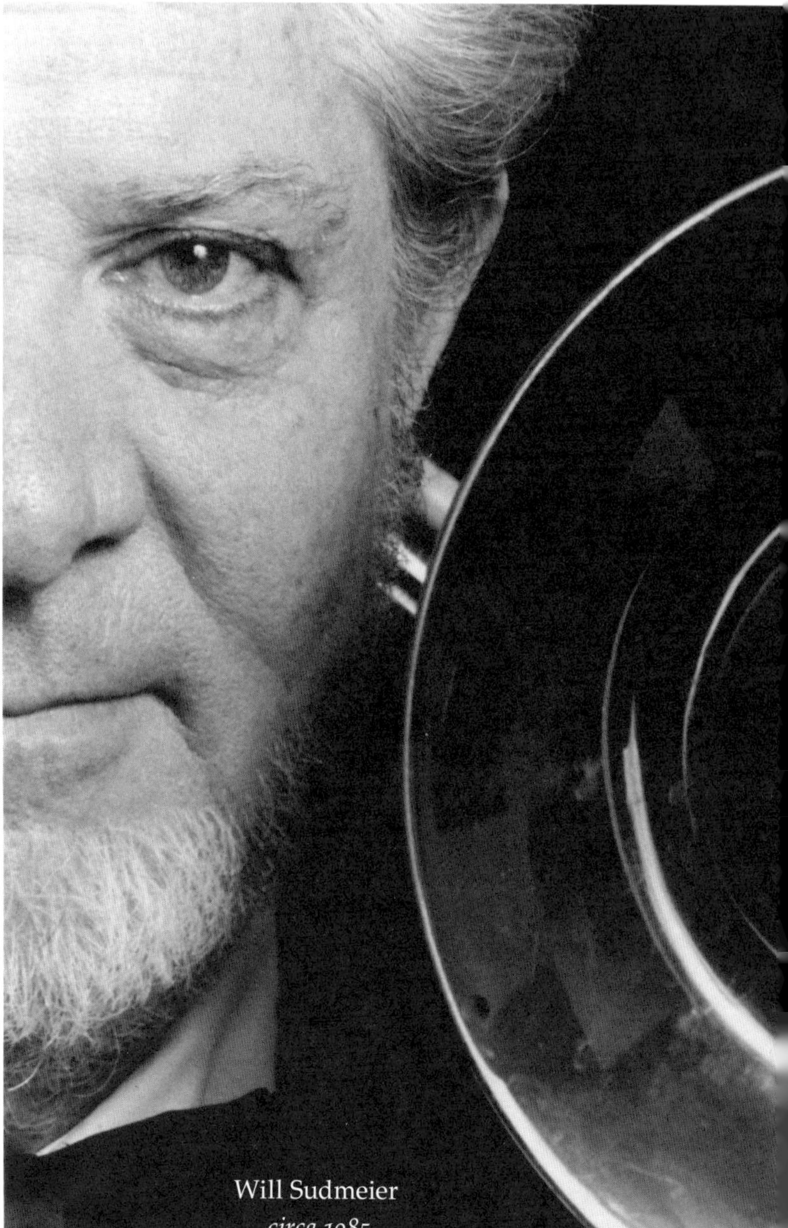

Will Sudmeier
circa 1985
Courtesy of Greg Sudmeier
anon

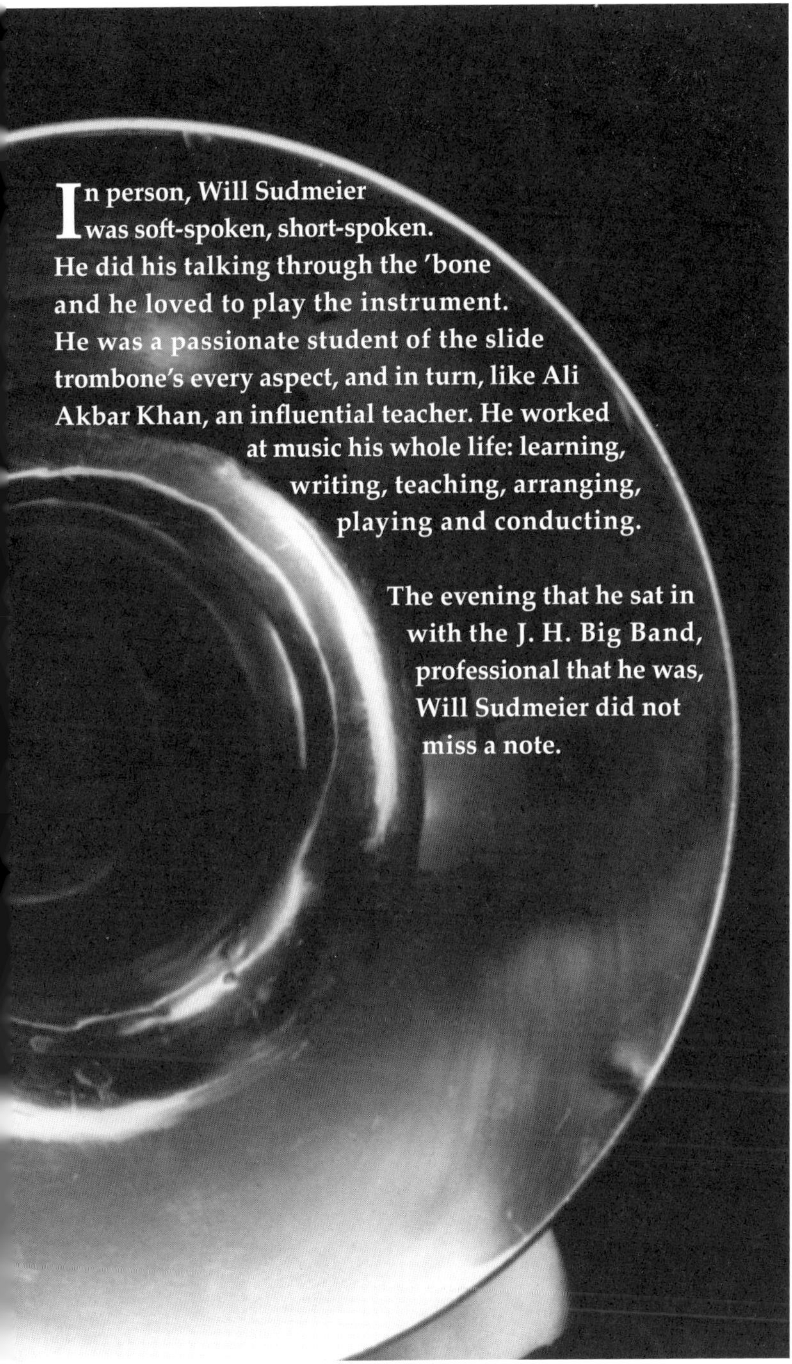

In person, Will Sudmeier was soft-spoken, short-spoken. He did his talking through the 'bone and he loved to play the instrument. He was a passionate student of the slide trombone's every aspect, and in turn, like Ali Akbar Khan, an influential teacher. He worked at music his whole life: learning, writing, teaching, arranging, playing and conducting.

The evening that he sat in with the J. H. Big Band, professional that he was, Will Sudmeier did not miss a note.

Pickin' for the Prez

On the afternoon of April 10, 2006, Doug Adamz called me. I play string bass in Doug's bluegrass trio, "Bravo!" a group that continues a tradition of bluegrass bands in California that started in the 1950s.

"Bill, do you have a minute? There's an upcoming gig I'd like to discuss."

"Sure, Doug."

"Is your wife out of the room? I wouldn't want her overhearing our conversation."

This was strange, being asked if my wife was out of the room, and visions of accompanying a lap dancer shimmied through my head. "Actually, she's out of the house, Doug."

"Good. So Bill, are you sitting down?"

This was bizarre. I could not imagine the gig that I would be better off hearing about seated, *and* with my wife out of the room.

"I'm sitting down," I said, as I stood up. "What's happening, Doug?"

"We've got a gig playing for President George W. Bush."

I sat down. "You're kidding me!"

"Nope. It's out on the Peninsula, at the home of George Shultz, Ronald Reagan's Secretary of State. It's a dinner party for fourteen people."

An hour-long conversation followed about the ethics of entertaining a President with whose politics we were both in sharp disagreement. On one hand, I did not want to entertain this president. On the other, I play music for a living. Turning down a gig, with the possible loss of other gigs from the agent or the Shultzes, is not how I put food on the table.

I went from, "Yes, I'll play the gig," to "No, I won't play it," to "Doug, I'll get back to you tomorrow with a decision."

"Fine, but don't spill the details of the job to anyone. If protestors found out, they could make life hell for the Shultzes."

"Sure, Doug."

That evening I called my friend Joe Armstrong, an older, wiser man than me. Joe has held the highest-level security clearance from the U.S. government, and yet has been a life-long Democrat. Without mentioning names, dates, or places, I communicated my dilemma to him.

He said he understood.

Joe rarely gives me advice; that's not his style. His method is usually more Socratic. That is, he asks me questions until, by my answers, I figure out the score for myself. But this time he went so far as to say, "If it were me, I'd take the job."

"You know Joe, sometimes, after a revolution, the revolutionary council sets up tribunals where people with even the least dealings with the old regime have their heads handed to them on bloodied platters."

He laughed. "Bill, I understand, but I don't think that's going to happen. I'll say this though. If you take the gig, be prepared: some of your friends are going to resent you for it."

When we hung up, it was midnight, a good time to quietly look oneself in the eye. This was a moral decision: to entertain or not entertain an immoral man. I wanted to pass it up, but I also wanted to play it.

At age sixty, having worked about every kind of gig there

is, I was facing one I had never played – for the President of the United States – and I was struggling with it. I wanted to turn it down, but realized that would not change Bush's mind about anything. It would impact me alone.

After a restless night, I called Doug back in the morning. "I'll play the gig, Doug. This is what I do for a living. I'll get to look Bush in the eye, take the measure of the man, maybe have a story to tell about it. And you know, it could be a hoot – a gig like I'll never see again."

"Fine," Doug said, "that's what I've decided as well. Now I need your social security number so they can run a security check on you."

I figured that would be the end of it for me, as Doug figured it would be for him. The number of marches and rallies we had both attended and petitions we had signed would certainly disqualify us both from playing this gig. We knew it was long odds that we would be sanctioned to play.

Five days later, a slim five days before the gig, Doug called to say we had been cleared. Either they hadn't dug deeply, or they were unintimidated by what they found: two native-born, non-Muslims who had never been arrested. Moreover, Doug had played for Shultz before, so maybe George had put in a good word for us. Still, passing the security check was a surprise to us both.

We discussed the gig's dress code, "formal country," and batted around a few ideas for tunes. I suggested we take a bluegrass look at "Hail to the Chief," which Doug, feeling strongly about how the 2000 presidential election had been decided, referred to as "Hail to the Thief." He did say that we'd likely play the Lone Star State's unofficial song, "The Yellow Rose of Texas," when Bush made his appearance.

"And by the way,: Doug added, "this is going to be an outdoor, strolling gig. So we'll be all acoustic, no amps."

Well, acoustic music is my favorite, so that was good.

But I tried to block out the strolling part. Playing a bass while you walk is an impossibility, unless, like the bassists in Philadelphia's Mummer Parade, you duct-tape the instrument to your body, something I was not about to do with my 130-year-old Czech bass. "Strolling is *not* going to happen," was the mantra I kept repeating to myself.

Finally the big day of the big gig arrived. I drove to Doug's where Russ Gautier (the third member of our trio) and I loaded our instruments into Doug's van and took off.

We arrive at the Stanford University campus, a few miles from Shultz's home, with forty minutes to spare. All three of us are jonesing for java, so we go prowling. It takes us a while to find a Peet's Coffee, and the line is out the door. By the time we're downing caffeine, we've lost all but five minutes of our forty-minute advantage.

We head out for the Shultzes', but are stopped within a block by Stanford University security. It seems that the President's conference at Stanford's Hoover Tower with the "Hoover Institution on War, Revolution and Peace," a conservative think tank, has been surrounded by a thousand demonstrators, and the police won't let us through campus. They give us an alternate route, and as we make our U-turn to find it, Doug picks up a cellphone call from our agent. She is on site, and anxious to know where we are.

We step on it and in ten minutes arrive at the Shultz residence, an old Cape Cod-style home in a neighborhood of beautiful homes, all on an acre or so. Our agent greets us at the foot of the driveway.

She tells us we're to proceed slowly to the top of the drive where people with guns will meet us. "Do whatever they tell you to do," she says.

This sounds like sage advice, and we grunt, "OK."

As Doug eases up the drive, we get our first glimpse of the United States Secret Service: eight guys in dark-blue suits, white shirts and ties, each with an earbud in place and a coiled wire running under the collar.

We eyeball them carefully as we slide up the driveway, and thankfully, they eyeball us carefully. Should push come to shove this afternoon, we want them to know we are the good guys, as in, "Don't shoot, we're the good guys."

Sure enough, armed White House guards meet us at the top of the driveway, and tell us what to do. We're to bring our instruments to poolside in the back yard where we'll be playing, and then exit the premises. They'll sweep our instruments (scan them with metal detectors) sweep us, and then let us return to the back yard when the moment to begin playing arrives. Doug is told to park his van back out in the neighborhood.

We offload our instruments, cart them to the bandstand, and return to the top of the driveway. There Russ and I hang with the catering crew (who are on pause until the cocktail hour begins), as Doug climbs into his van and drives off to find a parking place.

Then this meticulously planned afternoon starts falling apart. Since demonstrators have blocked access to the Hoover Tower on campus, it has been decided that all fifty conferees will be bused to the Shultz's home where they will meet in the living room with the President. An intimate dinner party for fourteen has ballooned into a conference for fifty. The schedule has been put back an hour, we are told. Actually, the pushback turns into almost two hours, and proves a nightmare for security.

One of the guards tells me, "A home in a neighborhood is tough to secure. All the surrounding homes have to be checked out and patrolled throughout the day." Sure enough, we spot armed security guys patrolling the perimeter of the Shultz's home. One has taken a position behind the oak tree in the back yard, a submachine gun cradled in his arms. Two Apache helicopters circle high overhead. Bringing in fifty more people is going to add to the difficulties.

So, the Chief of White House Security decides to put the home into lockdown. No one is allowed in or out.

Ten minutes later it occurs to me that Doug has been gone for twenty minutes, and that he's likely been caught outside the locked-down home, unable to get in. I mention this to our agent who brings it up with a secret service agent. He's wired for communications but refuses to do anything: they're in lockdown. During the next hour she approaches a number of the security personnel with the same plea: "Can you get our leader through?"

The answer is the same: "No, we're in lockdown."

These are a tiring two hours for us. It's chilly, and there are few places to sit down. But as uncomfortable as it is for us and the catering crew, we at least are inside the lockdown. Doug is outside, standing at the foot of the driveway just twenty-five yards away, hidden from our view by shrubs. Sure enough, they are not letting him near the house.

A guy in a suit grabs Doug's coat as he approaches the Shultz home. "You can't go in now," he says. He doesn't explain that there's a lockdown. As the suit leaves his post, he tells the guy from the California Highway Patrol (CHP) who replaces him, not to let Doug in. The CHP guy tells Doug to step back. Doug is actually losing ground now. He tries to tell the patrolman that he belongs there – "I've got a job to do here too!" – but the CHP guy says Doug's credentials aren't cleared.

This puzzles Doug; his credentials *have* been cleared. But he moves back; outgunned, he has no choice. So Doug downshifts into waiting mode, meditation mode.

But now a Special Weapons and Tactics team member, a SWAT guy, dressed head-to-toe in Kevlar and bristling with weaponry, replaces the CHP guy. He seems fairly friendly, tells Doug his name, gets Doug's name. Doug tells him he's a musician in the band that has been hired by the Shultzes to play for the President, and that he must get in. The SWAT guy says he knows who Doug is, but can't let him in.

Now Doug's afternoon takes a dive. A squad car of four CHP guys pulls up. One of them sees Doug standing there, and takes him for a protestor. This 6′ 4″ deeply beefy patrolman strides right up to Doug, plants a menacing scowl on his mug, and shoves it into Doug's face, nose to nose.

This purposely-provocative act is referred to as "in your face," and that is exactly where this CHP guy is. For thirty … sixty … ninety seconds … he locks Doug in a Sonny Liston staredown.

Fortunately, Doug, who has a brown belt in karate, is an unflappable guy. He doesn't move, he doesn't flinch, he doesn't utter a word. He just calmly looks back at the guy. I would not have managed the same even response, and my hat is off to Doug for handling a difficult situation well. One wrong word and he would have been *way* out of there.

Finally, one of the Secret Service guys who had eyeballed us when we pulled up the driveway sees this standoff, walks over to the CHP guy, and tells him that Doug is a musician playing for the Shultzes. The big guy stands down.

Doug takes a deep breath. He will later tell me that this one-hour stretch locked out on the sidewalk is the most unforgettable part of his entire afternoon.

Our agent borrows a cellphone – hers was in her purse, inside the home – tracks down Charlotte Shultz's number, calls her and tells her the story. Charlotte tells her husband, George, and George tells the Chief of White House Security who personally walks out and escorts Doug back in through the lock down.

Doug joins us and takes a seat off to the side. His face is pale and he holds his head in his hands.

"You OK?" I ask.

"Yeah, I'm fine," he says.

He is not fine; he is visibly shaken.

Now the presidential limo arrives, drops Bush at the front door, and pulls into the driveway, next to the band and catering crew. It is the only vehicle they allow to remain in the driveway all day. Incredibly, the driver leaves it running the *entire* afternoon and evening!

Doesn't he know this is California?

The caravan of unmarked vans carrying the fifty conferees starts arriving. It is accompanied by hundreds of security personnel in squad cars, unmarked cars, Humvees, military vehicles, motorcycles, ambulances and fire trucks. They hang out on the street that fronts the house, looking like a multi-force security expo.

Finally, the conference inside the Shultz home starts closing and the events coordinator moves us into position. Once again the uniformed guard sweeps us. We charge up the flight of ten steps that leads from the driveway to the backyard ... but now there is another hold. The conference is not over; we are not going on.

So we're stranded on this outdoor stairway. I'm standing two steps beneath the upper landing where a Secret Service agent is stationed, guarding entrance to the grounds. He wears the regulation dark-blue suit, white shirt, tie, and deadpan.

Because I am two steps below him, I'm eyeball even with his tie. There's something about it that I recognize. It's just a business tie, a small red motif repeated on a gray background, nothing wild or crazy. But it looks familiar. I know this tie ... I think.

"Ah, excuse me sir, but is that a Jerry Garcia tie?"

He face pales, his jaw slackens, and without saying a

word, he flips the tie over to show me the Grateful Dead logo on the back. He leans in towards me and whispers, "No one *ever* gets that!"

Knowing the Dead's reputation, deserved or not, for sex, drugs, & rock 'n' roll, I ask, "Does your boss know about this?"

His non-answer screams, *"No! And I don't want him to!"*

So I say, "Are you a fan of Jerry's?"

"Well, kinda. Of his early work."

Well that's interesting, because the neckties are definitely Jerry's later work. The agent sounds like he's trying to distance himself from Jerry.

"A few years ago, I played some bluegrass with Jerry. I wrote a story about it that's in a book of stories that was published recently. If you'd like, I'll give you a copy when we leave."

Before he can answer, the events coordinator gives us the green light to enter the grounds. We have ten minutes to uncase our instruments, tune up, and get ready to play. Doug has his guitar, fiddle, and harmonicas. Russ has brought a guitar, fiddle, banjo, and mandolin. Ten minutes is cutting it short.

We are staged on an upper patio, on the same level as the pool and the pool house where the dinner party will be held. Our bandstand overlooks the lower patio where the guests, including the President, will exit from the conference and congregate for hors d'oeuvres before strolling over to dinner.

With only one instrument to prepare, I have a few minutes to look around. The grounds, on a sloping hillside, are impeccably kept. The old oak tree that dominates the back yard is particularly well maintained. The park benches look sleek and sculpted, contoured into their corners of the yard. The poolside lounge chairs and chaises are quietly tasteful. A housekeeper sweeps the patio of the vegetation that has fallen in the last fifteen minutes. Another caretaker skims a half-dozen leaves from the pool's surface. The joint is immaculate.

With two minutes to spare, I make a dash to the only bathroom in the vicinity, in the pool house. There I pass by the table where the guests will be dining. I've seen some beautifully set tables at gigs I've played for the 1%, but this is the most breathtaking. The sparkling gold-ware and the gold gilt-edged chinaware on the dining room table glisten so brightly you could imagine human hands have never touched them. The Austrian crystal stemware rainbows the afternoon light. A fan-folded, floral-print linen dinner napkin has been set above each plate. At each setting is a small gift, and above, a hand-lettered name card. There is one for George and another for Charlotte, and many that begin with the title "Professor" for their Stanford faculty guests. The overall impression is of precise elegance in the setting of a classic California pool house.

I return to the bandstand just as the conference is breaking up. Charlotte gives us the signal to begin playing, and we tear into a medley of Irish fiddle tunes. Watching through the home's back window, I see that the conferees are exiting through the front door, Bush and the Shultzes wishing them farewell. Finally, the doors to the patio swing open and we segue into "The Yellow Rose of Texas."

One, two, three, four professors exit the house, and then, there he is, the Decider of the United States of America, arguably the world's most powerful man.

George W. Bush is wearing a grayish-tan suit with an American flag lapel pin, a blue vertically pinstriped shirt with red horizontally pinstriped tie, and black shoes. The tie and shirt, their pinstripes colliding at a ninety-degree angle, don't necessarily harmonize, but Bush distinguishes himself as the only man there who is not wearing a dark jacket, and as the only guy who did not sleep in it. He looks tailored and pressed; the professors, true to rumpled type, do not. For a moment I wonder, Did they tell these guys to all wear dark jackets so Bush would stand out? Nah, impossible.

Bush steps onto the patio and hears the music. He looks up in our direction, and our eyes lock.

He nods to me. Thank you for "Yellow Rose of Texas."

I nod back. You're welcome.

And now he beelines for the bandstand. As he walks across the lower patio towards us, he extends his fist – it clutches a brown bottle wrapped in a white paper napkin (probably a zero-alcohol beer) – slightly to his right. This must be a signal, because instantly, and magically, an anonymous hand darts out and takes it from him. This little transaction makes me aware that Bush is being watched constantly, and by many people.

Bounding up the four steps to the upper patio, the Prez is suddenly with us at the bandstand. "Thanks for coming out and playing music for us today, guys. I really appreciate it."

He extends his hand to Russ who is playing mandolin. Russ stops playing – Doug and I keep the music going – shifts his flat pick to his left hand, shakes the president's hand, and says "How do you do."

He reaches for my hand next. Well, when the bass player stops playing, the music is over. So, the "Yellow Rose of Texas" fades on the bush as I shake hands with *the* Bush.

"How do you do, Mr. President. Welcome to California. I hope you're having a good time."

"I am. Ya know, being out here, my outlook is better already."

Well, that's what visiting California is somewhat about: a better outlook. For a moment I envision him, under

California's balm, joining the Green Party and renouncing war.

OK. It's a brief moment.

Now something unexpected happens. After shaking Doug's hand, the President starts to walk *in to* the band, between Doug and me.

I had heard Bush was an amateur guitarist, so as he takes these steps, I say, "Mr. President, would you like to sit in with the band?"

"Naw. I want to have my picture taken with you!"

He steps between Douglas and me, and turns to face the same direction we are. The White House chief photographer, Eric Draper, charges up the steps, puts his camera to his eye and frames a shot.

It's an awkward moment for me. The shot will be on my left, but the bass is in the way. I swing it from my left hand to my right and step forward, but my left foot collides with the bass's endpin, pitching me forward. I'm going down.

Now this, in a millisecond: the Secret Service agent with submachine gun standing behind the oak tree; the dozen armed servicemen patrolling the home's perimeter; the three assault weapon-wielding agents on a neighbor's rooftop watching us; two Apache helicopters circling overhead; the half-dozen sharpshooters who have me in their laser sights. Fall down on my thirty thousand-dollar bass, splintering it loudly and bring Bush down as well. Or catch hold of his shoulder and save my instrument. That feels wrong, life threatening, and like bad protocol. *Don't do it!*

But the survival instinct kicks in. I grab Bush's shoulder, catch my fall, close my eyes, cringe, and wait for a shout, the crack of a rifle, a blurred rush, a numbing headlock.

But nothing happens.

I stand up, ecstatic to have saved my bass and relieved just to be alive as Draper clicks off a shot on his DSLR.

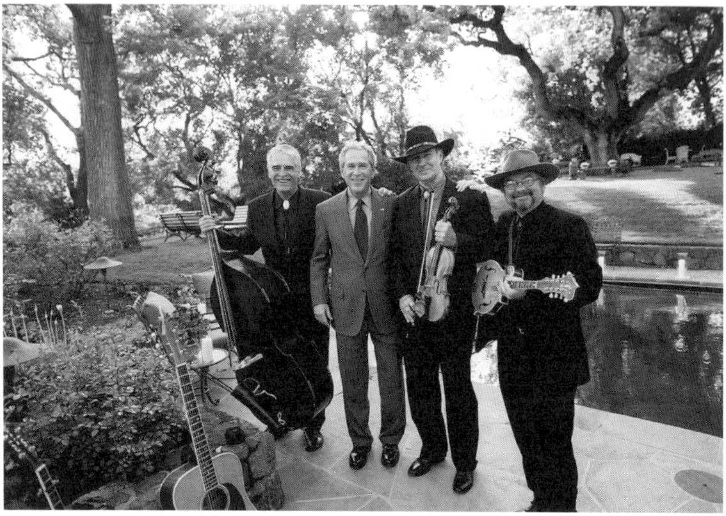

The bass, the bass's endpin, the author, the Prez, Doug, Russ
George & Charlotte Shultz's back yard · April 21, 2006
By Eric Draper

Bush and the band break our pose. He says, "Thanks again, guys."

"You're welcome, Mr. President. Is there anything special we can play for you?"

"You guys are doing great. Just keep doing what you're doing."

He starts walking away, but after three steps he turns back to us and says, "I didn't know they had bluegrass in California."

I'm lost for words. Finally I blurt out, "Of course we do, Mr. President!"

"Naw. You guys must be from Kentucky."

Well, bluegrass was born in Kentucky, so if you're a Republican you're probably thinking, He's paying the band a compliment. But if you're a Democrat you're thinking, He *is* out of touch.

Then the president trots down the steps and rejoins his dinner companions.

Bush looked fit, trim. He was pleasant in a goofy, I-didn't-know-they-had-Bluegrass-in-California way. He acted the politician well. He didn't have to come over to the band, thank us, shake our hands, or have his picture taken with us. But he did. There couldn't have been much in it for him, except maybe a chance to get away from the dark suits and thick talk that must have been going on for him all day, or, in his wildest dreams, to win us over to the dark side.

Although he possessed Texas ebullience, he was perhaps short on charisma. When he rejoined the other guests, they didn't crowd around him as people do for ex-presidents Clinton and Carter. The quests had broken into four groups of two to five people each. His group numbered four. It was interesting to me that most of these professors, who probably saw each other on a weekly or even daily basis, had more to discuss with each other at that moment than they did with the President of the United States. Minutes later, during a break between tunes, two of the professors started a conversation about California wine grape-growing with me – a hireling – and they were standing ten feet from the President of the United States.

Bush seemed to like music, to have an appreciation of it; he noticed it the moment he stepped onto the patio.

His declining to request a tune was the right move. Asking for a song that was not in our repertoire could have caused an embarrassing moment with benefit to no one.

Bush did not seem to be a serious person; he was all laughs. His eagerness to joke seemed like an unpresidential eagerness to please. I had expected that the United States President would possess a certain gravitas that rippled underneath everything he did, one that came with his day-job. But there was none of that in Bush, none that he displayed to us at any rate.

We pick up a new tune and continue playing for another twenty-five minutes. Then we get the sign from Charlotte Shultz that her guests are going to walk to the pool house for dinner. She signals that we are to lead the group. I had envisioned following the group, so I hesitate for a moment. But she makes it clear we are to lead … *now!*

The moment to stroll has arrived. Yikes! I pick up my bass and gamely try to walk and play at the same time. Since my left hand is committed to holding the bass and carrying its weight, I can only pluck open strings with my right hand. But the chord changes don't call for open strings, so it's a cornpone sound and a three stooges sight as I waddle towards the pool house with Doug and Russ. I look over my shoulder, and Bush is right behind me.

He notices my predicament and says, "Walking and carrying that bass, why you must have good upper body strength."

For the second time today he has me at a loss for words. The best I can muster is, "I guess doing the stroll is part of my job today, Mr. President."

I see a clear slice of patio off to the side of the path we're on, the last place for us to comfortably pull over and play while the guests walk by us to the pool house. We take our new position and tear into "Cluck Old Hen", expecting the crowd to walk on. But no, Bush stops to listen, so the whole crowd stops to listen to us sing and play this old-timey song.

My old hen's a good old hen
She lays eggs for the railroad men
Sometimes one and sometimes two
Sometimes enough for the whole darned crew

Cluck old hen cluck and sing
You ain't laid an egg since late last spring
Cluck old hen cluck and squall
Ain't laid an egg since late last fall

They stay awhile, bobbing their heads, tapping their feet, and then disappear into the pool house for dinner. It's the last I see of the president.

We play another tune and then get the signal that dinner has begun; the gig is over. We've played for maybe thirty-five minutes. We pack up our instruments and begin the trek across the patio to the top of the staircase.

I've got my gig bag and books with me now, so as we're about to exit the grounds, I turn around to find the Garcia neck-tied security officer.

There he is, twenty-five feet away from me, guarding the entrance to the pool house. Now *our* eyes lock, and in this moment his face is a rictus of dread.

I drop my gaze down to his tie.

Get this!

He has taken off his Garcia necktie and swapped it out for a plain ol' blue polka-dot number, definitely not Jerry's creation.

He doesn't want to risk confronting me and being outed as a Dead Head in front of his colleagues or, worse yet, his boss.

So Jerry … you can rest easy. I guarantee you he'll never wear that tie of yours on the job again.

I told this story on Ray Edlund's KPFA radio show, "Pig in a Pen," where Ron, an old friend, heard it. He lit into me: "Why in God's name did you perform for Bush, the biggest calamity to ever happen to the United States, unless you turned it into a political statement by unfurling an anti-war banner? Don't you think Bush has cannibalized the constitution enough – including wiretapping Americans – to be impeachable, is responsible for killing thousands of innocent people in the Middle East, set the stage for economic disaster for our kids and grandkids by eliminating taxes on the rich, and led the world into a tipping point on global warming, to name a few?"

Well Ron, thanks to Joe Armstrong, I heard you coming. And I want you and the Revolutionary Tribunal to know: I understand your concerns.

"Belly dancing is a woman's dance."

—Middle-Eastern saying

Great Spirit!

The Bush gig saw the American President, fifty Hoover Institution professors, two Apache helicopters, and two-hundred fifty armed personnel in a mashup that must have cost taxpayers a half-million dollars. It was a high-tension scene, and I was concerned that for raw excitement, gigs might be all down hill from there.

Then, on July 13 and 14, 2007, I played a belly dance show at a restaurant in Lake Tahoe, a benefit for Lou Gehrig's disease sufferers. You see, Doug Adamz, besides leading "Bravo," also works the belly dance-band business. Over the years, he and his music sidekick, Russ Gauthier, have cut half a dozen albums of original Middle Eastern-style music that he sells around the world to troupes of belly dancers.

We are called "Light Rain" when we perform this music. It's the same three guys as in Bravo, playing pretty much the same instruments – Doug, violin; Russ, mandolin and 5-string banjo; and me on electric bass – but applied to the sinuous rhythms and modes of Middle-Eastern music.

The Joffrey Ballet picked up the rights to three of Light Rain's compositions, choreographed them, and started performing them on tour. They dance to one, "Rabekin," in the 2003 Robert Altman film about them called *The Company*.

With help from the Joffrey Ballet and Altman's film, Light Rain's music is heard around the world.

On the Tahoe gig, wunderkind percussionist Tobias Roberson augmented us on dumbek (a hand drum), cajón (a box drum that the player sits on), and zills, also called finger cymbals. At twenty-six, Tobias, extremely talented and in demand as a percussionist, has played hundreds of belly dance gigs, and rates as a young old-hand at this music. As a newbie to Middle Eastern rhythm sections, I looked forward to his presence in the band.

We arrived at the venue, the Sawtooth Ridge Restaurant in Tahoe City overlooking "The Lake," as Californians call Lake Tahoe, early Friday afternoon. Chris Karnofsky, the champion of this two-day event, met us as we walked into the club.

When Doug introduced us, she said, "Bill, I'm so honored that you could come and play music for us. I'm thrilled that you're here. I cannot thank you enough for joining us."

Honored? Thrilled? I looked over my shoulder to see if there was some other Bill she might have been addressing, but only The Lake looked back. Having made me feel like royalty, Chris had won me over completely.

As we offloaded our equipment into the club, we watched the restaurant's stage, dance floor, and dining room being transformed into a Turkish nightclub. Waiters were clearing the silverware and plates, removing the tables and chairs. Workmen were putting in a nightclub entrance at stage right, fashioning it from two-by-fours, cardboard, paper mâché, and buckets of paint. The walls were being hung with middle-Eastern tribal cloths, the ceilings draped in multi-colored silk parachutes.

As we set up our gear, the cast started arriving. Dressed in street clothes, their costumes packed into wardrobes, it was impossible to say who played what role in the show. Chris was the calm center of this gathering storm and she managed our endless questions with gracious patience. Maintaining stillness at a cyclone's eye, absorbing frenetic energy and redirecting it to focused goals are skills not quickly learned. Chris had done this before.

Later that afternoon, we gathered on the dance floor for rehearsal. Everyone was in costume, and I now saw that the people I had identified as workmen building the set were in fact all cast members. We were two belly dance troupes; four solo belly dancers; a male belly dancer, Kamaal; a magician, Majinga; stand-up comedienne Joy Michiela; and the great Ali Baba himself with his harem of six women. And oh yes, guarding the harem were four eunuchs – I didn't ask and I didn't look.

There were also two sets of musicians: our group, Light Rain; and a group that called itself "Abdul and the Night Visitors," with musicians Victor Torres, Neil Hutchins, and Sebastian Williams. The Night Visitors billed their sound as "ethnic," but these guys made ethnic sound smooth. They were tribal – mountain tribal – in the oldest, dustiest, and best sense. With the zurna, dumbek, and tabla drums (traditional instruments played in this music), they took me to ancient lands I had never been to, and if they take me again, with all respect, I will be wearing earplugs.

It's about the zurna.

Their leader, Abdul, played this instrument, one that is described as a double reed, conical wind instrument. Blowing into the double reed drives its nasal honk into a metal disc. The metallic amplification of the honk creates what is commonly called a "piercing" tone. But calling the zurna "piercing" is like calling a root canal "pinching." The sound of the zurna is a shrill, high-noted, whiney, saw-toothed, screechy, yakety-yak, eardrum-drilling yowl.

What's more, a zurnaist plays tortuously long yowls between very short breaths. Actually, the best zurna players practice circular breathing. They breathe out the air stored in their cheeks while they breathe into their cheeks through the nose, making one long, uninterrupted yowl that lasts the entire tune.

What's worse, the zurna needs a lot of air to get it vibrating, so zurnaists always play it *loud*. Every time Abdul lifted the instrument to his lips, I flinched. (Later on, I'll tell you what I really think about the zurna.)

By the way, I am not alone in this zurna-phobia. Doug said, "I would rather have a rock 'n' roll drummer living next door than a zurna player."

Finally rehearsal began. The director told us there would be no stopping. She wanted it to feel like an uninterrupted production. But it was rough going. Two or three key players were absent. We needed to stop and talk things out, but instead we barreled through to the finale without interruption.

So our first performance in front of paying customers that evening became our dress rehearsal. We put our hearts into it, but there were some awkward silences, miscues, and segues that did not flow as scripted, and that's being charitable.

Leonard Nemoy, famous for his role as Dr. Spock in the *Star Trek* television series, was in the audience. As he exited the house, he turned to a few of the cast gathered in the lobby and said, "Great spirit!"

Aargh.

"Great spirit" is *not* what a performer wants to hear. It implies that good intentions were evident, but the execution had failed.

Nimoy's comment led a few of us to huddle for a post-mortem. We agreed that the spotlights – all reds and blues – were too dark. With the addition of strobe lights – *too much* with the strobe lights – plus the carbon dioxide smoke of a fog machine – *way* too much fog – the stage was under-lit, too difficult to see. And the Night Visitors! Abdul, could you dial down the zurna, please? Way too shrill.

"Great spirit" did not cut it. The audience was paying seventy bucks a head to be entertained. We *had* to pull off Saturday evening's show, our last. We said good night and left for our various homes-away-from-home, pooped after a long drive, a short rehearsal, and a stumbling performance.

Saturday evening arrived, and with it the troupe in an upbeat mood as we met backstage. New costumes appeared; old ones had been cleaned and pressed. Last night's performance was not mentioned because it was in the past.

The show began with a procession of the cast through the audience, led by Abdul and the Night Visitors. We were a bright parade of sensuous women in thinly veiled dance costumes, musicians dressed like a desert village's unemployed (only with silk scarves), scimitar-schlepping palace guards, an overindulged-and-lovin'-it Ali Baba and his overindulgent harem, followed by four limping eunuchs.

Abdul and the Night Visitors were particularly animated this evening, the A-man himself a player possessed, blowing zurna furiously. Fortunately, Abdul was at the head of the procession and we were at the rear, a few yards behind, so the volume of the zurna was not so bad for us. But we saw that the Night Visitors were setting the tone for an uninhibited procession.

A loosey-goosey feeling filled the company. We were relaxed, even carefree, and way past inhibited. The girls were graceful, chastely flirty with the guys in the audience as they paraded by, and breathtaking in their tribal costumes.

An old theatre superstition has it that "A bad dress rehearsal guarantees a great opening night." If yesterday's show was our bad dress rehearsal, this parade felt like tonight could be our great opening night.

Finally, we reached our places on stage alongside Ali Baba, his harem and their eunuchs. The performers took their places on the dance floor in front of us, two feet below stage level, ... and the show began.

The opening monologue, delivered by Ali Baba in Turkish – or was it gibberish – was translated into English by His Royal Interpreter. It was a honking introduction, thick with political barbs aimed at President Bush (then at a 33% job-approval rating) that set even this staunchly Republican audience to howling.

We were on a roll.

The segue to the first dance number, which last night fell on its face and then puddled, was seamless tonight. The girls were delightful to behold, and their ensemble work had gelled. In the audience, men's eyes rolled like ball bearings.

The show was flying. The first act was a leap up from last night's performance and a huge success with the crowd. Backstage during the intermission, the troupe was jubilant. The girls fled to their dressing room, a large canvas pitched in the parking lot behind the restaurant that they dubbed "the red tent." Flushed with success and with makeup reapplied, they emerged even more effervescent and rosy-cheeked. We were all primed to take the stage for the second half of the show.

Act II jumps out of the gate, and changes as quickly. The first dance number, which sees one troupe of girls accompanied by Light Rain, ripples, and then flutters. The room's energy surges, and the women dance more sensuously as the band's rhythm hits a deeper beat. Unable to keep their seats as the music intensifies, the second troupe of women, who had been sitting on the sidelines watching, gets up and joins the first on the dance floor.

I look down at the script. This is not in the script.

The two troupes of girls are intermingling, inspiring each other's creativity and sensuality. This is way hot.

Now Abdul and the Night Visitors pick up on this vibration, take up their instruments, and start playing along with us.

I don't have to look down at the script. I *know* this is not scripted.

Ali Baba's harem girls, who have been peeling grapes for the pasha and otherwise fawning over him like in his dreams, abandon their posts and join the others on the floor. Now twenty-five women are dancing.

The eunuchs jump off the stage – that's got to hurt – and join in, followed by the Great Ali Baba himself. Now the entire troupe is belly dancing. This brings the audience to their feet. With arms raised, they start shimmying at their seats to the music.

Everyone not bolted down to the floor is gyrating in the strobe-raked room. The bartender behind the bar, the director, script discarded at her feet, the light and smoke people – everyone is trance dancing, visibly transported.

We are way off the script, beyond the show, and into

a happening. The room throbs to ancient Middle Eastern tones as a transcendent moment arrives and stretches out into long minutes of sustained bliss.

Immersed in the red spotlights of passion and the blues of mystery, I now *get* the lighting. The strobe lights and twisting smoke shred the dark, revealing and then masking the dancers' moves, just as the girls' floating veils reveal and mask them. The pulsing music and the dancers, their graceful movements lit in stroboscopic clouds of blue and red, have created a reality jump, a magic slice of slipped space that boils around me, enveloping me.

And the zurna.

What a beautiful instrument! The zurna's sharp wail, its sound as old as the wind, breaks through the drums and cymbals, spiriting us to old-town Istanbul. With three drummers from two bands, the zills of a dozen dancing women, and the bass thundering beneath, we are an exercise in musical antiquity.

I close my eyes and slip into this exotic vortex.

Towards the end of this heavenly dance, I lean over to Tobias, sitting in front of me on the cajón, and tap him on the shoulder. He leans back.

"Tobias, are all your gigs this crazy?" I ask him, expecting an off-the-cuff answer, a laugh and a nod.

But instead, Tobias turns to survey this epic scene – more female flesh than a man might see in a year of Saturday night lap dances, the din of two bands, the keening of twenty-five women, the clouds, the strobes, the dancing audience – and reflects on this insane divinity playing out in front of us. He nods in appreciation of what he has seen and turns back to me.

It seems I will hear a considered, perhaps wise response.

"No, not this crazy … " he says.

He looks out at the dancers … and then back at me.

"But sometimes more women!"

This transforming dance slowly comes to an end, and two numbers later the show closes to tired but prolonged applause.

The cast gathers 'round for group photos and then for a delicious performing arts tradition, the after-show hang. When artists come together to create a show, there is a palpable collective tension. You want to do your best, to create "art" with your colleagues, and you pressure yourself to rise to the occasion. The tension escalates through rehearsals and the opening night curtain. Working towards a goal together, the troupe bonds. When the final curtain falls on opening night, the tension is released, to everyone's relief. The cast party that follows opening night always sees a major celebration, and often, long discussions. Intense conversations about the art of making art and the work and politics of art, are the subjects of this interlude. Creatively engaged people, devoted to the arts, love talking with each other about what they love to do, even though what they do – singing, dancing, acting, playing music – may differ. Our talk about the heart of making art goes on for an hour.

Finally, the troupe starts to say our good-byes. The band has much equipment to pack out and load into the van, so we are the last to exit the room. As Doug starts the engine, he asks me to go back in for a "sanity check," a final look-see for any equipment that may have been left behind.

The room is dark except for a lone work light that stands at stage center, barely enough for me to get a look around. I hear scratching from the corner of what had been the dance floor and is now again the dining room.

It is Chris, broom in hand, sweeping up.

This exotic evening showed me the Bush affair for what it was: a political function where music was an incidental handmaiden to the event. At the belly dance performance, artists worked together on a show that overflowed the script and created a transcendent experience for all who were there.

I wish Leonard Nimoy had been in the house the second night. That show had Great Spirit.

The strobe lights and twisting smoke shred the dark, revealing and then masking the dancers' moves

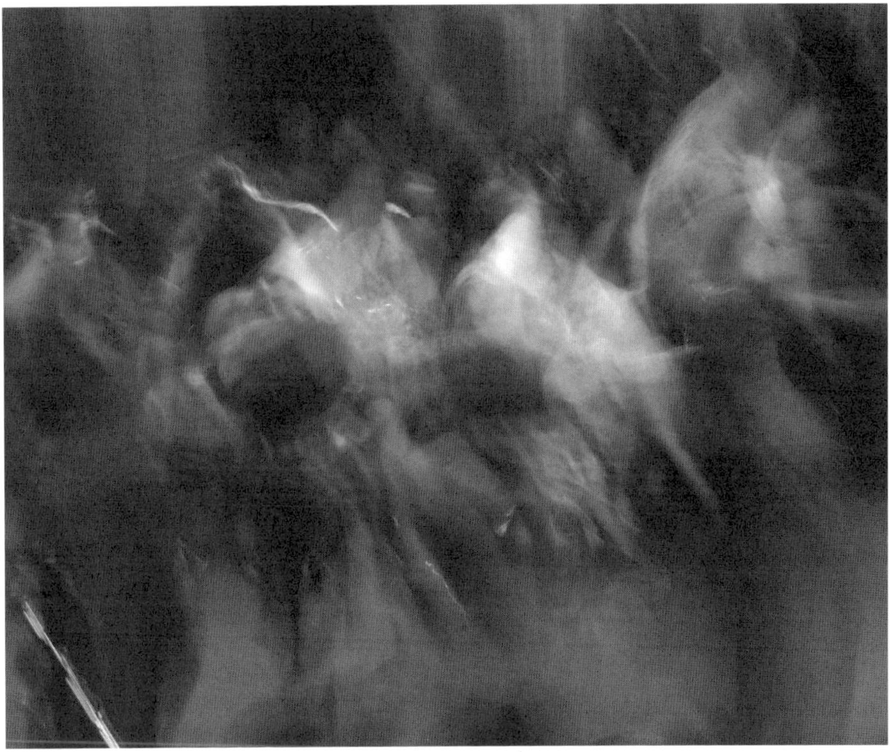

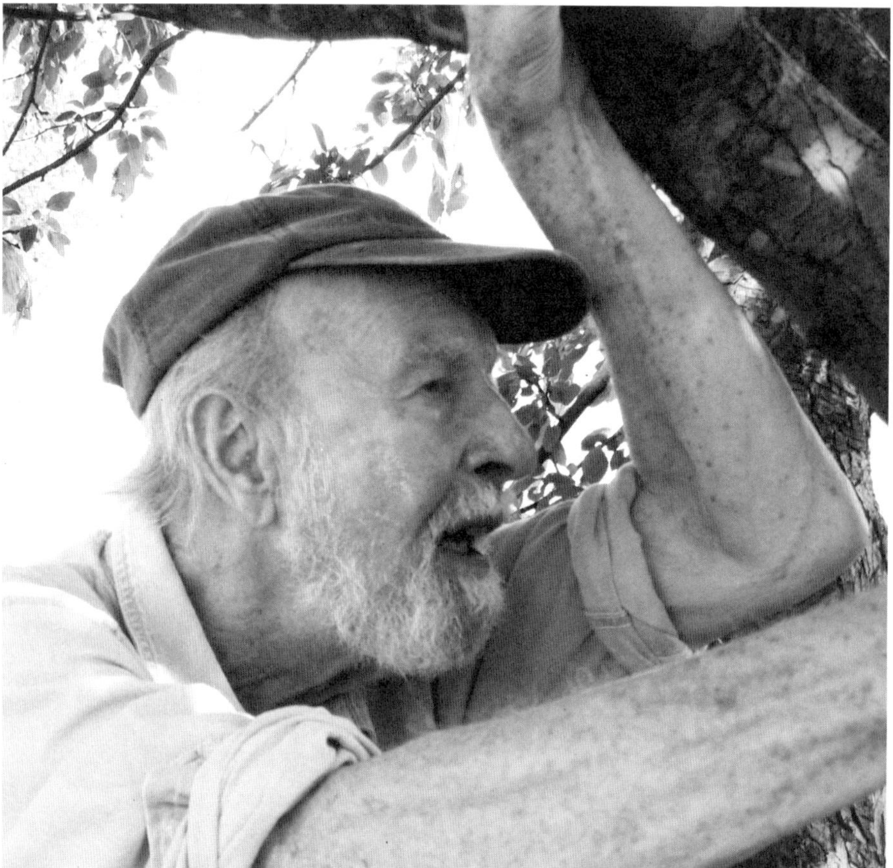

Pete Seeger
Beacon Strawberry Festival, New York · June 15, 2008

Pete

Dad called him "Pete." All the other Greenwich Village musicians we knew he'd usually call by their full names. But Pete Seeger was always just plain Pete. I used to think dad was alone in this, but I discovered some time later that everyone who knows Pete, everyone who reveres him, refers to him by his first name.

I remember him singing in our apartment on Bleecker, Street many times, alone and with the Weavers. I remember him playing 4-hand piano with Lee Hays on my mom's Chickering piano, and stopping by with his wife, Toshi, and their children.

Our two families moved from the Village, ours to Sunnyside Gardens in Queens, and his to Beacon, New York. There, Pete built a log cabin home on a mountaintop. Broke his leg doing it. I remember going to the housewarming party that Toshi and Pete hosted.

When Pete came into the city for a gig, he'd sometimes stay with us in Queens. When I saw his coffin-shaped banjo case sitting in the dining room next to mom's piano, I knew there would be some good music in our home that evening.

Dad was his biggest fan. Pete once sent him one of his books for copy editing. Dad went to it with his usual focused fervor, and sent the document back to Pete when he was done. Pete said that of the three copy editors he had given the book to, my dad had caught *by far* the most errors. My father couldn't have been more pleased.

So who is Pete Seeger? The many books about him, plus the video, *Pete Seeger: The Power of Song,* take an inspiring look back at Pete's long career. The film mentions an important part of who he is: Seeger's penchant for playing a peace-making role, of wanting and working for peace between all. In it, Pete says of two old political adversaries, "I'd really like it if I could get them both in the same room talking to each other."

Peace is central to Pete Seeger's thinking and wishes.

The movie also captures a telling moment as Pete and Toshi are walking hand in hand through New York City's Washington Square. A woman, also walking through the Square, recognizes Pete. It is clear she is not an acquaintance, just one of millions who has seen him perform, who knows his work.

She rushes over to him, puts her hand on his back, looks up at him and says, "Thank you. I have to thank you for everything: for your life; for my life; for my children's life. Thank you. You have been absolutely extraordinary. Thank you so much."

Then she walks away.

This is an example of what may be Pete's greatest accomplishment, his inspiring of people to better lives: inspiring them to sing out in harmony, to fight for peace and justice, to do good. It is his effect as an inspiration that is hardest to tally and tell, but it is monumental.

Pete Seeger is a singer and songwriter of inspiring songs. Alone or with others, he wrote "Where Have All the Flowers Gone," "Oh Had I a Golden Thread," "Kisses Sweeter Than Wine," "The Water is Wide," "Guantanamero," – *'With the poor people of this world I want to cast my lot,'* its last verse sings – "Waist Deep in the Big Muddy," and "Turn, Turn, Turn".

And incredibly, especially in this era, he never introduced any of his songs with a nod to his own authorship. I never head him say, "Here's another one I wrote." I didn't know he penned some of these songs until I started researching them.

Pete co-wrote, "If I Had a Hammer" with Lee Hayes in 1949. Although the tune was not a "hit" for the Weavers when they recorded it, it was nonetheless a very popular song in America and elsewhere. It has been recorded by over a dozen artists over the years, including Trini Lopez, whose recording reached number 1 in thirty-six countries.

Peter, Paul & Mary recorded "If I Had a Hammer" in 1962. In their hands it eventually reached number 10 on the Billboard charts. They did a great job with this song, an excellent job, but I've always liked Pete's original version just as much.

But this is what Pete had to say, in his usual self-deprecating, self-effacing manner, about "The Hammer Song," as it is sometimes called: "I made up a tune, but it wasn't really that good a tune. Seven years later Peter, Paul & Mary rewrote my tune and then it took off."

"It wasn't really that good a tune," he said.

It was and still is a *great* tune, and for its time – singing about justice, freedom, and love, as it did – a daring tune. But Pete, true to his humble self, transfers the glory to someone else.

Seeger is a master instrumentalist, fearless, confident and driving in his playing. He knows the 5-string very well, and has poured thousands of hours into unlocking its secrets. He has shared his knowledge of the banjo as a writer of the first modern 5-string banjo instruction book (100,000 copies and counting). He is a master of the 12-string guitar. By his playing Pete showed us how to play this two-fisted instrument, and he co-wrote an instructional book about the 12-string as well. His book, *Steel Drums: How to Make Them and Play Them,* played a pivotal role in bringing the pans (as steel drums are called), out of their obscurity in Trinidad and into the world of music from Broadway to jazz fusion.

Pete is America's first and foremost folksinger (he has been called "Mr. Folk Music" and "Folk Music's High Priest"), and was a founding member of both the Almanac Singers and The Weavers. The latter are America's first contemporary folk music group and are acknowledged as the founders of the American folk music revival of the 1950s and '60s. So, Pete was the creator of that renaissance, and by extension the folk revivals of the 1970s, '80s, '90s, double-aughts and beyond. He is the person most responsible for showing America the music of her roots.

He is a social and anti-war activist (on the rim of his banjo head he has written, "This machine surrounds hate and causes it to surrender"), environmentalist, outspoken political progressive, member of the US Army from 1942 to 1945, peacemaker – I already said that – and, importantly, American patriot. On this score, Johnny Cash said, "The Pete Seeger I know, and the Pete Seeger that [my wife] June and I have come to love, is one of the best Americans and patriots I've ever known."

The television show Pete hosted in the mid 1960s, *Rainbow Quest,* featured some of the most outstanding country and city folk of the era. It was the first time I ever saw bluegrass greats The Stanley Brothers on television, possibly the first time I saw them anywhere. Other guests included Johnny Cash and June Carter, Mississippi John Hurt, Reverend Gary Davis, Brownie McGee and Sonny Terry, Doc Watson, Elizabeth Cotton, and Judy Collins – all icons of that rich '60s folk era.

Pete created a new style of banjo picking, "Seeger picking." Truth is, he created a number of right-hand techniques, most of which have not been given names. He coined the terms "hammering on" and "pulling off." Pete added three frets of length to his 5-string banjo neck, enabling him to play in more keys, and in keys that were more compatible with the guitar. It's called the "Seeger neck."

My wife and I saw him perform on June 15, 2008, at the Beacon Strawberry Festival in upstate New York, when Pete was eighty-nine. He took the stage and started to play the melody to "This Land Is Your Land" on the 5-string banjo; the audience broke into applause. Then he led us through singing the song, feeding us each line before it arrived so we could sing it back to him. He told about two new verses, recently re-discovered, while he kept his banjo ringing. Through the choruses sung by the crowd, you could hear his voice singing, wobbly but confidently urging us on. He roused us to a fortissimo final chorus, and brought the house down with a hammered "this land … is made … for you and me."

It was a bravura performance by a senior artist who put every fiber of his body into his art. And it showed off Pete's special talent with the sing-along.

What he did with the crowd – teach the words, lead the singing, teach the harmony, teach the song's history, teach about Woody Guthrie, get everyone singing along, bring the tune to a round-house finale – is something that no one else does so successfully. It was a master class in leading a sing-along, led by a master teacher, the Dean of American Folk Music.

Pete has also perfected a technique of segueing songs together during his shows, one that robs him of applause in the short run: After he has sung the last chorus of a song, he keeps the banjo going and starts talking to the audience about that song, or about the next song and how the two are related.

Then, still talking, he stops playing, re-capos and re-tunes the banjo, and launches into the next song. By making this move, he misses out on applause for the first tune.

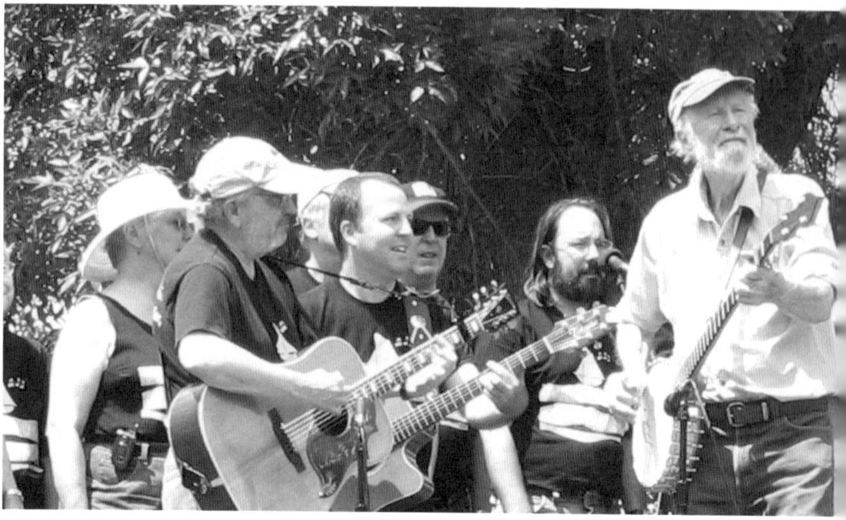

He finishes this second song similarly, and segues into a third tune, depriving himself of applause yet again. Finally he brings the third song to the close the audience had been waiting for, one they greet with explosive cheering.

I believe this practice stems from Pete's humility, and a wish to avoid repeated applause. But it also puts the focus on the songs, their words and messages, which is where Pete wants it, I'd imagine.

Pete was responsible for adding music to the Civil Rights movement of the 1960s, popularized "We Shall Overcome" and introduced it to Dr. Martin Luther King and the movement with verses that Pete had created (*"We'll walk hand in hand,"* and *"The whole wide world around"*).

With Toshi, Pete started "Hudson River Sloop Clearwater," a non-profit that cleaned up New York State's Hudson River (*after* the Federal government had declared it an industrialized river). He doesn't smoke, drink, or chase women (just political causes), and he has never sold out.

But he has also taken it on the chin for his beliefs and left-leaning politics. Pete was hauled up in front of the House Un-American Activities Committee, branded a "Red," blacklisted from TV, and marginalized by the mainstream

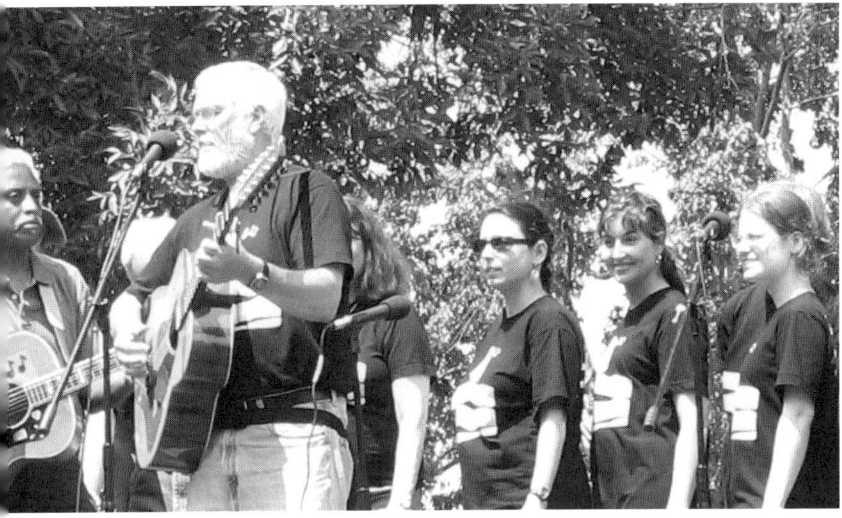

media. He made his mark outside the main, until the main finally recognized him.

In 1994, Pete was awarded the Kennedy Center Honor for lifetime contributions to American culture and the performing arts, at the Kennedy Center in Washington, D.C. Introducing Pete for the award, President Bill Clinton said: "He was an inconvenient artist who dared to sing things as he saw them. He was attacked for his beliefs; he was banned from television. Some artists make musical history. Pete Seeger made history with his music."

Times have certainly turned when a United States President gives Pete Seeger an award.

I can't imagine that anyone has memorized more tunes than Pete, or played more benefits. The last time I saw him perform was at a benefit for the Woody Guthrie Foundation, in September 2009, when he was ninety. He played standing up, proud, brave, and true to his generous convictions. It was as memorable as the first time I saw him play, in our living room on Bleecker Street in 1946.

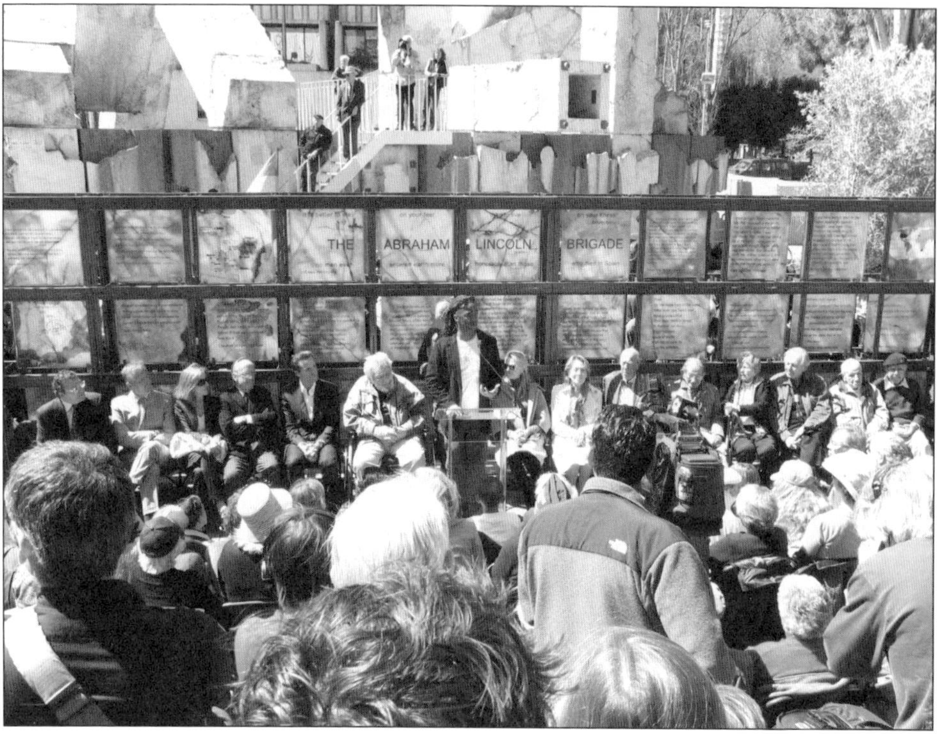

The Abraham Lincoln Brigade Monument
with the Vaillancourt Fountain behind it
March 30, 2008

The Vulcan and the Patriot

On March 30, 2008, Noni and I went to the San Francisco unveiling of a memorial to the veterans of the Abraham Lincoln Brigade, the 2,800 Americans – my uncle included – who volunteered to fight fascism in the Spanish Civil War from 1936 to 1939. Nine hundred volunteers died there. An old family friend had made a donation to the monument in my father's name when my dad passed in 2007. I wanted to be at this event.

The City of San Francisco erected the Lincoln Brigade monument at the foot of Market Street on the Justin Herman Plaza, a high-visibility spot. It fronts the Vaillancourt Fountain, a jumble of a dozen twisted, fallen pipes that spew streams of water into a pool. It has never been San Franciscans' favorite public sculpture, one can safely say. And then came September 11, 2001. In its visual evocation of 9/11's Ground Zero, the Vaillancourt's muddle of fallen infrastructure never made so much sense.

The Spanish Civil War Memorial, a panel of 45 two-foot-square onyx plates that sits just east of the Vaillancourt, stands 8 feet tall and spans 40 feet. The east face displays quotations about the war, while the west shows photos of troops, tanks, and battles. The first national monument to the Abraham Lincoln Brigade (technically, the "Lincoln Battalion"), its details demanded an inspection and reflection that would have to wait. It was already getting crowded when we arrived.

A blue-sky day of Bay winds chasing slips of clouds found a crowd of 1,200 gathering for this unveiling, most of them "greatest generation" and baby boomer progressives. But next to me was a twenty-something guy.

"Why are you here?" I asked him.

"My grandfather fought in this war. He told me his stories."

My sense was that everyone there had a story to tell.

The Musicians' Action Group played the songs of the era, notably "Venga Jaleo" and "Vive la Quince Brigada." Everyone within earshot sang along with these songs that are passionate as the Spanish are: wildly passionate.

"Viva la Quince Brigada" sings of the 15th Brigade, one that included the Abraham Lincoln and George Washington Battalions from the United States, and the mostly Canadian, Mackenzie-Papineau Battalion. "Long live the 15th Brigade", the lyrics proclaim, "Covered in glory." Each line alternates with a hip-churning "Rumba la rumba la rumba la!"

Eleven Lincoln Brigade vets, including well-known social activist, Abe Osheroff, were in attendance. In their nineties, most sat in wheelchairs or leaned on canes, so it took some time for them to settle into chairs on the slim walkway that fronted the memorial. There were only thirty-nine American veterans of the International Brigade who lived that day. Having eleven of them there felt like a record, and also, like the end of an era.

Peter Carroll, head of the Abraham Lincoln Brigade Archives and the Master of Ceremonies, began the event by introducing the dignitaries who had gathered: the eleven Lincoln Brigade veterans and two volunteer nurses; San Francisco Mayor Gavin Newsom and his fiancé; the Director of the San Francisco Arts Commission; Spain's Ambassador; and, possibly because of the Ambassador's presence, San Francisco's "Chief of Protocol and Director of Special Events," Charlotte Shultz.

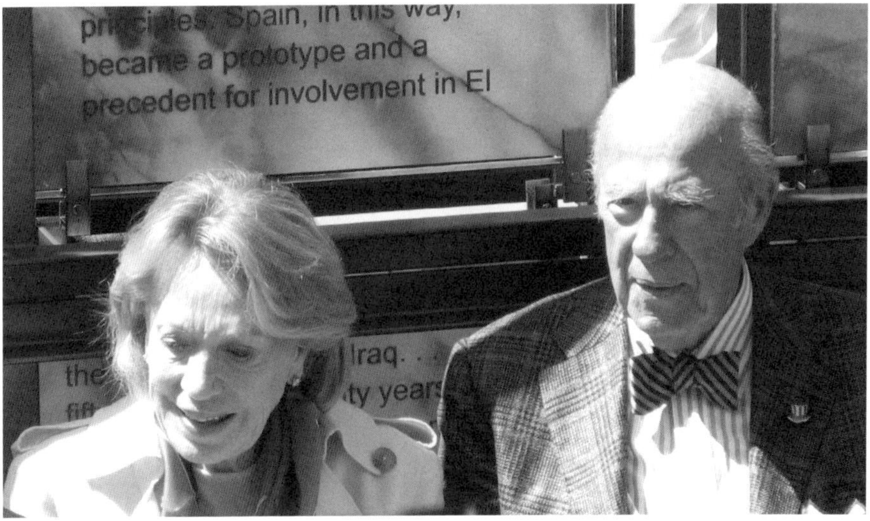

Charlotte and George Shultz

Also there was Charlotte's husband, George Shultz. I had played music at the Shultz's a few times by then. George was associated with the "Vulcans" as Condoleezza Rice called George W. Bush's foreign policy team. Some presume he was their supervisor. At his parties I have heard him proudly say that he backed Bush in his White Hour run, and Schwarzenegger in his bid to become California's governor. George was not well loved by this crowd.

Shultz, looking like a lion in winter who has faced a few safaris in his day, was introduced by the MC to a prolonged chorus of hearty boos. As the jeering was about to die, a man in the crowd shouted out, loudly, clearly, unmistakably:

"MURDERER!"

It was an electric moment. Everyone heard it. We stopped breathing and looked at the shouter, a dockworker, brawny arms folded across a barrel chest, leading with an unapologetic chin.

No one was going to mess with him.

As for Shultz, this was not the first time this bona fide conservative had been dissed in public; he's been booed before. But I wondered what he was thinking at that moment. Maybe it was, This is the last time I let Charlotte drag me to one of her "Special Events" again.

Then Peter Carroll introduced San Francisco's Mayor, Gavin Newsome. The guy looked movie star handsome: square-jawed, healthy, and brightly lit. An impressive figure, he has genuine charisma and, some say, presidential potential. Newsome has done good things for San Francisco as far as The City is concerned, including allowing gay marriages. His "Care-Not-Cash" program tries to get homeless people into city-assisted care.

Whatever his accomplishments, they were not enough for this crowd. The MC brought him on to begrudging applause from a decidedly tough room.

As sharp as he looked, it was Newsome's speechifying that was most impressive. He started by saying that only in San Francisco could this monument have been erected.

As Bay Areans, everyone there, I sensed, proudly agreed.

The mayor said that in San Francisco "we can disagree" – and here he looked right at the guy who had called Shultz a murderer – "without being disagreeable."

We recognized that as well, with a murmur that rippled through the crowd; the dockworker's epithet had been a down moment in an otherwise upbeat day.

Newsome spoke on the Spanish Civil War without notes for a dozen minutes, no small feat in my book. It was a

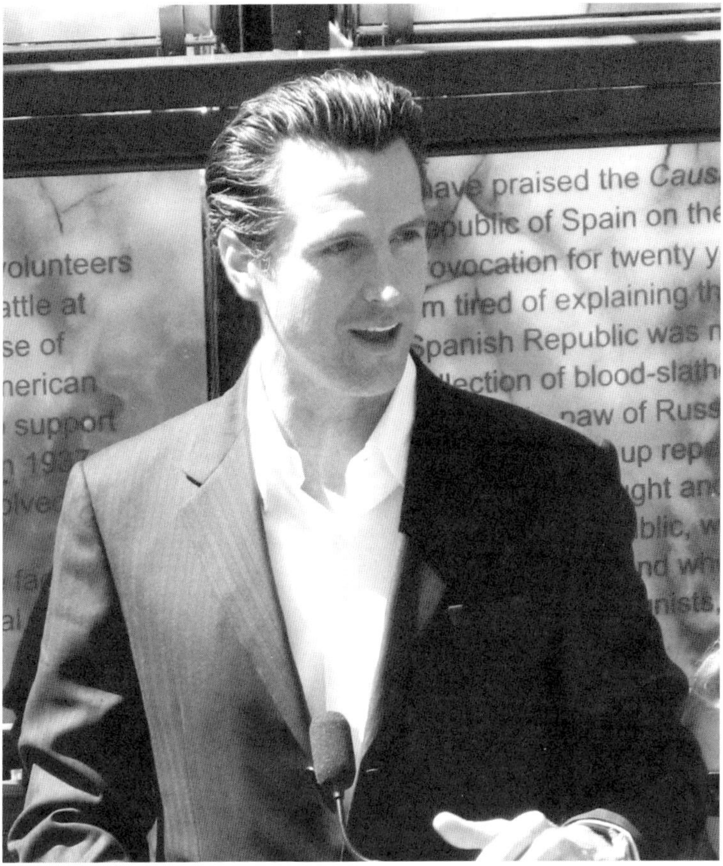

San Francisco Mayor, Gavin Newsome

well-organized talk, commandingly delivered and easily understood; it gave me a good impression of the man as a speaker and as a human being.

His aside to the dockworker required both a setup ("in San Francisco we can disagree"), and a punch line ("without being disagreeable"), and was delivered off the cuff. It constituted a publicly administered rebuke by The Mayor of the town, a rebuke that the crowd tacitly approved of,

I felt, because we agreed with it. The mayor's remark demonstrated his presence of mind, his command of himself and his audience. No one was going to mess with the dockworker, except the mayor, and he did it decently. Newsome departed the podium to a longer and louder hand than the pale applause that greeted his arrival.

One of the veterans who spoke, Abe Osheroff, is a renowned, life-long social activist. From age twelve he worked tirelessly for the disenfranchised, organized evicted tenants' and miners' unions, and raised aid for striking workers. When the Spanish Civil War arrived in 1936, Abe signed up and was wounded at the Battle of Belchite. Soon after, he enlisted in the U.S. Army to fight the Nazis in Europe.

Holding a microphone in front of him as he sat in a wheelchair was his companion, Gunnel Clark. Abe said:

"To me, being an activist has always been a special privilege. It's a wonderful job, you never run out of work, you meet the nicest people, and the pay is very high."

The audience laughed. We knew better.

"Yes it is, if you value the love and respect of the people you work with more than you do money and physical things … then the pay is very high."

We applauded.

"There is this incredible feeling that the stuff we're made of never goes away. Because the bastards will never stop their evil and the decent human beings will never stop their struggle."

The crowd cheered.

"I'm not a San Franciscan, I'm a New Yorker. But I can't imagine any other city where this could have taken place, except San Francisco. Because in many ways San Francisco is one of the greatest crossroads of growing culture, of advanced ideas, that has appeared on the map. So I salute

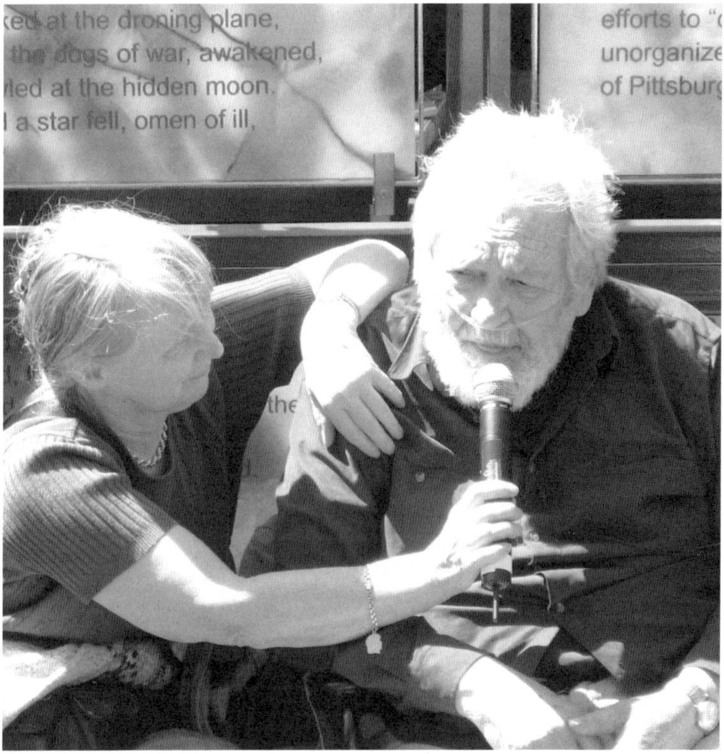

Abe Osheroff with Gunnel Clark holding the mic

all you San Franciscans, and I thank you on behalf of the Abraham Lincoln Brigade for making us immortal."

Oshoroff brought the house down with an inspiring speech, spare on words and generous with emotion. We were on our feet, many of us in tears.

~

When the official event came to an end, people gathered, hugged, got autographs, thanked the veterans and nurses, congratulated them, and finally dispersed.

Then we walked around the monument. Its onyx façade shimmered in the late afternoon light that penetrated its translucency and cast shadows of the overhanging trees on the memorial's egg-white face.

On the center four panels of the monument, we saw

THE ABRAHAM LINCOLN BRIGADE

boldly lettered. Directly below that was Hemingway's famous quotation:

> *"... no men ever entered earth more honorably than those who died in Spain."*

It seemed so simply sure, like Hemingway himself.

Three days later, Abe Oshoroff died at his home of a sudden heart attack. On April 7, just over a week later, two more veterans died, Abe Smorodin and Ted Veltfort, both ninety-two. Thirty-six Lincoln Brigade veterans remained at that moment.

~

I wrote up this event as a three-page story that included some photos of the memorial, and sent it to a few politically inclined family members, to Pete Seeger, and to my cousin Kathie Sarachild. (Known as a theoretician of the feminist movement, Kathie coined the expression "Sisterhood is powerful.")

Four days later the phone rang. It was God calling.

I've known him all my life, or, more accurately, he's known me all my life. His strong baritone voice rang out:

"Hello, this is Pete Seeger."

Pete would be the first to object to being deified, but to many folks he is a living saint, and I believe it was Bob Dylan who said that in so many words.

Though he's been a life-long family friend, and played music in my father's house on many occasions, this was the first time he had telephoned me. Slack jawed, I sat down immediately.

Pete was calling me that afternoon to say thank you for sending the story about the unveiling of the memorial, and for the photo of his longtime friend, Faith Petric, who had been there that day. I took it that he would have loved to have been at the unveiling. Certainly he would have enjoyed this historic event, the likes of which will not be seen again.

Then he turned the topic.

Pete said, "If I had been there when that man shouted 'murderer' at Shultz, I would have walked right over to him, looked him in the eyes and said, 'We're all murderers. What we've got to do is sit down and start talking about our differences.' "

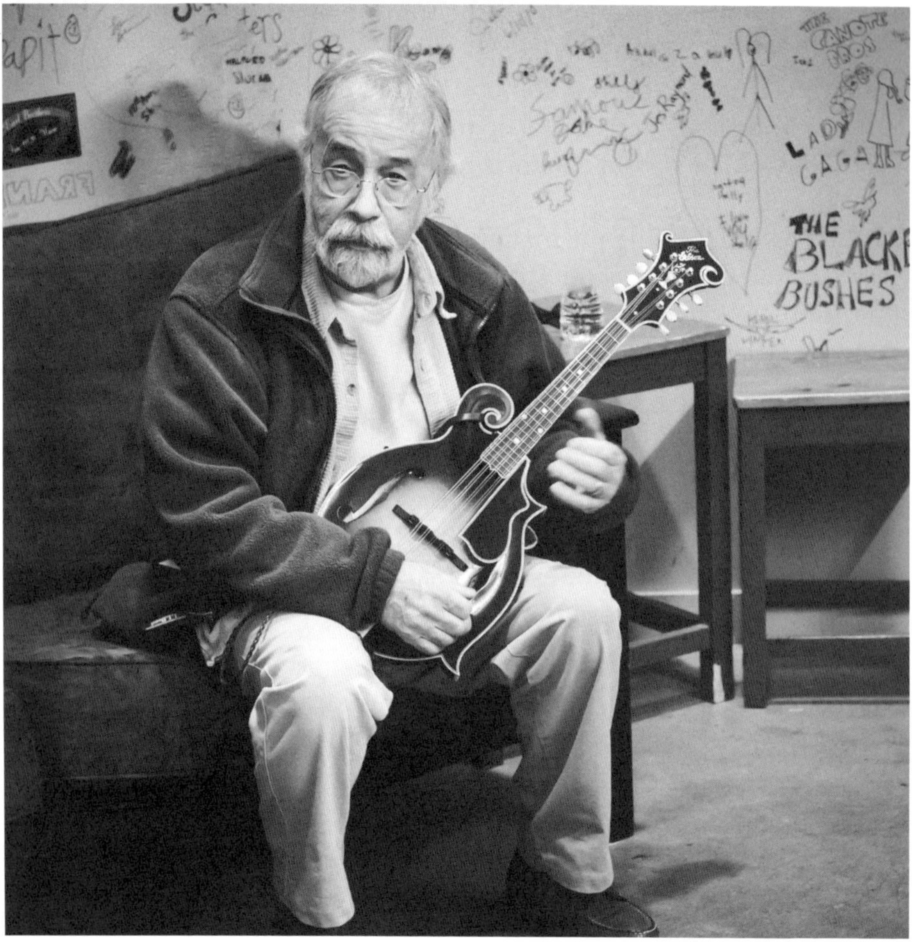

Roland White

Freight & Salvage Coffeehouse, Berkeley · February 22, 2012

By Mike Melnyk

Roland White
~ Heart Behind the Holler

Roland White is a sweet soul. A warm, genuinely modest and much-loved guy, he is a blessing in the life of everyone who passes through his.

As a mandolinist, Roland is bluegrass royalty. He rose to this station by pickin' and singin' in a parade of often historic and always top-notch bluegrass groups for fifty years. In the 1960s he played mandolin with his brother, legendary guitarist Clarence White, in the Kentucky Colonels. He worked with Bill Monroe and His Blue Grass Boys and with Lester Flatt and the Nashville Grass. In 1974, he joined the progressive bluegrass group, Country Gazette, and played with them for thirteen years. In 1982, he teamed up with Jerry Douglas and Bela Fleck to form a band they called "The Dreadful Snakes," named after the Bill Monroe song, "The Little Girl and the Dreadful Snake." The Snakes synthesized trad-grass and their ironic view of it, in what might have been the first post-modernist take on bluegrass. In 1987, Roland joined the Nashville Bluegrass Band, a state-of-the-'grass group that won two Grammy awards for

Best Bluegrass Album during his tenure. Currently Roland leads his own unit, the Roland White Band. It is a tribute to Roland as a picker and singer that he has played in so many historic bands, both traditional and progressive.

Roland and I were both teaching at the 2009 Summer Camp sponsored by the California Bluegrass Association (CBA), and sat down one afternoon for a chat. There was something I wanted to ask him.

"Roland, I know Tony Rice's story about the 1935 D-28 Martin guitar your brother Clarence used to own. What is your story about it?"

As I recall, his response was, "That piece of crap!"

Then he explained this colorful remark.

Roland said that he and Clarence – this was 1958 or '59 – cruised the L.A. pawnshops the first Monday of each month, the day the pawnbrokers tried to clear inventory by offering deals on goods that were freshly out of pawn. Nothing showed up for the brothers, so they trooped over to McCabe's Guitar Shop in Santa Monica. Finding zilch in the showroom, the brothers wandered back to the repair shop.

There, in a corner, standing upside down on its peg head – in pieces – was a 1935 Martin D-28. The instrument was unstrung. The pick guard had started to peel off. The top had been egregiously, perilously, sanded down. The fingerboard had been lopped off at the high end by two frets' worth so the O-hole could be enlarged; that oversized O-hole became the instrument's most remarkable feature. The fingerboard had been removed and taped to the neck to keep it from wandering off. To paraphrase Bob Dylan, I still can't remember all the worst things Roland said about this instrument. Its beat-up condition was why he called it a "piece of crap."

The brothers asked McCabe's what they wanted for the guitar.

"What do you boys want to offer?"

"Twenty-five?" the brothers said hopefully.

Glad to get this clunker off their hands, McCabe's let the instrument go and threw in the case as part of the deal.

So here's an historical point about this renowned instrument, one that I have never seen published. It wasn't Clarence who carved a bigger O-hole in top. When he bought the guitar, the O-hole had already been enlarged by the previous owner, name unknown.

Roland and Clarence took the guitar home, and showed it to their dad, Eric, who was the luthier for the family's instruments. He took one look at it and said, "Sure hope you boys didn't pay anything for this."

The instrument's repair was beyond the father's scope, so they brought it to Southern California's "guru of guitar repair," Milt Owen. Owen took one look at the Martin fingerboard that had been taped to the instrument and declared it beyond salvation. He pulled out a radiused Gretsch fingerboard blank, sanded the arch flat, fretted it, and glued it in place. The whole job cost twenty, maybe twenty-five dollars. "That's the way I remember it," Roland said.

Owen strung the instrument with light gauge strings. He told Clarence that the guitar's thin top would balloon out if he put heavier strings on it.

When he got home, Clarence, true to teenage male type, put a set of Gibson heavies on it. Sure enough, the top ballooned out, making the action high and the guitar difficult to play. Later on, he put medium-gauge strings on the instrument, but the ballooning that the heavier strings had caused did not reverse itself.

In March of 1964, Clarence married Julia Hackney. "Susie," her friends called her. He got into electric guitar around the same time, and needed some money to finance these transitions. This is where Joe Miller entered the story.

Joe had been a fellow student of Clarence's at UCLA and was involved in Miller's Liquors, his family's bottle-shop chain. Joe was also a folkie, and he loved Clarence's ol' Martin. He had told Clarence that if he ever wanted to sell the guitar, to let him know. Remembering this offer, Clarence picked up the phone – this was 1965 – dialed Joe and told him he was selling the Martin. Miller asked him what he wanted. Clarence said $500.

Joe accepted the offer.

Bobby Sloan, fiddler with The Kentucky Colonels, was present for this sale and mentioned it to Tony Rice in the 1970s when they played together in "J.D. Crowe and the New South." Tony was a big fan of Clarence, and he wanted this guitar very much, so he bird-dogged Joe Miller.

Evidently there were many Miller's Liquors throughout the state in the early '70s. Tony knew that Joe lived in Pasadena, so he phoned the Miller's Liquors at North Lincoln Avenue and Figueroa Drive, and after a couple of tries, reached him. Tony said he wanted to buy Clarence's guitar.

Joe wasn't using it, so he agreed to sell the instrument to Tony, after he'd had it appraised. Tony's story here, as I recollect, is that Joe took the guitar to a violin repairman who appraised the instrument at $300, which is what Joe sold it to Tee for. When I mentioned to Roland that $300 was less than Joe had paid for it, Roland answered, "Well, the guy wasn't using it." That is, it had no value to him.

Tony has had much work done to this instrument by various luthiers over the years. I take it that as a result, the guitar is not as difficult to play as when Clarence owned, hated, and shot at it.

Tee used it religiously when we were in the David Grisman Quintet together, taking it to all our gigs and playing it on the first DGQ album. Then he started experimenting with an Ovation guitar because its narrower dynamic range made it a more suitable instrument for recording.

Wire-rimmed glasses frame Roland White's Lincoln eyes. At seventy-three, his full, neatly trimmed white beard and slowly thinning white hair outline a most gentle smile. On stage, he takes one purposeful step for every three meanders that most of us take; this somehow seems to be less about economy than wisdom, and Roland is a wise man. Born in Maine to French-Canadian parents, Roland was brought up speaking French and didn't start learning English until the second grade. He moved to Southern California in 1954, so his accent blends these influences.

Roland is generally a man of few words, another wisdom he has learned along the way. When he picks up his mandolin, one that Gibson custom-made to his specifications in 2004, he plays with a loose right wrist, his power coming from his forearm and waving hand. His tone is both meaty and trebly. The fingers of his left hand crawl low over the fingerboard, seeming to make one move for other pickers' many.

At the 2009 CBA Summer Camp, Roland quietly and effectively led the tunes he chose for the instructors' set – a performance by the teachers at the Fathers' Day Festival that followed the camp. For the finale, he rehearsed us in a medley of "New River Train" in E-major, "Y'all Come" (also in E-major), and "Orange Blossom Special," which begins in E-major and modulates up to A-major.

A little background on these tunes:

"New River Train" was first recorded, and likely written, by Henry Whitter of Fries, Virginia in 1923. In calling this song, Roland was digging deep into American music history, before bluegrass, and into the hillbilly era for this three-chord song, with its tongue-in-cheek cautionary lyrics:

Darling you can't love one,
Darling you can't love one,
You can't love one and have any fun,
Oh darling you can't love one.

Subsequent verses warn against loving two (*can't love two and let your heart be true*), three (*can't love three and still love me*), four (*can't love four and love me anymore*), and in Roland's rendition, five through ten as well. On the New River Train you just can't win in love.

Arlie Duff wrote "Y'all Come," the next song in the medley, in the 1950s. Even if you've never heard "Y'all Come," you know it; the tune is in America's genes. But a few eyebrows in the band rose as Roland called this somewhat non-bluegrass song.

When Roland sang "Y'all Come," the lyrics seemed like a Norman Rockwell painting from a long time ago. The song evokes a too-old-to-be-true phonograph record of neighbors and kinfolk gathering for a lively dinner at Grandma's house. Grandma's shout-out to the audience to drop on by, to "Y'all come," is one that the band and audience – actually everyone within earshot – should respond to with a hollered, "Y'all come!"

Roland's gentle French-Canadian-Maine-California accent, his unadorned expression of the line, his coming from a place of "y'all come," of openhearted welcome, was spot on. The entire audience and band shouted a "Y'all come" back at him, every time. Roland brought it off with the heart behind the holler: we love ya, neighbor. Come on over.

Roland said that the third tune in the medley, "Orange Blossom Special," (known by its initials, "O.B.S."), should end after the first chorus. He knew that after the multi-verse rendition of "New River Train" and the full-tilt arrangement of "Y'all Come," we could only touch briefly on O.B.S.

This scorching instrumental modulates up a perfect fourth to A-major for a fiddle solo that immediately climbs up another perfect fourth.

Its success relies partially on the Blue Grass Boys' original recording of this classic, and fully on said fiddler's rendition of it for an all-horses-in-full-gallop exit from the arena. Our fiddler, Paul Shelasky, rose to the occasion. O.B.S. drove home a masterfully arranged medley that brought the house down.

Roland had booked a concert at The Palms Playhouse in Winters, California, the next year, following the 2010 CBA Winter Camp. He had hired on Laurie Lewis, Keith Little, Jim Nunally, and yours truly to join him. Roland wanted to give the band a title that mentioned all our individual names, but Dave Fleming, The Palms' owner, insisted on "Roland White's All-Star Bluegrass Band." This troubled Roland's humble nature, and he called me up – he called all of us up – to apologize for it and get our OKs. None of us objected because his name alone in the group's title was in fact the right thing to do.

The five of us had never played together and we were looking forward to rehearsing at The Palms at three that afternoon. I arrived five minutes early, and when twenty lonesome minutes had passed, called Roland on his cell.

Roland had been nursing a cold and seemed sluggish. The previous night, he had slept in his car under a bridge in the freezing cold after getting lost on his way to Jim's house. The following morning at Nunally's, he fell down and couldn't get up for fifteen minutes. He drove to the Palms gig with Jim, sleeping most of the way. My call woke him up and he didn't sound too good. But yes, he said, they were on the way, running a half-hour late.

Roland arrived fifteen minutes later with his chin on his chest, looking wobbly on his feet. He called his wife, Diane, who wisely insisted that he go to a clinic for a checkup. We took him to the Winters Healthcare Foundation, three doors from The Palms. They admitted Roland quickly and assessed his vital signs. Falling down gets low points from doctor types, so they recommended that we immediately take Roland to the Sutter-Davis Hospital, a half hour away.

In the meantime, Keith Little's wife, Phyllis Polito, had arrived and volunteered to drive Roland to Davis. As we bundled him into the car he turned to me and said, "Gettin' old is the pits."

Then Keith, Jim, Laurie and I walked back to The Palms, went backstage to the dressing room and rehearsed. Since it was Roland's gig, we decided to perform his songs as homage to him. So we went over "Darling You Played with a Toy Heart," "I Might Take You Back Again," "Satisfied Mind," "I'm Blue and Lonesome Too," and other tunes Roland is known for.

There is a certain Nirvana that pickers seek. We wish to surround ourselves with sound, drench ourselves in music. At the rehearsal, Laurie, Jim, and Keith stood in a half circle. I took a seat in front of them, leaned forward, and closed my eyes. They sang down the songs, working the tunes to the way Roland performed them, focusing on the vocal parts. When Laurie sang the lead, she knew the harmonies she wanted to hear with it. She sang the baritone part to Jim: a slinky, would-break-a-snake's-back-to-sing-it part. And he sang it right back at her, perfectly. He understood – all of them understood – the roll each of the three vocal parts played, and how each is created.

Bluegrass has a strong element of the blues in it, the bending of the 3rds, 5ths and 7ths of the scale. It was particularly sweet to hear the bent blues melodies harmonized by lines above and below. The three of them worried the blues notes, tuned them and re-slid them, sharpened their singing, synched their breathing and shaped their dynamics. They dug into the lyrics – "What are the words Roland sings right there? … You say what?" – and worked on creating vocal beauty, all in my immediate surround, a sonic delight.

In the meantime at the hospital in Davis, Roland was initially diagnosed with pneumonia. We tried to reassure ourselves that this was not the worst news. After all, pneumonia is treatable. But more tests and an x-ray pointed to bronchitis. No fun this bronchitis either, but the medicine men put you on antibiotics that do their job fairly quickly, we reassured ourselves. They started giving Roland the meds an hour after he arrived at the hospital.

Phyllis brought him back for the second set and he sat in an easy chair off to the side of the audience, quietly sawing serious wood.

At the end of the gig, Laurie retrieved the musician's share of the money that David had collected for the show. She counted up the greenbacks. The four of us agreed that Roland should receive not only an equal share, but also a leader's take on top of that. Laurie divvied the dough that way.

Roland went back to Jim's house that evening, and flew back to Nashville on Sunday. I called him at his home on Monday.

"I'm fine," Roland said, "just fine. I'm so sorry I missed the gig. Thank you for covering for me. And thank you for the generous split. I didn't deserve my cut."

March 5, 2011

I was fortunate to play a Northern California tour with Roland this past week. On Friday, after our show at Bernie's Guitar in Redding, we drove up to Linda and Bruce Wendt's 100-acre ranch above town where three of us in the band were staying the night.

We awoke the next morning in a country home overlooking a vista of cows, chickens, pigs, ducks, vegetables, and fruits. Bruce was in the kitchen cooking up chilaquiles, a Mexican egg dish, and Linda was preparing the dining table for company. We took seats and Bruce served us the eggs. As we started wolfing down what may be the tastiest breakfast I've ever had, in walked the Wendt's daughter and son-in-law, Tom, and their three grandkids. As coffee and O.J. started around, a genuine breakfast party got under way.

Their neighbor from down the road dropped by for a cuppa joe, wouldn't you know, and everyone shook and howdied with him. Laurie, Patrick, and their hosts arrived and joined in. Then the gal who lived across the way, Tom's sister, stopped by. We were a family of sixteen people, many of us related by blood, and all of us related by music.

When an old Flatt & Scruggs tune came on the satellite bluegrass channel, Roland told a story about playing with Lester:

"We walked on stage at a Tennessee schoolhouse with eleven people in the audience. I said to Flatt, 'I guess you don't draw much here, Lester.'

"Flatt shot back, 'This is *your* crowd, Roland.' "

And then Roland, Laurie and Patrick sang a gospel chorus that hushed the room.

So there it was, a real, live "Y'all Come." Grandma and grandpa, kids, grandkids and neighbors, in-laws and outlaws (that would be the band), singin', pickin' and storytelling around a groaning table in a country kitchen, with cows mooing and chickens scratching just outside the window.

The last line of "Y'all Come" is "Y'all come to see us when you can." And the last words Bruce and Linda said as we left were "Please come again, any time."

~

It is possible to hear variations on the Clarence White D-28 Martin story; it has benefited from the folk process. I have told it as I remember Roland (and Tony) telling it to me, as faithfully as I can.

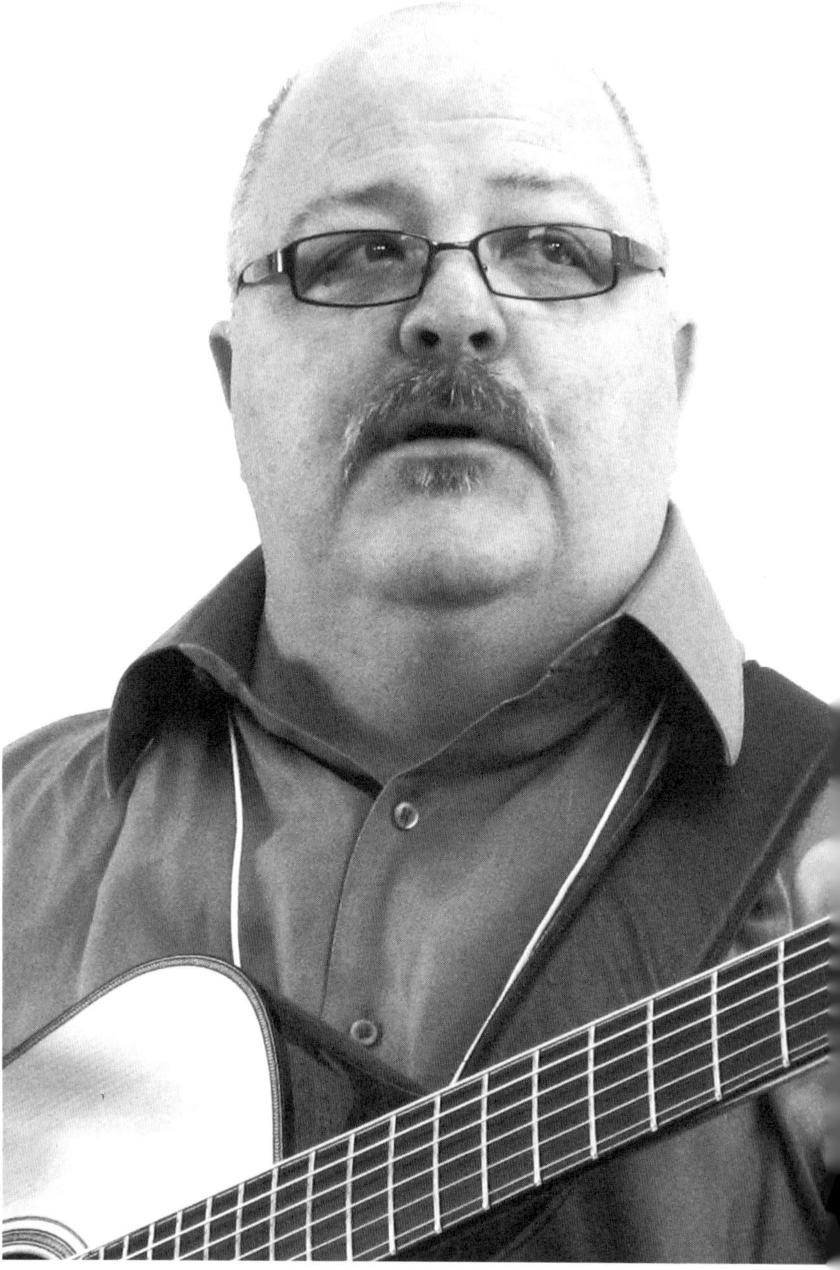

Jim Hurst
Sebastopol Community Center Youth Annex · March 12, 2011

Jim Hurst
~ On a Changing Road

He said he was working hard on that, on being his own man, finding his own guitar voice. But it had not been easy.

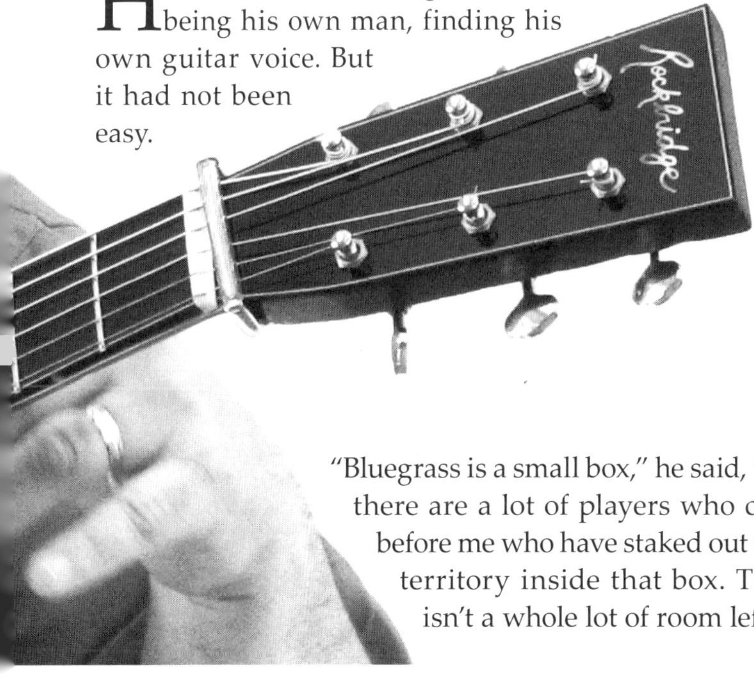

"Bluegrass is a small box," he said, "and there are a lot of players who came before me who have staked out their territory inside that box. There isn't a whole lot of room left."

Jim Hurst is a master of the acoustic flattop guitar. He's more than a "flat-picker" because he also fingerpicks the guitar using many right-hand techniques that pull a rich tone pallet from the instrument. If you haven't heard him play yet, then please seek him out and give a long listen. Jim Hurst is on his way to being the next acknowledged great on the acoustic flattop guitar.

We met in 2004. Jim was slated to play Santa Rosa on August 13 of that year, but his bassist had double booked herself that evening and felt obliged to play the other gig. I got the call to fill the bass slot. Jim's reputation had reached western shores. It sounded like fun, so I said, "Sure."

I met Jim and his band the afternoon of the show, backstage at the New College of California. He had Megan Lynch on fiddle, Steve Smith on mandolin, and Bill Evans on the 5-string. We only rehearsed the tunes once or twice each, but the band had high spirit and tight ensemble. Jim flat-picked bluegrass style on all but two tunes, so it was a bluegrass band putting on a bluegrass show. Our performance that evening was unusually hot and the audience felt it.

Jim has been back to Sebastopol a few times since, in a number of configurations. He has played here as a sideman with the Claire Lynch band, as a solo act, and as a trio that included me on string bass.

And in December 2011, he was in town as a duo with Dobro dog, Rob Ickes. They were hotter than Fukushima. On that gig, seven years after the first time I had seen him, Jim flat-picked bluegrass style on just two tunes – a 180-degree flip from his first Sonoma County show. So his picking and his music interests are hardly strictly bluegrass. He is evolving away from 'grass, towards wider pastures.

The bluegrass audience is also evolving. Younger people are not setting out lawn chairs at bluegrass festivals as many of their parents did, preferring "jam bands" over traditional bluegrass acts. These groups, like the prototypical jam band, the Grateful Dead, usually feature *long* solo sections played over rhythm grooves. Although jam bands have roots in different soils, the one planted in bluegrass is called "jamgrass."

Poor Man's Whiskey, a Bay Area jamgrass band, sports the instruments of traditional bluegrass – mandolin, guitar, banjo, string bass, plus – gasp! – drums, but their music is as untraditional as their addition of traps. PMW's biggest hit, "Dark Side of the Moonshine," is a takeoff on rock band Pink Floyd's "Dark Side of the Moon."

Bill Monroe invented bluegrass music, so his proclamations on the genre carry weight. He had a well-known putdown of anything that was not bluegrass. "That ain't no part of nothin'," he'd scorn. To Bill Monroe's ears, I reckon, both Pink Floyd and "Dark Side of the Moon" would be no part of nothin' no how.

After his duo gig with Ickes, Jim and I sat down at a Sebastopol watering hole to talk. Jim, a serious and long-time student of the guitar, acknowledges three major influences, Chet Atkins, Doc Watson, and Jerry Reed, and three minor ones: the fabled Lenny Breau; Tony Rice; and Travis-pickin' Merle Travis. Jim seems to study a guitarist by listening to his music and learning his techniques. You can hear a picker's playing seeping into Jim's, and then you hear it disappear. I don't hear much of Chet, Doc, or Jerry directly in Jim's playing, or Lenny, Tee, or Merle for that matter. I mostly hear Jim playing Jim, as informed by all of the others.

Yes, you can hear him tip his hat to an influence. He will play a Lenny Breau-ish cascade of melodic harmonics, for instance, but the choice of notes is Jim's, not Lenny's. He loves the sound of Breau's chiming waterfall, but puts his own melody to it.

Jim said he had found it difficult to book himself as a solo act into bluegrass festivals, or even as a duo. "Bluegrass promoters want bluegrass bands, and they want those bands to play the traditional tunes. And it's worse in California than anywhere else!" he said.

True enough, I know. For a historically progressive state, this is hard to understand, and not a good sign.

Jim proved to be a serious student of 'grass's turning path as well. "Bluegrass is struggling to find a new identity. Young hotshots are coming along who in some cases don't know who Flatt & Scruggs were. But the old guard wants to keep that Bill Monroe, Flatt & Scruggs kind of feel, which is vital to the art form. The old guard feels that anything recorded past 1958 or 1960 just ain't bluegrass.

"Other factions in the bluegrass community are reaching out to new ideas, inviting folks of other races, other cultures, to be part of bluegrass. But the old guard doesn't want anything to do with that. Not because they're bigoted. They just feel like, 'That's not bluegrass over there; this is bluegrass over here.'

"I'm sure there's some bigotry as well. There's some bigotry not only with skin color but also with regions of the country. There are different ways to avoid inclusivity by being exclusive. So if you're from Virginia, anyone who is west of the Mississippi River can't be bluegrass. North Carolina, Virginia, Kentucky, Tennessee, some parts of West Virginia: that is the nucleus of bluegrass to those people's minds.

"Chris Pandolfi, banjo man with the Notorious String

Dusters, gave the keynote speech about that same thing this year at the International Bluegrass Music Association (IBMA) Business Conference. He essentially said, 'We love Flatt & Scruggs; we love bluegrass. But we're not them. You need to give us a chance to be ourselves and do what Flatt & Scruggs did, which is jump out and do our own thing.'

"So there is this struggle to figure out what bluegrass is and what it isn't. There are youth who are coming in who have all this energy, all this desire to play bluegrass, but do not play it like Bill Monroe or banjo man Eddie Adcock. They want to play it their own way, even though some of them have been close to traditional bluegrass.

"So it's changing because of the advent of youngsters such as multi-instrumentalists Michael Cleveland, Josh Williams, and Cody Kilby. These young hotshots are dynamic people on their instruments; they have opened up the game in a different way than Sam Bush's New Grass Revival did. When New Grass Revival came along, maybe some first-generation fans felt they were being slapped in the face, even though Bill Monroe was one of Sam's biggest heroes. The band never intended to be disrespectful, but I think that some people who were watching them take the stage in T-shirts got offended."

I asked Jim if jamgrass bands figured in these equations.

"Yes, it all figures, but I think that jamgrass is having a minimal effect at this point because those bands have more of a cultish following. It's more of a 'this-is-cool-so-I'm-going-to-like-it.' The New Grass Revival's music was top-notch. But with some of the jam bands, it's not great music sometimes. It's really not.

"And while they're more successful than I may ever be, it doesn't mean that it's cutting edge music. I've been around some of the jam grass guys, and while they seem to all be fine people, it's a different kind of culture, which I know how to do, because coming from an Appalachian mountaintop, we were different right from the top. We talked different, acted different, and had a different style of walking. But you can tell knowledge on your instrument pretty quickly, and some of the jamgrass guys ...." His voice trailed off, but what he had left unsaid was understood.

At his performance that evening I had been struck by how thoughtfully Jim approached and explored the guitar. His versatile right hand techniques – flat-picking, modified chicken-pickin' (or flat-finger-picking as Jim calls it), Travis picking, palming the strings, harmonics, pinch harmonics – came from years of learning what other people have done, and applying it to his own style.

But he said the he feels stymied now. He has a lot to say on the guitar, but has found it difficult to get his music out to the public. CD sales, we all know, are way down. The bluegrass festivals, as he mentioned, don't want a solo act. "And folk music festivals have no idea who I am," he said, "and are not really looking for a bluegrass soloist anyway." Teaming up with another picker, as he had done here with Rob Ickes, helps at the door, but half their door does not necessarily give him the all-the-door take of playing solo.

As we downed the last of our pinot noirs, Jim said, "I don't know where I'm going next." He walked out into the night, got in his SUV rental, switched on the GPS, and drove off to his next gig.

October 20, 2012

Jim came back to town to play a solo show this evening, so we had breakfast together earlier this morning. He said that every year the IBMA World Of Bluegrass convention has a number of official showcases where a select group of artists are invited to present their acts to the public. Historically, these have *always* been bands. This year they invited eighteen acts. Seventeen of them were bands. One of them was a solo act, and that was Jim Hurst. This in itself was a breakthrough for him, and a turn of the road for bluegrass music. Kudos to the IBMA for showcasing a solo artist.

Jim more than held his own at this performance. According to folks on the bluegrass listserv, he was "extraordinary" and "masterful." One gal said that the only way Jim's show could have been better was if it had been twice as long.

After his IBMA performance, his booking agent, Liz DiSessa, stepped into the elevator where two festival promoters were standing. She asked them what they thought of Jim's performance. They both loved it and said they were going to hire him. As an upshot of his showcase, one festival has already signed Jim, and five others are in negotiations.

Moreover, he has played five festivals as a solo act since I last saw him. The promoters and audiences appreciate the respite between bluegrass acts that Jim provides. When there are two or more stages going simultaneously – fairly common at most festivals – a stay at Jim's tent is the pause that refreshes. And of course, being the monstrous guitarist that he is, he pulls in the guitar fanatics, of whom there are many, to his show.

Jim has also clarified who he is and what he's trying to do inside the "small box" that contains bluegrass. He is not a band, not another singer/songwriter, and not a comedy act. He is a guy with a guitar trying to present something of value: songs that the audience enjoys. In this, he is following the tracks of John Hartford and Doc Watson, two performers whom audiences always enjoyed hearing.

His show tonight manifested this clarity. When Jim played the guitar, regardless of the tempo or rhythm, he got the audience's toes tapping, putting them on his side from tune one. His guitar playing was stunning, but did not draw attention to itself. He avoided playing chorus after chorus of pyrotechnic solos, and usually kept it to one or two solos interspersed in the song. He did play a few instrumentals during his show, most of them medleys that grabbed our attention and kept us interested.

His between-tune patter had also evolved. He'd follow a medley with a Q&A about the tunes he had just picked. "What was the first one? ... Right! And what came after that?" Or he'd tell a story about the guitar he's playing, made to his specifications by Gallagher Guitar, a small guitar maker in Wartrace, Tennessee. They only make a half dozen so-called signature guitars – guitars made to the specs of and named after famous guitarists. One of them is the Doc Watson Model, another, the Jim Hurst Model.

His rap also showed a growing self-awareness. When his introduction to a song was running a little long, he ended it with "That might be too much of a buildup," which brought a chuckle from the room as he immediately launched the tune.

Once again I was entranced by Jim's playing. His right hand was noticeably all over the instrument, harvesting a bushel of tones from the guitar. But his playing, like the playing of all the great instrumentalists, showed economy of motion. A little movement created a lot of sound. He made the instrument look small in his hands.

His technique continues to expand. He used his right hand to spank harmonics out of the instrument. Pretty astonishing. He picked a Jerry Reed song, "Lock on Me," that at times sounded like more than one person was playing. His rendition of John Cadley's "Mist of Memory" was breathtaking, and riveted the room, as did an unexpected instrumental rendering of Joni Mitchell's "Both Sides Now," one that made me hear that song with fresh ears.

So again, I urge you to catch him next time he's in your 'hood. To hear Jim Hurst play is to witness a major and evolving talent, a man exploring both the guitar and himself.

Facing Race with Eric Bibb

The evening of July 27, 2008, found me sitting in the back of our band's SUV as we arrived at a Lake Harmony, New York, tollbooth. Our driver, Sari Bibb, white wife of black bluesman Eric Bibb, handed the attendant double the toll as she pointed over her shoulder at our harp player's station wagon. "And that's for the guy behind us," she said to the toll taker.

As Sari pulled away, Eric, riding shotgun and with tongue firmly in cheek said, "That was mighty white of you!"

An "Ooooo-eeee" was heard from the white bass player sitting in back. "I don't think that's what Obama meant when he said Americans should have a conversation about race," I said.

So Eric and I had that conversation, one that took place over four 1-hour web chats. Transcribed, it ran seventy-two pages.

But I've jumped ahead of my story again. Let me back up to our first meeting.

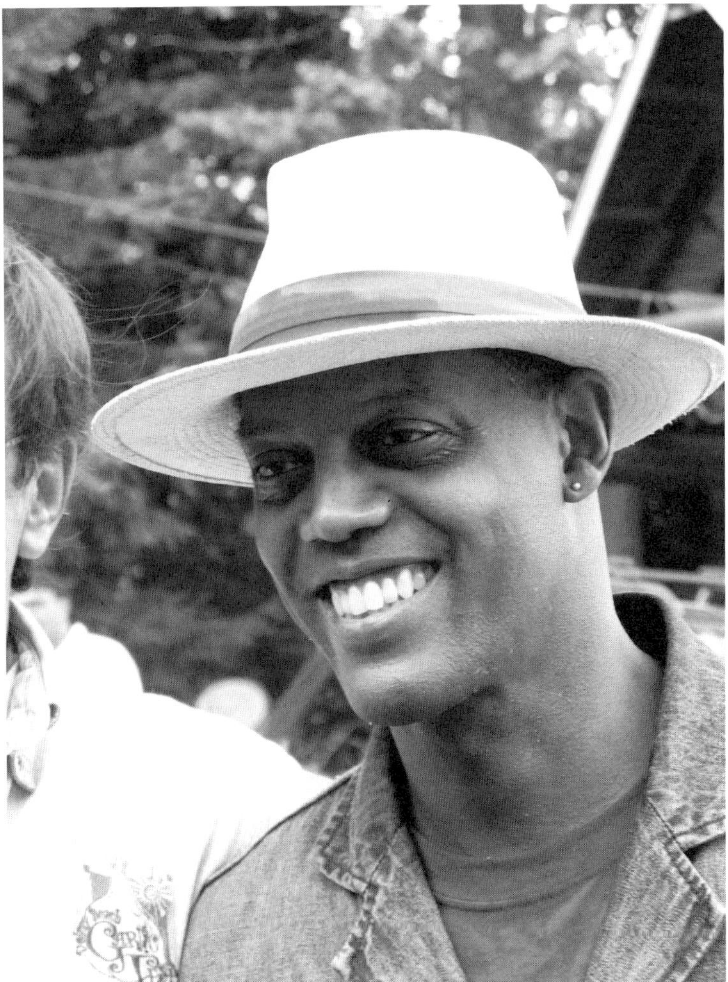

Eric Bibb

Lake Harmony Blues Festival · July 27, 2008

In 1999, Eric Bibb played the Kate Wolf music festival outside Graton, California, where I was backing Peter Rowan. Born in 1951 to folk-singer Leon Bibb, Eric took up the guitar at age seven. He released his first album in 1997, and has released over twenty albums since, many of them featuring or honoring the artists he grew up on: Bukka White, Paul Robeson, Pops Staples, Curtis Mayfield, Taj Mahal, Odetta, and others.

During his festival set, Eric, a country blues and gospel singer-songwriter, deftly fingerpicked his acoustic guitar – a gently thumping bass line underscoring lacework chording – sang soulfully, and spoke briefly but intimately between songs. The tunes he wrote and sang broke the blues mold – no small achievement. His performance, both passionately musical and deeply spiritual, riveted the audience. Eric had a quality beyond charisma that all performers seek. Eric had magic.

I remember thinking, It would be a treat to play music with him some day.

Eight years later, we met briefly at a gig he played at the Sebastopol Community Center, and subsequently stayed in touch about playing together the next time he toured Northern California. That opportunity arrived when Eric invited me to accompany him at his March 2008 gig at the Freight & Salvage in Berkeley. The day before the show he e-mailed a list of tunes that I practiced as best I could in the little time that remained. But driving to the gig the next evening, I felt under-prepared.

Arriving at the Freight, I found my way to the backstage dressing room. Twenty black people were there chatting away amiably. I was the only white person in the room. This scene had me smiling. Cool.

Eric introduced me to his traps drummer, Larry Crockett, and percussionist, Linda Tillery, both African-Americans. Though I've played with black people in bands through the years, this was the first time I'd been the only white person in an otherwise all-black group. This too was just fine, though a tad intimidating. African-Americans created the grooves of blues and soul, and remain its most adept practitioners. Miles Davis said that the musicians he most enjoyed working with were the ones he learned most from. I knew that working with this band was going to be enjoyable.

Rehearsal began, Eric counted off the first tune, and sixteen bars into it, I understood that Larry Crockett is a so-called "pocket drummer." His playing is so simply solid, so metronomic, that it creates a pocket, a safety zone, for other players to play in. No matter what excursions through space a soloist takes, he knows that the beat will be waiting for him when he returns because the pocket drummer will be holding it there.

Put at ease by the steady time, I released my underpreparedness anxieties and dropped my bass parts into Crockett's pocket.

Eric played the first set solo to a packed house. Afterwards, he sat at the "merch" table to sell and sign CDs – his merchandise – to the line of enthused fans that wound down one side of the room and across the other. I've played the Freight a number of times, but have never seen so many people buy an album from the performer. Eric's show, musically and spiritually captivating, makes you want to take it home with you to relive his spell.

The band joined him for the second set, playing Eric's "Destiny Blues," "Get On Board," "Needed Time," and others. The audience received our music loudly, and their long ovation brought Eric back for two encores.

Afterwards backstage, the band was buzzing. Eric thanked me effusively, much more than I deserved; it was his artistry that made the show. We shook hands, parting with many thank-yous and let's-do-it-agains.

A week later I got a call from his agent. Eric wants you to join him on an East Coast tour in July. Can you make it?

In one regard, this tour was a repeat of what I had seen at the Freight. Backstage were mostly black faces, and in front of the stage, in the house, predominantly white faces. At our last stop, at Pennsylvania's Poconos Blues Festival, the folks backstage were Eric's fellow performers: black bluesmen, some of them twenty years Eric's senior, who had hoed a long blues row. I felt they were there to catch Eric's show, but more importantly, to pay tribute to him as a dedicated fellow bluesman.

After our set, the MC took the stage and pointed the crowd to the merch table where Eric would be signing albums. He said that in the fourteen-year history of the festival, Eric held the record for most albums sold.

That afternoon Eric probably bested his own mark, signing and selling his CDs while the rest of us packed up the SUV and station wagon. An hour later, we hit the road and soon arrived at the Lake Harmony tollbooth where this story began.

~

Our discussion about race covered many topics, but these interested me most:

Eric said, "The civil rights movement, which had been on a roll, was derailed with the assassination of Dr. Martin Luther King. The change that Dr. King was talking about was shortchanged, and there is residual anger and rage even in African-Americans who have accomplished a lot economically and educationally.

"That rage is expressed in sophisticated ways by educated people, ways that are not destructive to their own livelihood and well-being. And it is present in the attitudes and actions of people who live on the street: a defiance, an anger, a feeling that it's basically a loaded deck.

"In America there are so many contradictions. We talk

to the rest of the world about being the voice of democracy, and we want to police the world and dictate that other countries should be free like us. But the United States is still a place where injustice occurs on a daily basis.

"Our justice system is not just. It is highly prejudiced against black people. There is a schizophrenic system in place where skin color still plays a huge role in what your fate will be if you end up in the courts."

I took a breath, changed the subject. "Eric, it's understood why black slaves would adopt Christianity, the religion of their masters, while they were on the plantation. Once freed from slavery and plantation life, why would they continue to embrace their enslavers' religion?"

His answer surprised me: "The African-American version of Christianity is heavily informed by the African-American experience; it is not the Christianity of the slavers. The stories of the Old Testament and the teachings of Jesus, which were heavily marinated in a philosophy of love and compassion, resonated with slaves, enabling them to make direct contact with their Maker by reflecting on these stories and contemplating the person of Jesus. That lent tremendous strength and spiritual sustenance to people in distress. The colonizers' Christianity was bereft of integrity, because there were too many contradictions.

"So I think that Christianity was redeemed – salvaged, in fact – by the African-American experience because it was embraced by a people who could really live it. Turning the other cheek and embracing forgiveness, a philosophy of life for some, became, for African-Americans, as slaves and descendants of slaves, a survival strategy. It was a way to feel personal power and pride at being superior to the people who were oppressing you.

"I'm sure there were many slaves who had personal

epiphanies, spiritual revelations, visions. Once they could accept that there was some truth and some goodness in the world, and that it was personified by Jesus, then people began to have personal experiences which let them know: Hey, it's all right, this is a passing thing. This is the way it is, and for whatever reasons, we need to keep our hands on the gospel plow.

"So I think that Christianity, true Christianity, was embodied, was experienced directly in the African community over and over again. Their faith was not just a repetition of hymns, but really belief. Faith."

Eric said that in America, when black people get together, they talk about racism. "It's a paradox. On the one hand, African-American people, like all folks, have lots of things to share, and much of it does not have specifically to do with race. But on the other hand it always comes up because we, as people of color, are living in a world dominated by people who don't look like us, and who moreover have a cultural dominance.

"So it comes up as a way of deriving collective strength from sharing experiences of survival. We talk about sharing your particular handle on getting through a lot of chafing experiences, and that becomes a bond. It also becomes a crutch, a whining common denominator that in some cases dominates too much. It becomes an excuse for not getting on with things, and not prioritizing more important things, even though it's a very vital issue."

I asked him how he felt about white people singing the blues, a genre created by black Americans from their struggles in white America.

"You realize that there's something universally appealing about this expression, this language that was developed in the African-American experience. And I feel a certain pride, a certain victory even, in having something that was created out of so much suffering, appeal to so many people around the world. It's almost as if there's a cosmic revenge. It is a balancing experience that a music expression created in a community of suffering, amidst great oppression and degradation, could touch so many people. It tells you that there is hope, there is some kind of order in the universe, and that out of suffering could come unification, harmony, and a collective awareness of our connectedness.

"The message of the blues and its related music genres – spirituals and gospel – is a unifying message. That the African-American experience of such suffering could produce a language that unifies the world is a wonderful thing to realize, be a part of, and be an exponent of. It's a privilege to be connected to a tradition that has such a lofty mission in the world."

Towards the end of our talk, Eric said, "The discussion of racism and the issue of white supremacy and all the assumptions that accompany it, should be more of a topic in any American's conversation because it's vital to confront it and get through it with some healing experiences. White people, for their own sake, I feel, should talk about it more, because it's a haunting specter that needs to be revealed and dealt with so that everybody can live more productive, peaceful, anxiety-free lives."

Our conversation was illuminating; it showed me an African-American's personal view of racism. (And please remember that what you have read here constitutes less than ten percent of our conversation.) Eric's perspective took me by surprise, opened my eyes. It changed me.

It's not that I was unaware of black rage; the Rodney King riots of 1992 are a reminder of that anger. But Eric, a sharp, knowledgeable, articulate world-traveler, has seen and felt racism on both hemispheres. Hearing the story of a black man with a lifetime of racial experiences brought me face to face with racism. He showed me the outlook in the black back of America's increasingly multihued but still majority (72%) white bus. I heard Eric's personal story of what being his race in America (and in the world) meant to him.

As we came to the end of our discussion, I said that I wanted to walk away from our talk with action. "What could you and I do," I asked him, "to change the face of racism?"

Eric had a remarkable idea. He said that at music festivals, the promoter often stages a round robin. The principal performers take seats on the stage in a half circle facing the audience, and each in turn sings a song, going 'round the circle a few times.

Instead, Eric said, "Let's put our instruments down and say, 'This is going to be a very special workshop about another kind of music. No instruments, guys; just bring your hearts and your experience. We're going to talk about race, in front of an audience, at a festival.' "

"Do you have the clout to do this, Eric?"

"Yes, with some promoters at some festivals, yes, I believe I could bring it about."

My idea for action was that each February (African American History Month), the media – newspapers, magazines, websites, social networks – should devote themselves to a discussion about race. There could be articles, essays, writing contests, diatribes, rants, blog posts, public forums, chat room chats, … whatever it takes to engage the public in this topic.

I said that my discussion with Eric had changed me. Besides making me more aware of racism, it has made me more open to discussing race with people of color. When I'm at a party or club, I'll sometimes seek out an African-American and start a conversation on this topic. Reactions have always been welcoming, and the ensuing discussions, enlightening.

It starts by looking the other person in the eyes. To lock eyes with a person of another race is to meet in a place where color does not exist, where only humanity lives; it sets the stage for a frank discussion.

Sure, your views on race may be more conservative, or more radical, than Eric's. You may love or resent people of another color. Understood. But whatever your views and opinions, all of us should start talking about race.

Get together with one or more people of another color. Someone goes first. Say what your race is and then talk about what it feels like, what it has meant, to be that race living where you live. Then the next person does the same.

Now is the time.

~

Backing Eric Bibb was more than a treat. Making music with him and his talented sidemen and -women, connecting to his generous spirit, and talking with him about race, were an immersion in African-American culture and a consequential experience for me.

Playing on stage with Eric reminded me of why players seek playing out. It is when, giving the best we have, we are most alive.

Epilogue

I'm grateful to have found the string bass and played at so many events where people fell under the spell of song. Magically, the heartbeat of a bass causes smiles to appear, toes to tap, and heads to bob.

Playing music that people sing with and dance to, pray with and sway to, is to love and be loved. It is the gift my parents gave me.

About the Artists

I am delighted to have so many fine photographers and artists represented here. My thanks to each of them for their kind permission to publish their works in *Acoustic Stories*.

Danilo Amílcar — Danilo Amílcar works as a freelance photographer, and at the School of Design at Mexico's National Institute of Fine Arts and Literature. He has documented his country's rock culture, dance, and the daily lives of Mexicans. Danilo is currently developing *Las Hijas del Máiz,* comprised of portraits of Mexican women. In 2013, Mexico awarded him an artist's grant. His work is at daniloamilcarfotoartvi.blogspot.com/ and at facebook.com/daniloamilcar.lasjijasdelmaiz.

Gilles Boisvert — Gilles Boisvert studied at the École des Beaux-Arts in Montreal in 1958 and 1960 before studying engraving with Albert Dumouchel from 1961 to 1964. In trips to New York he discovered action-painting artists, and then pop-artists. During the '60s, he was at the forefront of young artists who advocated democratization and deregulation of arts. At the Museum of Contemporary Art in 1966,

Boisvert created what can be considered one of the first, if not *the* first "environment" in Quebec art. He co-founded the Media Gallery in 1970, and in '73 created a mural of integrated architecture at Montreal's Maison de Radio-Canada. Other architectural projects followed as well as works of monumental sculpture throughout the 1970s and '80s. In 1983, he produced a series of lithographs accompanying poems by Michel Beaulieu for the artist's book. In over forty years, Gilles has presented his work in more than 200 solo and group exhibitions in Canada, the United States and Europe. His work is at miximages.com/boisvert/ .

Patrick Ciocca — Patrick studied the upright bass at the classical conservatory of Lausanne, and has played Europe with Bill Keith, Peter Rowan, Jim Collier, and Pierre Bensusan, among others. He has done sound design, light design, and audio engineering for dozens of acts, touring in China, Thailand, Egypt, Canada, Brasil and the USA. He is currently Technical Director of the *Octogone Theater* in Pully, Switzerland.

Eric Draper — Eric Draper was the White House Photo Director under President George W. Bush for the entire eight years of Bush's presidency, photographing him daily in his activities at the office, abroad and in his personal life. Draper was named Special Assistant to the President, and is the first White House photographer to be named a commissioned officer to a U.S. president. During his tenure, Draper directed the photographic and archival conversion of the White House Photo Office from film to digital and took nearly one million photos documenting the presidency.

Linda Emme — "I am both painter and photographer; with infrared film, both mediums converge. The painterliness of light flairs abstracts the image, while the softness with which it records people, pushes the images toward painting. The hard edges of digital black and white somehow offend my eye. While I taught Photoshop, Illustrator and InDesign for fourteen years at Art Center College of Design in Pasadena and free-lanced for twenty years, I have always kept my photography as my own special space to be myself. I took this shot of Bill to see what I'd get with very little light in a very dark space." Her work can be seen at emmeinfraredphotography.com

Marshall Freedland — A professional banjoist and guitarist, Marshall toured with the Robert DeCormier Singers in the 1960s, joining legendary bassist Bill Lee for their New York appearances. His photographic education began in 1964 at Goddard College with mentor John Mahoney.

FRETS Magazine published work from Marshall's 40-year oeuvre of bluegrass and folk masters, which included Libba Cotton, Mike Seeger, Brownie McGhee, Peggy Seeger and Ewan McColl, Dave Van Ronk, Merle Travis, and Doc Watson.

Michael Ferguson & Alton Kelley — These two gentlemen co-created the New Riders of the Purple Sage logo. I was told that Michael Ferguson drew the original design, which Alton Kelley then edited and colorized.

Michael Ferguson was the pianist and a vocalist in The Charlatans, a seminal San Francisco rock group. Along with George Hunter he created a poster for the group's first gig at the Red Dog Saloon in Nevada City. It is considered America's first psychedelic rock poster and became known as the "SEED" due to its pivotal importance to this art form.

Alton Kelley arrived early on the Haight-Ashbury scene and was one of the founders of the Family Dog in 1965. He went on to create many landmark posters for the Dog and for San Francisco rock groups, both alone and in collaboration with Stanley Mouse. Alton emerged as one of the foremost artists of the psychedelic era.

Al Hirshfeld — Al Hirshfeld's drawings graced the entertainment section of the *New York Times* from 1928 to 2002. Your name may have been in lights on the Shubert Theater's marquee during this era, but you had not arrived on Broadway until Hirshfeld had drawn you. He drew artists with often a few lines and sometimes many, but Hirshfeld always distilled and captured them. His style was unique, and it can be said that he created his own genre. His works are in the Smithsonian Institution, the National Portrait Gallery, the Metropolitan Museum of Art, the Museum of Modern Art, and the Lincoln Center Library, among others.

Annie Leibovitz — Annie is most likely the best-known portrait photographer in the United States. She cut her teeth working for *Rolling Stone* in the '70s where she defined rock photojournalism. When she left, I thought, Where will she go now? The answer was: everywhere. In the last three decades she has shot dozens of covers for *Vanity Fair,* including the beautiful portrait of the beautifully-pregnant Demi Moore. The photo of Aretha was the last she took during our afternoon together. We were about to leave when Annie asked Aretha for one final shot, walked right up to her, put the camera to her face, and took this insightful portrait.

Karl Leopold Metzenberg — An L.A. photographer, Karl taught B&W darkroom technique at the *New Communicators* school, shot objects for catalogues and heads for actors, and through a series of fortuitous accidents provided the "open road" shot on the cover of Jackson Browne's album *Running on Empty.* He lives in Santa Barbara.

Mike Melnyk — "As a teenager I worked as an assistant with an advertising agency. Later I studied photography as both fine art and trade. It wasn't until about twelve years ago that I found an interest in working with artists, primarily musicians. There's something about what they do and how they live that continues to interest me. My work is not only a document of their world, it's also a means for me to live and work in my own creative way." He is on the web at mikemelnyk.com .

Jon Sievert — Jon wrote and published the book *Concert Photography: How to shoot and Sell Music Business Photographs,* the bible of music photography. He was also staff photographer and editor for *Guitar Player Magazine.* His photos have appeared on more than one hundred magazine covers, dozens of album/CD packages, and in countless books and publications worldwide, including *Rolling Stone, Musician, People, Acoustic Guitar, The New York Times, Entertainment Weekly, Guitar World, Vanity Fair, Newsweek,* and *Fachblatt.* He can be found on the web at HumblePress.com.

E.K. Waller has been teaching photography since 2004, guiding students on a creative path to realizing their vision. She is an advertising photographer, shooting for advertising and editorial clients, specializing in food, product, and people. She is also a fine art photographer who loves to scout and wait for the "decisive moment" in her fine art "Street Photography." E.K. is Fats Waller's granddaughter.

Acknowledgments

I could not have completed this work without the help and support of my wife, Noni. She is my first-line editor, story confidant, and the originator of some of my tales' best titles. Moreover, I'm nuts about her. Thank you sweetheart, very much.

Flatpicker and scrivener Rick Jamison reviewed and edited the entire manuscript, and then patiently answered my stream of questions that followed. Thank you very much, Rick, for your editing expertise, insights into music and musicians, and your unflagging enthusiasm.

Many people read individual chapters in the book and gave me their feedback on them. Many thanks to Brian Boldt, Linda Jay Geldens, Arthur Goldstein, Bob Jenkins, Jim Marcolina, Laurie Reaume, and Lynne Terry for their editing and feedback.

I am grateful to Steve Gorn for telling me so much about Ali Akbar Khan, and to Alam Khan, David Trasoff, and George Ruckert for their stories about the master.

My thanks to Rick Dougherty, Gina Sutton, and Ramon Sender for their insights into Lou Gottleib.

A big thank you to Jeff Barnard, Greg Sudmeier, and Floyd Reinhart for telling me Will Sudmeier's story.

I am grateful to vexillologists Rob Raeside, Peter Hans van den Muijzenberg, T.F. Mills and Esteban Rivera for their help in leading me to a positive identification of the flag and people involved in the wreath-laying ceremony at Ranville, France.

Book design master, Pete Masterson, has been unstinting with his time and expertise, providing perceptive answers to my questions about content, type, typesetting, design and layout. Thank you, Pete, very much.

Likewise, Desta Garrett, a book designer of long experience and huge eyes, was more than generous with her feedback about the appearance of this book. Thank you, Desta.

And a big thank you to book-art designer and poet, Ama Bolton, for her review of galley proofs and her thoughtful, insightful reflections that followed.

And finally, I am much obliged to Doug Adamz, Bill Bradbury, David Aks, J Brown, Kristi Buffo, Patti Collins, Richard Hoover, Stan Jay, Chris Karnofsky, Primo Kim, Charlie Pearson, David LaPlante, Jim Nunally, Peter Nye, Pamela Poland, David B. Teague Sr., Gary Wagner, and Roland White for providing details that have enriched these stories, and to Seth Evans for managing the VineyardsPress.com website.

Permissions

The author tried diligently to obtain the permissions and releases necessary for publication of the material in this book, and for the protection of the sensibilities of the people it depicts and names. If anyone mentioned or depicted in *Acoustic Stories* is in any way embarrassed, violated, or offended by finding himself here (or by not finding himself here), the author apologies sincerely and profusely.

Many thanks to Paul Tannen for permission to use the lyrics to Bill Monroe's

"The Little Girl and the Dreadful Snake."
Used by permission, Tannen Music,
A Division Of New Media Music Inc.

A big thank you to Mitchell Greenhill for permission to quote the lyrics of:

"Your Long Journey"
By Rosa Lee Watson and Doc Watson
Copyright Hillgreen Music (BMI)
Used by permission

I am grateful to Linda Emme for the infrared film photo she took of me at Rancho Nicasio.

Many thanks to Mike Melnyk for his photo of Roland White.

I am grateful to Danilo Amílcar for the concert photo of Steve Gorn playing the bansuri flute.

My thanks to Karl Leopold Metzenberg for permission to publish his delightful photo of Kate Wolf.

Thank you to Deborah Kohler, Assistant Director of Public Relations at Delgado Community College, New Orleans, Louisiana. The cover of the Buddy Bolden jazz funeral program is used by courtesy of Delgado Community College.

Many thanks to Andy Braunfeld and the Philadelphia Folksong Society for permission to reproduce the Society's flyer for Bob Dylan's May 1963, concert.

For permission to reprint the NRPS logo, created by Michael Ferguson and Alton Kelley, thank you, John Dawson.

My thanks to Jon Sievert, for his permission to use the photos of Peter, Paul & Mary, and Jerry Garcia, and to Patrick Ciocca for permission to use his photo of Bill Keith's Bicentennial Bluegrass Band.

My sincere thanks to the anonymous photographers and artists whose works are in these pages.

Ordering Acoustic Stories

If you would like to order additional copies of *Acoustic Stories,* please visit us at VineyardsPress.com. There you may place an order for a signed or inscribed copy of the book.

You can get in touch with us, or get on our mailing list to hear about Bill's upcoming projects and tours at

info@vineyardspress.com